CRIME AND ITS CORRECTION

BERKELEY AND LOS ANGELES

CRIME
AND ITS
CORRECTION

An International Survey
of Attitudes and Practices

by JOHN P. CONRAD

UNIVERSITY OF CALIFORNIA PRESS 1970

UNIVERSITY OF CALIFORNIA PRESS
BERKELEY AND LOS ANGELES, CALIFORNIA
UNIVERSITY OF CALIFORNIA PRESS, LTD.
LONDON, ENGLAND
© 1965 BY THE REGENTS OF THE UNIVERSITY OF CALIFORNIA
THIRD PRINTING, 1970
ISBN 0-520-00265-2
LIBRARY OF CONGRESS CATALOG NUMBER 65-13768
MANUFACTURED IN THE UNITED STATES OF AMERICA

To Charlotte

FOREWORD

It is rare, indeed, that an intelligent, thoughtful, and responsible person comes into intimate contact with offenders processed through our criminal and juvenile courts without experiencing a sense of frustration and dismay; dismay that there are so many and frustration that the society we have created has learned so little about the forces that created them, and even less about constructive responses to the problems they present.

As long as public leaders regarded the offender as an inevitable product of original sin calling only for retributive punishment, little was expected of penal and correctional administrators. The maintenance of order and the efficient operation of the "system" seemed enough. But with the wider acceptance of reformation, rehabilitation, and restoration of the individual offender to normal responsible membership in the community, the correctional field was confronted with a new set of challenges infinitely more complex and difficult.

Faced with these new goals and aspirations, both scholars and administrators are looking to the methods of scientific investigation for ways to ask meaningful questions as well as to find useful answers to both new and old queries.

It was with these ideas in mind that we of the California correctional system formed the Institute for the Study of Crime and Delinquency to provide a vehicle for study and research in corrections without reference to the jurisdictional barriers of the all-too-numerous bureaucracies of public administration.

The Ford Foundation agreed with us that a proper starting point would be to review in as systematic a way as possible the attitudes and practices in several leading countries of the world.

This report, published under the auspices of the Institute for the Study of Crime and Delinquency and financed by a grant from the Ford Foundation, is, we believe, a readable and revealing analysis of this international survey which sets forth in broad outlines the status and the dynamics of the correctional effort in these countries.

Dr. Clyde Sullivan and Mr. John Conrad were the principal observers both in America and Europe. They, with other staff, made exhaustive reviews of the literature and official reports.

The writing in this volume is that of Mr. Conrad. The Board of Directors of the Institute for the Study of Crime and Delinquency is grateful to him for the monumental effort that he has put forth.

RICHARD A. MCGEE

CONTENTS

I

INTRODUCTION

For about seventy years, the life of the California prison at San Quentin was dominated by a jute mill. Huge, dirty, noisy, and dangerous, it kept thousands of inmates busy at labor regarded as hard. As the decades of the twentieth century passed by, it "progressed" from obsolescence to obsoleteness. The engineering firm in Scotland which built the original machines, discontinued the manufacture of spare parts. The mill, always unique in California, had to become self-sufficient to survive. Parts were fabricated in a prison foundry established for the purpose. Inmates were trained in the maintenance of looms the like of which could not be found elsewhere in the Western Hemisphere. As the years passed, the burlap sacks produced by the mill were priced higher on the retail market than those imported from India, despite the low prison wages. It did not matter that the mill was uneconomic as well as obsolete. It kept inmates busy, if resentful. Its capacity to create secondary work was considered an advantage.

In 1951 the mill burned down, in spite of great precautions against fire. The cause of the fire will never be known for sure. In due course, a modern cotton mill replaced it. The new mill incorporates labor-saving devices undreamed of by Scottish loom designers of the Victorian era, but it keeps San Quentin inmates busier than ever.

The hideous memory of the San Quentin jute mill is resurrected not for its moral, if any, but for a parallel to the present plight of corrections. Inertia abetted by tradition, the law governing prison industry, and the need for work for inmates to do kept the looms clattering. Most changes in the routines of the mill were in response to the aggression or resistance of the inmates, not from concerted plans by management to improve its operation. Only a destructive event brought about its replacement by a modern and economic mill. No one defended the mill, except as being better than nothing at all. There were many on the San Quentin staff who saw the harm the mill did and thought it exceeded its benefits. No one studied the matter. To this day, no one has any way of appraising the effects of this variety of punitive hard labor on inmates. This is regrettable, for the jute mill offered an incomparable laboratory for the study of differential punishments inflicted on adult offenders of many categories.

Most parallels to the system of corrections are obvious. Inertia, the law, and the inherent bureaucratic resistance to change preserve not only the physical structures but also the ideas, the organization, and the expectations of the system. The ramshackle aggregation of lock-ups, jails, reformatories, camps, and penitentiaries was improvised from the mixed motives, the speculations, and the *a priori* notions of the nineteenth century. So, too, probation and parole were brought into being to improvise an amelioration of justice. Because no one has thought of instruments of control, change, retribution, and deterrence which could replace these social institutions, they survive. An uneasy interdependence is established; because the whole consists of many parts which interact well or poorly depending on design and maintenance, we have chosen the term *the correctional apparatus* to refer to the system.

As we shall see, the condition of the correctional apparatus varies greatly from community to community. Typically the operation of the apparatus is much like the old jute mill; obsolete, unreliable, unchanging except as offenders themselves force change on the system which holds them.

Here and there, exigency and leadership combine to produce planning to replace witless drift. From this conjunction this study had its origin. The years which followed World War II brought to California the expansion for which ambitious interests had longed. With the doubling of the population in a decade, special pressures were brought to bear on the ancient correctional apparatus. New prisons were built, sleepy part-time probation departments turned into bustling, overworked casework agencies, and a pair of professionalized administrative structures, the Department of Corrections and the Youth Authority, were created to operate the state programs for adult and juvenile offenders.

Expansion on this scale demands organizational changes, systematic planning, and good reasons for doing what is proposed. In 1957, at the behest of the legislature, research divisions were installed in both agencies to enable all concerned to evaluate the progress of the correctional programs proliferating where so little had gone on before. From this beginning, an appetite for research and development soon developed. What kinds of typologies could be constructed to facilitate treatment and prediction? What kinds of program made a difference with what kinds of inmates? How much difference was needed to make a new program pay off? How are results measured? If by recidivism rates, what kind of event constituted recidivism? Both research divisions found themselves heavily engaged with new inquiries of their own. Foundations made funds available for special investigations designed to improve the correctional apparatus. The resemblance to the jute mill and other infamies vanished. The vision of a new profession, a community service rather than a blunt instrument of repression, dazzled the staff both old and new.

Nevertheless, though optimism pervaded the organizations, questions arose about the directions in which the apparatus was developing. Though resources for research were increasing, a general strategy was needed which would divide the labor, prevent unnecessary duplication of projects, and provide for the development of investigations which a public agency could not undertake. Discussions of future research investment began to provide for the organization of a research institute which would, among other things, carry out certain projects which were recognized as basic correctional research. When members of the two research divisions explored with the staff of the Ford Foundation, it was seen that a preliminary survey of trends in practice and research was needed. On such a survey the program of the institute could be based.

It was agreed that the staff of the survey would inform itself regarding the present state of the theory of corrections and its application to practice in as wide a range of cultures as could be arranged. The task was to examine "what the doers were thinking and what the thinkers were doing" about correctional advance. Perhaps, if the examination were perceptive enough about the gap between these closely related activities, some steps might be taken to bring academician and administrator closer together.

For it was readily apparent that the gap between thinker and doer exists and that it handicaps practical progressive steps. Harried prison wardens and probation officers have little time to read and to listen. To continue doing what has always been done is the reliable plan under the circumstances. A better idea may exist up in the sky, but a tightly budgeted organization is in no shape to bring it down to earth.

Similarly, there are many social scientists with validated research to impart to administrators and untested ideas to investigate. Their impatience with the necessities of the established order is easy to understand. Nobody seems to be listening. The same old mistakes are being made, and mistakes in this particular field are expressed not in mere inefficiency but in human waste and tragedy.

From the opposition of doer and thinker comes inaction buttressed by the recriminations of both sides. Observers during the past two decades are painfully familiar with this opposition and its consequences. Its effects were expressed, after the inception of this survey, with querulous bravado by the sociologist Donald Cressey:

> The decisions a warden makes on a day-to-day basis are limited in scope and are attempts to solve immediate, pressing problems; they are only remotely related to general theory or ideology. A social scientist's notions about government, about prisons, or about rehabilitation, then, are likely to be considered unrealistic or idealistic because they do not contain explicit directives for handling a variety of daily administrative problems. We once asked a warden about the value of sociological training for prison workers, and he responded, "It is like I say around here. A man is tearing up his cell and has just attacked an officer. So I say, 'Well, let's go over here to the shelf and get one of these criminology books and find out what we should do.' There's nothing there." There never will be anything there. Nevertheless, the detailed insights by the authors of this volume show realism and concern for the practical implications of social science theory for those decisions. The authors probably know more about prisons than do most wardens, and their research *can* be put to administrative use by men who are skilled in solving the day-to-day problems of government.[1]

But if Cressey's analysis of the resistance of the old-line warden to social science ideas is correct for many places, there are other places where the social scientist has an attentive audience of administrators. Our task was to learn what happens to the correctional apparatus when the scien-

---

[1] Donald R. Cressey, *The Prison* (New York: Holt, Rinehart and Winston, 1961), p. 10.

tist and the administrator work in harness on the design of prison communities in which cells will not be torn up and officers will not be attacked.

To bring doer and thinker closer together, the Institute for the Study of Crime and Delinquency was formed in late 1959. The prime movers of this new agency for correctional research were Richard A. McGee, then Director of the California Department of Corrections, and Heman G. Stark, Director of the California Youth Authority. The Ford Foundation made a grant to carry out the survey of correctional trends which appeared to be the first order of business. Two investigators were appointed, Dr. Clyde E. Sullivan and the present writer. Sullivan had been Director of Guidance and Research for the Alameda County Probation Department, one of the most advanced in California. A clinical psychologist, he brought to the survey a wide experience in the application of behavioral science to the gritty realities of treatment in corrections. This writer, a social worker by training, was the Supervisor of Inmate Classification of the California Department of Corrections. In 1958-1959 he served a year as Fulbright Research Fellow at the London School of Economics, in the course of which he became familiar with the administrative problems of a rapidly expanding correctional apparatus in England, problems which were excruciatingly similar to those with which he had dealt in the apparatus in which he regularly worked.

We started in January, 1960. It was from the outset clear that our task would be no more than a reconnaissance of the correctional world. No more could be accomplished in the allotted two years than an attempt to bring into communicable order the state of correctional theory in the hope that the chasm between doer and thinker might be narrowed.

This volume is the report on what we saw. A later report on the condition of correctional theory will be the second product of the survey. However, progress is never made by books alone. For movement ahead in a field in which movement is glacially slow, there must be some determined workers with ideas. We hope that from this book and its companion ideas will be spread which will accelerate the glacier.

SOURCES

In a year of travel even the most indefatigable observers can only see a finite number of institutions and agencies. We decided that the correctional world could be trisected, though not into equal parts. The first sector was the traditional correctional apparatus which has sur-

vived thus far into the twentieth century and in some surprisingly enlightened places. In its corruption, its inefficiency, and its primitive
brutality it has for generations offered a target for the humanitarian
journalist. We decided to leave it to him, although we were aware that
there is still a job for a social scientist who should account rigorously for
its survival in terms of the strength and nature of the forces supporting
it; who should study its effects on the unfortunates who pass through its
lacerating machinery; and who should study the effects of such an apparatus on the community in which it is situated. Time may be running
out on the old ways in corrections, but while they are still practiced they
should receive more than denunciatory attention.

But we could not see that this was our charge.

The second sector is the standard practice of the correctional domain.
Since World War II, corrections has gone a long way toward professionalization. All cultures now show a general and official concern for humane and constructive treatment of the offender. The high-sounding
statement of purpose in the official regulations and the day-to-day practice of the average correctional employee show a willingness to meet the
correctional client half-way. His life will be made bearable, an effort
will be made to keep him constructively occupied, so far as a very difficult problem in public policy can be resolved, and, if he likes, he can be
educated and even receive some of society's most highly prized service,
psychiatric treatment. Differences can be found from nation to nation,
from state to state, and even from community to community. But the
core of standard practice is humane control. No matter who the correctional client may be — whether an inmate of a prison or a juvenile probationer — the community's objectives are to protect itself from the offender, and to set an object lesson to him and to his fellows of like mind
as to the consequences of crime. In many senses of the word, the standard practice of corrections as described in manuals and regulations and
as conscientiously practiced throughout the civilized world, though not
everywhere, is an astonishing testimony to the impact of humanitarian
ideals on the race as a whole. Solid cause for optimism about our future
may be found in the public willingness to spend so much concern and
money on those human beings who have deserved the least from the
community.

But having said so much in tribute to our colleagues in the profession of corrections we must confess that the territory which they occupy
has been charted too well to justify yet another report. Differences of

opinion still exist as to what may be expected of standard practice; bitter criticisms of its faults pour from writers. And a whole school of sociological analysis of the total institution and its malignant impact on its inmates has raised an unsettled theoretical question as to the futility of expecting a good outcome from any correctional program.[2] These are issues which ought to be resolved, but there are others better equipped to say what needs to be said. It is up to us to report on the prevalent operation of the field only to the extent that it limits the free development of advance.

We thought we could discern a third section of the field, an entering wedge, perhaps, rather than a well-charted area: the advanced practice of corrections. Good enough, so far, but how were we to distinguish the scouts from the troops? With a world to canvass, we had to have criteria. We began with society's assignment to corrections, its task as defined by a censensus of administrators and social scientists. This assignment we defined as *the social restoration of the offender.* From the interviews we conducted with administrators and from our reading of the literature, it was clear that the obvious conclusion had been drawn by virtually all correctional authorities from the fact that all but a handful of their clients come under control only to be released eventually. Therefore it could not be held that the correctional assignment was the control of the offender for the sake of control. It is the responsibility of the correctional apparatus to return the offender from his disadvantaged position as a member of a special, handicapped class, to full and unrestricted participation in the life of the community. How can this restoration be performed with the thieving, violent, lecherous, and muddled human beings who become correctional clients?

We could leave the problem in this state and proceed with our observation of the best answers as of 1960-1961. But it seemed to us that two preliminary problems had to be borne in mind. First, the experience of social degradation [3] produces effects on the offender. Many of these effects are extremely damaging. In bringing about the social restoration which we challenge the correctional apparatus to do, there must be a neutralization of the retributive sequence of arrest, trial, conviction, and sentence. So far as we have been able to see, there is little that the cor-

---

[2] Erving Goffman, *Asylums* (Garden City, New York: Anchor Books, Doubleday, 1961), pp. 3–124.

[3] Harold Garfinkel, "Conditions of Successful Degradation Ceremonies," *American Journal of Sociology,* 61:5 (March 1956) 420–424.

rectional apparatus can do to minimize the damage done to its clients before they are received. But the second stage in social degradation is the correctional experience itself. How can this be made benign? How can the damage so often reported by the critics of our agencies and institutions be offset by organization toward social restoration?

The correctional apparatus will not have reached its ultimate effectiveness merely by providing an intelligently humane place of confinement or by training staffs of tactful probation officers. The offender became a client from some sequence of cause and effect. Without prejudging how the task should be undertaken, something must be done to restore him to the community as a person less likely to offend that he was before received. Change, whether of people or of institutions, is one of the great unsolved problems of our time. But correctional administrators and clinicians must concern themselves with it every day. Some dismiss the possibility as too unlikely to lose sleep over. Others are preoccupied with the problems of change to a point where considerations of control recede to secondary importance. These were the leaders, we thought, whom we should seek out and whose operations we should report. We would not be able to pass judgment on the efficacy of their work. From familiarity with the difficulties in arriving at honest appraisals of our work we knew better than to expect that we could evaluate the programs of correctional apparatus in other communities and other cultures. But we could report what the doers were thinking and we might discern some trends.

The Institute enrolled a number of distinguished correctional authorities to act as an advisory committee. From correspondence with them, from a review of the literature, from observation it was possible to locate several places in which the glacier was in perceptible motion. Dividing the correctional world between us, Sullivan visited institutions and agencies in the Middle West and in France, Belgium, Germany, Austria, Switzerland, Italy, Yugoslavia, and Israel. This writer visited some institutions on the East Coast, and in Washington, British Columbia, and California. He also visited the correctional systems of England, the Netherlands, Norway, Sweden, Denmark, Finland, and the Soviet Union.

We interviewed persons engaged at every level of the correctional apparatus. Here and there, in the unlikeliest foreign parts, we found English-speaking inmates who could report on their impression of the correctional advances being experienced by them. We paid particular attention to "middle management," that class of correctional worker which is dedicated to transforming an idea into a practice: These were the captains, the supervising probation officers, the assistant wardens and governors, the vocational instructors. Almost everywhere, we managed to reach the highest echelons, the offices were policy is made. Sometimes we are able to trace the course of an idea in the headquarters office down to its actual impact on a correctional client at the other side of the country.

Early in our travels we discovered that what glitters is not necessarily gold. Intentions are the easiest aspects of the correctional apparatus to change. However valid they may be, management skill, money, and personnel are always required to put them into effect. These assets are never abundantly available, and ingenuity does not always cover the deficit. Some visits to well-known correctional innovations proved to be unrewarding. The innovating idea was there and so were the offenders to be corrected, but no connection had been made between the two. On the other hand, we think we made a few encouraging discoveries.

Our sources, then, turned out to be a selection of thoughtful and concerned people, well aware that they were engaged in an enterprise in which new departures are desperately needed but skeptically awaited. The reality of a rising volume of crime and delinquency confronts administrators in regions as widely separated as Finland and California. In the flourishing condition of criminal statistics, both threat and opportunity lurk. Numbers may swamp institutions and agencies to the extent that hard-won standards of service will be eroded. Where the masses of people to be dealt with obliterate the individuality of any, even well-trained staff members learn to be callous to the stereotypes into which they sort the population.

In the increased volume of crime many imaginative administrators and social scientists perceive their opportunity. A training school which is adequate to the demands made on it needs no change, it may be assumed. Something must be done about the hundreds of training schools all over the world which are so packed that the finding of space for new clients preoccupies the attention of the administrator. He will be aware that some options exist as to how much space might be designed. These options are based on choices about future program. From these chance materials most correctional progress seems to be made. It is not the elegant, carefully researched progress from analysis of a problem, through formulation and test of hypotheses, followed by adoption of a model which might characterize the design and building of an airplane. The correctional apparatus has only recently been thought of as an element of the social system worth tinkering with. Its designers must work after hours and hit-or-miss. But at least a beginning is under way, with the ominous tide of criminality propelling the correctional apparatus into change.

Change can be merely more of the same. Old prison designs can be taken from the shelf, with reinforced concrete replacing stone masonry. Parole agencies can add a new district office even more simply by renting space and hiring young social workers instead of old policemen.

But changes can also consist of new ideas which express the knowledge and spirit of the times. For this is the age when social science is making its first hesitant steps into maturity. The new ideas which it has so far generated are largely untested. But methods of studying social problems and gathering facts are now in our hands which make hopeful innovation possible. In every sphere of human activity innovation may express error, and often not even a novel error. We hope that in this book a structure may be developed by which the essence and consequences of hopeful innovations may be more widely and usefully communicated. The meager resources of the correctional apparatus should capitalize on gains wherever they are made; they must not be diverted into unprofitable channels charted by others. In a contracting world afflicted by social problems of great urgency, reconnaissances of this kind are increasingly needed. We hope that this volume will be the precursor of more comprehensive and informed comparative studies in this field.

So long as society consists of fallible human beings there will continue to be correctional clients. For centuries, we have single-mindedly punished each other with little profit. Reform has placed a limit on the permissible limits of punishment. Understanding has opened avenues to the limited help of offenders. We begin to see that the correctional apparatus, though it never can divest itself of its objective of punishment, can become a service through the application of scientific method to its tasks. To revert to our opening metaphor, the cruel waste of the jute mill is far behind us. The ideal correctional apparatus may not be in sight, but through analysis and experiment its dimensions are beginning to be known.

II

THE IRRATIONAL

EQUILIBRIUM

A PARADOXICAL DEFINITION

In the correctional world the standards set by policy makers and their day-to-day execution almost never coincide. Goals are described, but the roads to reach them are less easily charted. With graceful magnanimity and high purpose, Rule Six of the British Prison Commission prescribes: "The purpose of training and treatment of convicted prisoners shall be to establish in them the will to lead a good and useful life on discharge, and to fit them to do so" (1949).

Only an apologist could maintain that the mailbag shops and the coil-mattress renovation sheds, which are staples of British prison programs, are means consistent with these purposes. In every country there are similar contrasts between stated aims and actual means. The *Manual of Correctional Standards* (1959) [1] provides perhaps the most elaborate statement of aims and courageous prescription of means. But though these are standards to which most correctional administrations profess to adhere, examination of practice will uncover few institutions or agencies in which they are met. It would be wrong to draw invidious conclusions from this situation. The reasons for the cleavage between practice and prescription are not hard to find, and some of them will be studied in detail in this chapter. But the setting of standards spurs change, as the last two or three decades of correctional progress have shown. Throughout our correctional pilgrimage we encountered no ad-

---

[1] American Correctional Association, *A Manual of Correctional Standards* (New York: American Correctional Association, 1959).

ministrators who did not sincerely express their whole-hearted adherence to the standards, written or unwritten, of the prevailing correctional consensus. Not all their subordinates were as sure of the rightness of the aims or means; indeed there were few administrators who touched on their problems without frankly admitting difficulties in persuading personnel of the social truth and value of the new correctional philosophy.

A look at this philosophy and the uneasy balance of forces which it strikes accounts for the difficulties of its execution. The philosophy, as nearly as we can distill it from observations in eighteen countries, condenses into five postulates, taken literally by policy makers wherever we went.

Postulate 1: Offenders are social deviates; something is wrong with them.

Comment: We cannot generalize as to what is "wrong." In some cultures, notably in the United States, the notion is easily accepted that the offender is sick. By furthest contrast, in the Soviet Union, the offender learns that he cannot possibly be sick, but rather he is lacking in the moral education he needs for honest participation in a Socialist community. In the United States, the offender is likely to be an unfortunate person needing "treatment." In the Soviet Union he is, an unfortunate person needing opportunities to learn. Either way, something is wrong with the offender.

Postulate 2: Punishment exacted by the system is futile. Commitment to the system is punishment enough.

Comment: Wherever correctional practice has emerged from the age of legitimated sadism, this axiom has been accepted as self-evident. Whether the commitment is to prison or to probation, the punishment takes place in the court room where new conditions of existence are assigned. The aphorism of Sanford Bates, that offenders are sent to prison *as* punishment, not *for* punishment, is basic doctrine.[2] However, formidable elements of the general public are not in agreement; the enlightened principles of the new philosophy are still in jeopardy from the forces of darkness.

We were impressed, in this connection, with the aversion of correctional practitioners against the administration of any of the more obviously inhumane practices. In England, where corporal punishment is

---

[2] Sanford Bates, *Prisons and Beyond* (New York: MacMillan, 1936) p. 35.

perhaps a more lively issue than in any other Western country, its re-introduction is massively blocked by the unwillingness of any public agency, especially the Prison Commission, to administer it.[3] It is as though the correctional administrator, having shed the role of turnkey, finds his new role too attractive to return to old ways.

Postulate 3: During the period of commitment the correctional agency has an obligation to administer a regime which will equip offenders to "lead a good and useful life on discharge."

Comment: The regime consists of anything from analytic psycho-therapy to supervised athletics; it is purposefully related to an idea about change in attitudes or behavior. The obligation to treat implies an obligation to adopt a rationale for change. Though the rationales varied widely in sophistication, all administrators had one or more ready to hand. Few were tested in any way; there was general regret that neither method nor resources were available to evaluate and refine methods of treatment. Only in the Soviet Union, where a completed theoretical system is being applied, is the correctness of the treatment rationale considered certain. Data for conventional methods of analysis are not, however, made available to the foreign observer.

Postulate 4: Because the treatment required by the offender varies from individual to individual in accordance with what is "wrong" with each, the duration and circumstances of the commitment must also vary.

Comment: This principle is universally accepted, but opinions differ on how to apply it. Correctional thought is far from agreement as to who should prescribe treatment and when it should be prescribed. Concern for equity in sentencing and the state of public opinion heavily influences the nature of the treatment, whatever may have been prescribed.

Postulate 5: All correctional agencies have the obligation to maintain control over committed offenders.

Comment: Although obvious for correctional institutions, which must prevent escape, the obligation is not so clear-cut with the field agencies. But even if, as in England, the field agencies have been divested of all direct control requirements, many indirect obligations survive and are likely to continue to survive for a long time. The real nature of the relationship between probation officer and probationer cannot be evaded; whatever else goes on between them, control is the basic issue. Similarly, in the welfare schools of the four Scandinavian countries, though

---

[3] Advisory Committee on the Treatment of Offenders, *Corporal Punishment* (London: HMSO, 1960).

punishment is abjured and help is imaginatively proffered, control remains the essence of the relationship between the child and the school. The means of control may be more subtle than walls and surveillance — and in all observed institutions the direction of program was toward a parental quality of control — but, where necessary, walls, surveillance, and even physical isolation were made part of the control.

The obligation of the correctional apparatus to provide control of its clients is reflected in every phase of its operations. The probation officer may be an examplar of casework skill, but he still has his reports to the court to make. The chances are — in the United States at least — that he has a pair of handcuffs in his briefcase. The dilemma between control and change is at the bottom of the correctional muddle. It is often taken to be insoluble, and on that account many professionals are diverted from practice in the field. In Chapter V we have expressed our own optimisim about prospects for a creative resolution of the dilemma.

This series of postulates constitutes a correctional philosophy from which all sorts of applications flow. These postulates constitute a revolutionary change in the human race's notion of the obligations of the majority toward those who stray beyond the limits of its tolerance. Within much less than a century the administration of justice has shifted from its crude philosophy of individual and collective deterrence of criminals and crime. Throughout the world, those who administer the correctional apparatus assume control and change to be their proper task. We must credit this revolution to the educators and physicians who have seen crime as a problem to be solved rather than as a *casus belli* against those who prey upon their fellows. If the clergyman and the reformer put a floor under the depths of misery which the law could inflict, it remained for the social sciences to open doors through which the offender could emerge from the structure of misery altogether.

But, having congratulated civilization on the increasing disuses of barbarism as a means of combating barbarism, we must appraise the application of these changes. Though these postulates may be taken for granted by correctional leadership, though judges may espouse them and push for their implementation, practice falls dismally short of the humanitarian standards promulgated in model statutes and manuals, and the spirit of the rules and regulations governing official agencies. We can therefore define the standard practice of corrections as the *application* (*through the medium of the correctional apparatus*) *of individualized methods of change, under standardized means of control.*

The longer exploration to which we now proceed uncovers the old Adam lurking among the elegant concepts of the theorists and humanitarians. He no longer holds aloft the cat-o'-nine-tails, nor does he preside over a treadmill or a rock pile. But in the dual charge of chance and control it is the challenge of control which captures his imagination. He insists that offenders do not respond to absent treatment; probationers and inmates must be on hand to be changed. Between the ideas of the correctional theorists and their execution by uniformed personnel a many-faceted paradox is created. Though change is given verbal primacy by those who manage the correctional apparatus, their subordinates are absorbed in the issues of control. Here and there administrators concern themselves with the efficacy of treatment to the extent of heavy investments in research and demonstration. Probation agents, cottage parents, and correctional officers are trained in increasingly meticulous detail in every country we visited. The training of their supervisors is either taken for granted of left to convenience. Clearly there is no way to define standard practice without reference to the standards set. But we cannot fairly appraise the correctional system in terms of those standards nor in terms of the extent to which practice falls short of policy. It is only when we account for this gap, after having measured it, that we can generalize about the true state of corrections. If the future of corrections is to be wrested from the hands of time-servers and cynics we must discover why performance falls short and where new ideas are urgently needed. Standards have meaning only when they are met; when they are unreal, new standards will be established.

THE STRUCTURE OF CORRECTIONS:
CHANGELESS AND CHANGING

Whatever the changes in the philosophy and practice of corrections, they must be applied to massive old structures, not easily remodeled. Anyone touring the legacies of the Pennsylvania system which pervade the European correctional scene will know the magnitude of the task. To introduce group-influence methods in buildings designed to prevent the existence of groups requires a conviction sufficient to unsettle masonry and the mean spirits which have found sanctuary therein. The intricate skein of bureaucratic forms which make up the correctional apparatus discourages attempts to disentangle the irrational strands.

Just as the correctional task must be undertaken within the walls improvidently built by our ancestors, it must also be executed by staff and inmates living out roles and inured to relationships which have evolved over many decades. Some of these roles and relationships are essential to the survival of the correctional structure. Some are as witless as the fantasies of nineteenth-century prison architects. In a recent considera-tion of cultural evolution, the psychologist B. F. Skinner, points out:

The cultural inventor, even though relatively disinterested, has found it necessary to appeal for support to secular or divine authorities, supposedly inviolable philosophical premises, and even to military persuasion. Nothing of the sort has been needed for the greater part of physical technology. The wheel was not propagated by the sword or by promise of salvation — it made its own way. Cultural practices have survived or fallen only in part because of their effect on the strength of the group and those which have survived are usually burdened with unnecessary impedimenta. By associa-tion, the current designer is handicapped by the fact that men look behind any cultural invention for irrelevant, ingenuous, or threatening forces.[4]

What is there in the correctional apparatus which contributes to the strength of society? Can we identify the useless impediments which burden it and obstruct its effectiveness? If they can be identified, can they be jettisoned by a social order which may be attached to them from real, although irrational motives?

It is with institutions and agencies that the correctional apparatus must perform its tasks. It will not find other tools. The institution of con-finement will confine its captives, though its methods may be varied.

Basically, there is the model of the prison and the model of the field supervision agency. The former is found in any country with pretensions to contemporaneity. Probation and parole are less universal; cultural differences are more conspicuous. But this is the range of the means open to the correctional apparatus. They must be shaped to express a philosophy and to solve problems enmeshing human beings alone and in groups. The nature of the problem should shape the tools to solve it. But as in the penitentiary, the social order tries to solve today's correc-tional problems with yesterday's tools, too expensive to abandon as ob-solete, often too expensive even to modify. And some tools may have been shaped by a complete misunderstanding of the problem, such as an institution or an agency attempting to change its clientele through re-pression alone.

---

[4] B. F. Skinner, "The Design of Cultures," *Daedalus*, 90:3 (Summer, 1961), 544.

What has society made of that most ancient correctional tool, the prison? From the grim prototypes at Cherry Hill, Auburn, Dartmoor, and Fresnes, a prodigious variety has been generated. Nearly two centuries of evolution have been marked by two themes. First, the universal preoccupation with control for the sake of control and at any price and by whatever means. Second, there has been a flickering interest in humanitarianism, requiring that control methods approach the ethical standards of the general social order. The excesses which were licensed by the passing of control into the hands of the barbarous, the stupid, and the indifferent have thus elicited a fruitful conflict with the humanitarianism which is latent in every culture. Throughout this span of years, the questions which have collided in the minds of wardens and penologists have been: "How can I keep these unruly exiles in indefinite captivity?" and: "What are the conditions of life which I must provide for these prisoners to meet the ethical standards of the social order which has sent them to me?"

The structure of the correctional apparatus as it is found in every culture today has been shaped by these desperate questions. Crises have led to improvisations; the success of this device or the failure of that has led to a body of experience from which precedent for further improvisations could be drawn as the occasion arose. This accumulation of experience consists at its best of the reconciliation of the control and humanitarianism through the application of common sense. It has been common sense which has dictated the separation of the sexes, of the old from the young, of the first offender from the recidivist. It has been good common sense that economy, humanity, and control would all be served by the systematic classification of prisoners. Common sense has devised the expedient of probation as a means of removing from confinement inmates who could be as effectively and more economically controlled outside of prison. Through this reconciliation of control and ordinary kindness the primal congregate prison has been dispersed. This dispersion is the history of corrections. The women and children, the madmen and the imbeciles were removed from the merely vicious and consigned to institutions for their kinds alone. Later, the nuisances were removed, at least in principle, and placed on probation, leaving the menaces behind in prison. For the most part, the prison may gleam with devices of control but it remains a receptacle for the neutralization of the community's fear of the offender. How can it be made an instrument of planned change? Common sense will tell us that unless we can change the dangerous prisoners, we certainly should not release them. But it will take us no further. How to change the prisoner's behavior is the province of the behavioral sciences. In the fissions which have produced the juvenile institution and the probation agencies it has been possible for the behavioral scientist to make a beginning at developing systems for the planned change of some specific kinds of delinquents. Through applying these findings and these methods of extending knowledge to the entire range of the correctional apparatus, we may yet be able to organize its services to the advantage of each of its elements.

We begin with the present structure, fragmented as it is. There are three main divisions: the field-supervision agency (a term we adopt to embrace the function of after-care as well as probation), the juvenile training institution, and the adult prison. Though generally a division is maintained everywhere between the adult and the juvenile institution, this division is exceptional in the field service agencies.

What is the prevailing philosophy of each of these legatees of the common prison? To a degree which surprised us, the official leadership of each field in each of the visited countries expressed an identity of approach and idea. The five postulates advanced in the last section were accepted as self-evident in all of them. The correctional leaders of most countries are well acquainted with their counterparts in other countries. Perhaps the problems of crime and delinquency have characteristics which lead to inevitable solutions. For it is from the conjunction of the social expectations of the agency, the prevailing attitudes toward crime, and the state of our still scanty knowledge of ourselves and the springs of our behavior that we must assemble the materials from which we construct policy and practice. This conjunction may be more similar in the countries of the West than we might have expected. If the correctional apparatus constitutes an irrational equilibrium, as we believe to be true at present, then a finding that common features to the equilibrium exists throughout western society would reinforce the importance of confirming its nature and analysing its trend.

Correctional leadership speaks with increasing unanimity not only internationally but also concerning the three basic divisions of the correctional apparatus. Standards of practice and performance are not uniform, but the goals and the basic ideas of change are gaining general acceptance. Rehabilitation has for a long time been a hope in which few really had faith. Some used hopes in which they could not believe as instruments for obtaining compliance from their refractory charges. The sharpest illustration of this cynical process is reported by Cloward [5] in his account of the promise of restoration to duty held out to inmates of a military prison. Although the sharp definition of cause and effect is peculiar to the military situation because restoration is an actual transaction of record rather than a tacit attainment of status, we should not lose sight of the generations of officials who have blandly assured offenders that the key was in their hands to the gate through which they might return to accepted positions in society.

But cynicism seems to be giving way to the hope that rehabilitation may be realizable for more offenders than had been thought. Many influences have brought correctional leadership to this optimistic evaluation. For some, the observation that the mentally ill can be substantially helped has caused an infusion of optimism. For others, successes in their own field have made possible some hypotheses which they could hope to apply to other offenders. Still others have taken heart from the development of the social sciences to a level which made practical applications possible. Indeed, we might think of the current field of corrections as eagerly awaiting a new day. The returns are not in on a battery of inter-related experiments. Until they are, optimism is only a token of goodwill, a vast climatic improvement over the dour "realism" of the old-line correctional administrator.

It is easy enough to make altruistic statements about correctional principles. (It is difficult in these times to find a proponent of repression and punishment.) To make performance consistent with principle, however, is another matter. The social scientist formulating correctional policy must all too often execute his policy through inherited personnel. In addition to inspiring interviews with administrators of vision, our travels included encounters with old correctional journeymen, full of the spurious wisdom that flows from unexamined experience. They go about their admonitions, their investigations, their counts, and their records, persuaded that innovations are the afflictions of the young, that the more the system changes, the more it's the same, and that their bosses' speeches are either clever appeasements of the sentimental or (if they are really disaffected) conclusive demonstrations that the lead-

---

[5] Helen L. Witmer and Ruth Kotinsky (eds.), *New Perspectives for Research on Juvenile Delinquency*, U.S. Children's Bureau (Washington, D.C.: 1956).

ership is out of touch with reality. For them, corrections is a tough job of control, in which their hands are full with the required processes. We shall encounter them often throughout our report. We believe we can report some significant uses to which they can be put. But let us now proceed to the leadership and see what the journeymen have to put up with, and why.

THE FIELD AGENCY

Practice of corrections in the field is divisible into at least four parts: juvenile and adult probation; juvenile and adult after-care. Not all countries make all these divisions; a mild controversy simmers as to the merits of unifying services which rest on similarities of principle and practice. The issues at stake here revolve around the gaps between principles, as voiced by the theorists, and the limits of practice as described by those who are pushing doorbells, collecting facts, dictating reports, and trying to collect their thoughts sufficiently to be of some use to courts and clients.

We begin with the situation in the juvenile agencies, where the social directive is most clearly laid down. The establishment of the juvenile courts was enthusiastically greeted throughout the Western world during the early years of this century; and the ideas, sentiments, and practices which were set in motion are still proceeding in an evidently irreversible trend. Though the juvenile court and its counterparts in some countries where the very idea of a judicial process was abandoned (as in the four Scandinavian countries), were established to lift the blindfold of Justice in behalf of the young and immature, it is as though the blindfold, once lifted, never fell back in place. It is the juvenile field agency which has made possible the special orientation of the juvenile court. Because this orientation was so significant for the corrections as a whole, it is well to state its essence. Grünhut has stated it effectively:

. . . the orientation adopted involves three fundamental principles. First, the treatment — institutional or non-institutional — should be exclusively designed to pursue the juvenile's education and readjustment. Secondly, whether a particular measure is to be applied depends not on what the juvenile has done, but what is necessary and useful for him. Thirdly, even within a comprehensive system envisaged for all juveniles in need of social and educational treatment, the conception of criminal responsibility still obtains. Its scope and limits have been determined by law and this involves certain distinctions in the approach of the community to maladjusted children and juveniles.[6]

Without the establishment of a field service, the juvenile court's orientation would have remained pious and nominal. Though, as we shall see later, the field service provided to courts and authorities varies widely from country to country, and from village to metropolis, nevertheless lip service at least, and often muscle and devotion are given to the fundamental principles propounded in such statements as cited above. Atavists will plead in the correspondence columns of newspapers for a return to the birch and the woodshed and even for the observance of strict criminal responsibility for all children. Nevertheless, there is a solid acceptance by the official makers and administrators of policy that the traditional philosophy of the juvenile court must be inviolate. We encountered no exponents of an alternative, repressive orientation to supplant what has become an internationally accepted set of principles. But though the general outlines of the juvenile court's official emphasis on individualized treatment have remained unchanged for many decades, the demands of this approach on the capabilities of field services as provided have led to accommodations which are similar from country to country.

A significant example of such accommodations is contained in the comprehensive review of juvenile justice in California conducted by Shain and Burkhart in 1960. Though the objectives of juvenile probation as propounded by administrative, legislative, and judicial leadership were lofty, the means at hand were inadequate:

A study determined that the average juvenile caseload in the State was approximately 162 cases. Responses from individual probation officers responsible for supervising probationers were employed in arriving at this estimate. Information gathered in the commission's survey, based on estimates furnished by chief probation officers, suggests that there has been a slight reduction in caseloads. However, in many counties, probation caseloads are still at least two to three times as high as proposed by published standards of the California Youth Authority and the National Probation and Parole Association.[7]

---

[6] International Committee of the Howard League for Penal Reform, *Lawless Youth, A Challenge to the New Europe* (London: George Allen and Unwin, 1947), p. 22.

[7] I. J. Shain and W. R. Burkhart, *A Study of the Administration of Juvenile Justice in California* (Sacramento: 1960), p. 42.

The study showed further that the county with the lowest average caseload reported a figure of 70, that with the highest, 200.[8] The results of this allocation of work were what might be expected, though inconsistent with the stated goals of the juvenile court:

An attempt was made to determine the frequency with which juvenile probation officers personally contact their juvenile probationers. Probation officers in 16 of the 20 largest counties indicated that probationers are seen once a month while the remaining four indicated that contacts are made at less frequent intervals. In actuality, the size of the average caseload in these counties suggests that such supervisory visits do not take place as frequently as were reported. The more typical procedure is to contact a relatively small proportion of the caseload on a fairly frequent basis either because of further involvement in delinquent behavior or special interest in the child. . . . The survey data clearly reveal that in a 30-day period *most probationers receive less than one hour of casework per month.* For example, 10 of the 20 largest counties report that they spend 30 or less minutes per month with juvenile probationers.[9]

The authors conclude:

Observations of the level of casework and the degree to which these goals are attained in California's probation departments lead to discouraging conclusions. Probation personnel serving the juvenile courts of this State are supplying very little supervision and even less treatment. Only an insignificant proportion of probation cases receive intensive rehabilitative services. By and large, the services offered to juvenile probationers are minimal, superficial, and of dubious effectiveness. Several factors are responsible for this unsatisfactory situation. The level of skills necessary to render effective treatment is not universally available among probation officers; the small proportion who are trained and skilled are frequently thwarted by excessive caseloads and thereby are unable to render meaningful treatment services; and available treatment resources and placement facilities are in too short supply to provide the services required.[10]

The conclusion from the Shain and Burkhart study seems inescapable that regardless of the official principles of probation, its actual execution consists of whatever can be done by a modestly trained individual giving his attention to no less than seventy offenders per month,

---

[8] *Ibid.*, p. 43.
[9] *Ibid.*, pp. 43–44.
[10] *Ibid.*, p. 42.

allowing no more than an hour to each, and often a great deal less. It cannot be doubted that the allotted hour may be significant. Through the imposition and enforcement of limits, through his knowledge and use of community resources, through his accumulating experience in the constructive use of his time, the probation officer is in a position to make a powerful impact on his client. But the client must be in a position to benefit from this kind of service, and the probation officer must be able to afford it. In this conjunction of circumstances lie the limits of probation. The conjunction recurs again and again in field agency practice.

Shain and Burkhart were unable to arrive at a reliable evaluation of the effectiveness of these methods in terms of the subsequent delinquency of children on probation. In this respect, they were as baffled by methodology as their predecessors have been. A more conspicuous example of the difficulty of evaluating the results of probation is to be found in the Cambridge study published by Radzinowicz and associates,[11] which wrestled with the problems of defining success and tabulating it. But though crude data based on the simplest kinds of differentiations are conscientiously presented, the probation system of England was not equipped to account for different kinds of outcome in terms of the kinds of delinquents on probation and the kinds of treatment to which they were subjected. Perhaps more data might have been wrung from the official reports, but it would have added only to the demography of probation, not to an appraisal of its results. Methods of evaluation which relate a defined class of behavior problems to alternate methods of treatment and then to different kinds of outcome have yet to be elaborated by research technicians. With probation the problem is further confounded by the idiosyncrasies of individual court policies as to eligibility. Some courts restrict the award of probation to the sure successes; others make probation officers work adventurously. When the range of intake policies is so wide, comparisons of agencies will be meaningless as well as invidious.

Though the technical problems of evaluating probation have been elusive, we have heard no insistent demand from any quarter for their solution. The few studies of the subject that have been attempted or are under way seem to have been initiated as much on account of the inter-

---

[11] L. Radzinowicz (ed.), *The Results of Probation: A Report of the Cambridge Department of Criminal Science* (London: Macmillan, 1958).

est of the investigator as to satisfy the curiosity of the public, the court, or the probation officers. The absence of a demand for evaluation is a feature of the present system of probation which calls for an explanation — though, except for the difficulties of meeting the demand, none seems to have been attempted. But probation officers are busy, overworked and seldom skilled in research. A commitment to probation is cheaper than a stretch in a training school. Lastly, it may be inferred that the system succeeds simply because the community feels no special pains which may be attributed to it. It is scarcely justifiable to challenge a hard-working man whose services are an obvious economy to the community, especially when the community itself is unable to find that his work is ineffective.

The consequences of this failure to evaluate are reflected in two kinds of inertia. First, without systematic study of results it is impossible to improve the program. An example of this static quality of probation service is the universal uncertainty in the profession regarding the relationship of practice to results. This is sharply defined by Ralph England, reporting a study whose results were discouragingly like those described by Shain and Burkhart:

. . . a ratio of "contacts per month" was computed for each case by dividing the total number of contacts by the number of months actually spent under supervision. . . . The mean number of contacts was found to be .38 per month, or about one, every two and one-half months. . . . In view of the findings described above, it is difficult to reach any other conclusion than that the 490 probationers were not subjected to intensive, individualized social casework procedures, but were simply exposed to routine surveillance of slightly varying degrees of intensity. . . . Despite this apparent situation, only 17.7 percent of the probationers were found to have recidivated up to 1951. . . . [How] can the fact be accounted for that less than one probationer in every five is convicted of further offenses? One possible explanation is that the statistical observations referred to above are based on faulty manipulation; another is that the assumption is erroneous that the intensity and quality of the probation experience can in any way be assessed statistically; a third is that the probation theorists are mistaken, and that recidivism rates are not significantly associated with the quality of the probation to which offenders are subjected.[12]

---

[12] Ralph W. England, Jr., "What is Responsible for Satisfactory Probation and Post-Probation Outcome?" *Journal of Criminal Law, Criminology and Police Science*, 47:6 (March–April, 1957), 668–673.

If surveillance alone will achieve a success rate of more than 80 per cent, on what grounds can more sophisticated methods be introduced? Probation methods which actually introduced casework and concepts of planned change might make unnecessary many a term of institutional care. But we shall never know how many offenders can be kept out of institutions through improvement of practice until our studies are more systematic than they are now. Without a system of evaluation of results, we are not justified in crediting probation practice with results from any influence more refined than the process of intimidation through surveillance. We cannot even say how many probation successes were achieved *in spite of* the system rather than *because* of it. In turn, courts are not justified in assigning probation to offenders who cannot be safely controlled by such intimidation. An experienced American probation officer put it to us this way:

I like a slum caseload. You'll find that most experienced officers do. For one thing, you can cover everybody in a few blocks. For another, you don't have to deal with spoiled brats and neurotic mamas day in and day out. In the slums they're scared of you; they won't tell you much, but they know you know a lot about them — they don't know how much. I can cover 100 to maybe 130 cases that way. It's token supervision; I don't know how much good it does; I don't really know that it does any good.

It is obvious that the services offered to the community here are limited to surveillance. Though the officer had been thoroughly exposed to the in-service training program of his agency, and had indeed conducted some of it, his was the undifferentiated approach which makes virtually impossible even an analysis of the effectiveness of intimidation. Treatment does not enter into consideration as a realistic possibility, partly because it cannot be portioned out to the constituents of so large a caseload, partly because intimidation is easier. From the acceptance of these positions to an adherence to a model of probation as intimidation is only a short step. There is no rationale for intimidation by which practice improves. A program of investigation and supervisory contact will keep the officer convincingly busy. Neither the public nor the practitioner will reproach anyone but the probationer himself for the inadequacies of the system.

In the second form of inertia a more insidious process begins to invade the system. An excerpt from a valuable training manual will illustrate the preoccupation, with form at the expense of substance:

As a form of community treatment, probation can be defined as a means of protecting society by assisting individual offenders to make a more satisfactory adjustment to their environment. Adjustment can come about in two ways: (1) by integration and adjustment of the person; (2) by the relief of detrimental social pressures. The two are enmeshed.

To these ends, an understanding of the individual and his environment is necessary. This understanding must come from expert investigation. Without it, the court cannot make sound decisions and the probation process is stymied. The probation officer is charged by law with responsibility for these investigations. . . .

A probation officer is evaluated largely on the basis of his investigations and reports. He may be experienced, trained, and possessed of natural talent for his work, but if he does not communicate the results of his efforts, his work will be negated. He, himself, will be poorly regarded.[13]

None can question the importance of the well-communicated report nor the need for training probation officers in its preparation. But the probation officer who knows that his standing depends on the reputation of his reports will make sure that whatever else he does, his forms will be in order. The system will be likely to take greater pains to ensure that reports are improved, especially when made at the high pressures of an excessive caseload, than to examine the potentialities for the improvement of practice.

A second pattern of field-agency practice relies on the use of untrained volunteers. To varying degrees, this pattern is to be found in the Scandinavian countries and in the Netherlands. An enthusiastic but perceptive administrator of the system in Sweden, Sten Lilliehöök, Chief Probation Consultant of Stockholm, described the program to us. We draw on an extended discussion of Swedish probation as an example of the level of practice and type of problems occurring where the service provides for the predominant use of volunteers.

Lilliehöök sees as one of the strengths of the smaller Swedish communities the existence of a cadre of reliable and socially responsible business and professional people who are willing to assume probation responsibilities. Such people have the influence and initiative to act on the obvious environmental anxieties of probationers — the job, the housing, the debts. In the rapid communications circuit of the Swedish small town, a volunteer probation officer can keep thoroughly informed on the

---

[13] California Youth Authority, *A Guide for Court Investigations and Reports* (Sacramento: 1955), pp. 7–8.

activities of his client. Once such a relationship is under way, the professional probation staff in regional headquarters can ordinarily forget the case except for reminding the officers to send in their semiannual reports of progress. To maintain responsible channels, voluntary probation officers are paid 15 crowns a month (or $3) for each case supervised. Because this nominal fee is not intended to meet the value of the service rendered, the volunteers are discouraged from taking more cases than they can effectively supervise. People who volunteer for the money are excluded as soon as their motives are detected.

Probation officers are supervised by regional consultants. These consultants are responsible for week-end training courses, drawing on the resources of the Prison Department's in-service training program. The fairly recent development of such organized training has been followed by a considerable increase in the number of volunteers. Whether there is any connection is an unexamined but significant question.

The probation experience, when successful in any setting, is inconspicuous, and reasons for success are notoriously hard to assign. When the probationer fails, actions must be taken — sometimes immediate actions, sometimes tardy actions; and sometimes the action must be the resolution of an obstinate dilemma to which no good answer exists. In Sweden, much reliance is placed on the volunteer probation agent availing himself of expert help in a crisis. The expert help will be the regional consultant who may find that through his intervention as an additional environmental manipulator sufficient changes can be made to permit the original probation plan to continue. If the difficulties ahead are specially ominous, the consultant can arrange with the court for a one-week term of "probation detention." The probationer's uneasy course is interrupted; the entire situation is reviewed, and, Lilliehöök thinks, through a suspension of activity at critical times, the probationer can be diverted from a channel likely to lead him into further trouble. It was interesting to us to note that the facilities used for such detention are reserved for probationers only; the ordinary jails and the prison system are not used for these purposes.

Untrained but public-spirited lawyers, teachers, physicians, and businessmen are contriving with some official assistance to relate themselves usefully to fellow-citizens in deep trouble with the criminal law. The results are not tabulated; despite a highly developed electronics industry, Sweden has not yet applied the magic of the computer to

criminal statistics. Not even ordinary book-keeping methods are established by which the rate of recidivism can be used as a measure of success. Nevertheless, there are strains on the system which are forcing
modification, even though inertia may enable the basic structure to survive for a long time to come. We hope to make a case for such a survival;
the strength which the system draws from its pervasive roots in the life
of the community may nurture the development of a stronger superstructure of professional services. The strains seem to be met most
characteristically by the introduction of the professional administrator,
the psychologist, the social caseworker and by the dispersion of classes
of problems to special services. In this way, a grass-roots probation system is maturing slowly into an apparatus of diversified field services.

The first and most evident strain is occasioned by urbanization. It is
all very well in a cross-roads town in Dalecarlia or Värmland for a
schoolteacher or a grocer to supervise a young car thief or the rascally
scion of the community's leading problem family. But it is increasingly
clear that it will not do in Stockholm or Malmö. Out in the countryside,
the whole town can and will help the probation officer with information, at least, and maybe with constructive suggestions. But in the vast
housing developments of Sweden's great cities the transmission of information diminishes to an unreliable trickle. The businessman with an
office in downtown Stockholm and an apartment in a cooperative
apartment on the outskirts of the city will be hard put to it to find time
and occasion to see the miscreant for whom he agreed to furnish supervision. A telephone contact will be set up, supplemented by the occasional visit of the probationer to his supervisor's busy office. Even this
semblance of supervision is sometimes enough, Lilliehöök thinks, for
some kinds of uncomplicated cases where the awareness of a potential
figure of authority, however remote, is all that the situation needs. But
where mental illness or incapacity, alcoholism, or serious social problems are in.the delinquent situation, the need is felt for a trained and
fully committed probation officer who can keep in professional contact
with the client and his family, and who will be able to make necessary
referrals for other community services. Perhaps even the professional
probation officer cannot go much further, but this far the probation
service must go for this class of clients.

A second strain on the system is its responsibility for prison after-
care. Lilliehöök is keenly aware of a much more pressing level of responsibility for the released prisoner; he believes that no more than a

fourth of the parolees of Swedish prisons are appropriate for supervision by volunteer probation officers. Assignment to probation consultants has resulted in a reduction of the time available to the lay probation officers for consultation. Proposals have recently been submitted to the Prison Administration recommending the establishment of a special service for after-care within the prison system, to be staffed entirely by professional social workers.

The third strain on the system is the recruitment of volunteer officers. Difficulties in finding enough community pillars willing to prop up their most disreputable fellow citizens have taken increasing amounts of staff time. Some reliance has been placed on inviting probationers to nominate their own probation officer; within limits this idea is effective, but not every offender will have at the tip of his tongue the name of some reputable townsman who can be expected to give regular attention to the exasperating, time-consuming, and sometimes insoluble problems of the undeserving poor.

We have described the Swedish probation system at such length because it is not only typical of Continental probation practice in its use of lay volunteers but also in its step by step trend toward professionalization. We have noted the self-limiting characteristics of the American and English probation systems in which practice tends to be defined by what *can* be done by the probation officer. The potentialities seem to be limited to Investigations, Observation and Surveillance, Referrals, Employment placement, Advice, Crisis adjustment, and Report-writing. We do not doubt that often the basis for a casework relationship between the probationer and the officer is laid in the fleeting minutes allowed. But the standards of practice are established by time and numbers to be served, rather than the kinds of service required. In the Swedish system, a similar result is obtained by a different route. It is a system which is adequate to deliver the services listed above for some kinds of cases. Surprisingly, through its division between professional and lay arms, a second level of operation is at least made possible in which the difficulties of certain kinds of services are recognized as appropriate for the activity of a specially trained probation officer. In Chapters III and IV we shall consider the nature of such services. Here it is appropriate to mention the distinction as one which springs more directly to the eye in the comparatively unsophisticated Swedish system than in the more lavishly endowed English and American systems.

At the beginning of this chapter we referred to an irrational equilibrium in which a precarious and shifting balance is maintained between officially proclaimed objectives of rehabilitation and actual operations of control. As a figure of speech the irrational equilibrium will serve to remind us that we are balanced unreliably on an accommodation of an imperfect technique of behavior change to a system of control. We are not going to lay down as any consequence of our position that such an accommodation is impossible. Indeed, we believe that the opposite is true: that the problem of corrections today is nothing less than to make such an accommodation possible. But, to borrow Hannah Arendt's prodding phrase: "we must think what we are doing." [14] Whether in Sweden, or in the industrial north of England, or in the conflict-ridden streets of the new American slums, we must think of ways to differentiate, and ways to respond usefully to the differentiations which we have made. So long as probation is an activity by untrained officers carrying undifferentiated caseloads of a magnitude requiring an attention span to fifty and often well over two hundred reluctant clients, society is not entitled to more than "surveillance" or "token supervision." It will never know whether the efforts of the thousands of men and women of talent and goodwill who have engaged in this enterprise have been expended for any useful purpose.

The standard practice of probation is investigation and supervision, usually token but sometimes massive. Environmental manipulations occur, and it is not uncommon for creative relationships between officer and probationer to come about. We can easily find cases in which a direct connection can be traced between the officer's intervention and the client's successful outcome. We cannot produce a convincing technology which reliably guides us in making such connections. Under the circumstances, where probation officers pride themselves on their work, the pre-sentence investigations are usually stressed. This is the work which culminates in an official communication basic to a court decision. In the work of supervision the officer is anonymous. Neither his successes nor his failures are clear-cut. Within very broad limits, whatever he does is all right, and he can be excused for doing very little.

We have said nothing of the abuses which commonly vitiate the limited intervention in the offender's life, even as surveillance. Planless probation is easy to grant and as easy to conduct. The cynical use of the

---

[14] Hannah Arendt, *The Human Condition* (Chicago: University of Chicago Press, 1958), p. 5.

agency merely to collect fines and restitution debases the idea of probation. Too often the courts offer probation as a second, third, or fourth "chance" to breach a previously impregnable impasse. All these and still other abuses have been denounced from loftier rostrums than ours. They are defended only by casual improvisers, indifferent to standards but glib enough in the rationalization of expedients.[15]

Our strictures may seem harsh. They are addressed to the realities of probation rather than to its promise. Even at its present level of "supervision," its practice meets certain important social necessities. Whatever the specifics which are built into it, a system must exist to sort out those offenders who are to be controlled without confinement. Because of its indifference to matching standards and principles to the objectives of probation, society gets far less protection than it could and should have.

THE JUVENILE INSTITUTION

"I still think there has to be a better way to do all this. We haven't hit on the right answer yet." "By all this" was meant the institutional treatment of delinquents, and the sounder of this keynote was Heman Stark, Director of the California Youth Authority. His confession of uncertainty summed up half of the dilemma confronting him and fellow policy makers in this field today. The other half of the dilemma is the rising volume of delinquency in most industrial countries. Put together, the puzzle facing the judge, the theorist, and the policy maker is: "What should we do when we don't know for sure what to do, but nevertheless must do what we can for incessantly rising numbers of juvenile offenders?"

Going on with the dimensions of his dilemma, Stark told us: "I am opposed to many of the things that I'm forced to do. Just to keep even with what we're doing right now . . . we'll have to build a new institution every year for the next seventeen years, just to hold the line. That's a new institution for four hundred kids."

At the same time that buildings are erected and staff is recruited, California must find a program that works. It must hit on the right answer. Every year the number of minors arrested increases by thousands. Whether the rate of delinquency is increasing is a question we can side-

---

[15] For an impressive review of the abuses of probation, see Sanford Bates, "When is Probation Not Probation?" *Federal Probation*, XXIV:4 (December, 1960), 13–20.

step. The population explosion reverberates through the juvenile halls, the county camps, and the handsome new institutions of the Youth Authority. The reinforced concrete is freshly poured in most of them, expressing for many decades to come the best ideas, and the compromises of those best ideas in the interests of economy, about the treatment of youthful offenders. These ideas are effective with some, do no harm with others, and perhaps have delayed effects with still others. They do not avail to prevent the recidivism of perhaps half the children and youths committed.

What are these ideas?

It will be useful to say what they are not. Nowhere among the administration or staff did we find a self-confessed believer in the repression of the juvenile offender. Though spirits and confidence in treatment might be sorely tried, the day of the lock-step, the inmate cadet corps, the "duke," and the free use of the fire hose is gone. Practices survive which please no one. One superintendent of a considerately designed school for girl offenders took us to visit the basement room in which he had had to place a suicidal thirteen-year-old. Many things were wrong with what we were to be shown, he told us. The girl was too young for his institution. Her disturbance was so grave that she should have been in a hospital bed, but in his whole system no such bed existed. The basement room, which was all he could provide her, was dingy and usually very hot because of its proximity to the furnace. But no one could think of a better answer for this unhappy child than solitude in an uncomfortable cell. Two or three years from now, he hoped, the State would add a special treatment cottage which would give him facilities to see what could be done for girls like this. Meanwhile, all he could do with this particular girl was to hold her, to hope that with a psychiatrist's attention, his own genuine interest, and the patience of a tactfully watchful staff she would emerge from the basement and join one of the lively cottages.

In Denmark an enviable network of youth schools has been established by the Danish Ministry of Social Welfare. The objectives of the schools are so generalized that they include the social restoration of the entire range of children with problems, including those of delinquency. Much emphasis has been laid on the provision of comfortable, home-like surroundings for boys and girls in various kinds of trouble. Not only is the elegant Danish architecture applied to this problem, but a great deal of attention has been given to finding staff with warm, familiar attitudes and feelings. The headmaster of one such school told us: "Our boys have never had any experience of home life until they came to us; it is important that we give them as convincing an experience of home as we possibly can. We know we succeed because so many of them come to us in later years, long after they have left us, to tell us of a success or to ask our advice about a problem."

But even this thoughtfully organized chain of institutions has its weak link. Down a peaceful road on the east coast of Jutland we found a grim and battered collection of buildings known fearsomely throughout the land as the last stop before prison. A bluff former policeman, the superintendent, told us about his program and its problems. To him were sent the failures of the system, seventy rough young city boys of 17 to 20. Maybe a quarter of them might escape the suction of a further correctional career. For the rest, it was fourteen or fifteen months spent in vocational training under friendly but firm control — evidently pervaded with official pessimism. A tour of the institution took us through a pleasant enough cottage for prospective releases, an orderly but unmemorable dormitory, and shops for brickmakers, blacksmiths, carpenters, and painters. Finally we were taken to the closed unit, an old but stout cell block for fourteen. Here the refractory, the disturbed, and the overtly resistant were kept to "sit and think." Our genial guide became more careful. Each heavy green painted door was swiftly approached, unlocked and opened in one deft, rhythmical motion ending with the superintendent balanced on both feet and ready for anything. There followed a pleasant-sounding conversation, the superintendent's voice heavy but hearty, the lad's usually responsive to the humor of his official visitor. Obviously each lad was pleased to have his solitude interrupted. There would be few other interruptions. Meals would be served, and there would be some exercise provided. When he had sat and thought sufficiently, he would be moved to the open section of the institution to be placed in a dormitory. There he would accommodate himself to a raffish crew of peers, untidy in dress, alternately sullen and boisterous in manner, and each with good reason to know how little society thought of him. A staff of about thirty, including everybody from the superintendent to the cook, looked after them. Ruefully the superintendent described his plight as a commitment to control seventy of the most difficult youths in Denmark with whatever staff he could recruit with low wages and the prospect of hard and thankless work. For professional assistance he had an occasional visit from a psychiatrist who was required to see each boy at least once. He also had it firmly in mind that he was in a transition from the "authority system to the modern system." For him, this meant that the staff was no longer to tell boys what they must do. Somehow, with each of these ugly young customers a friendly relationship was to be developed. Maybe they would become less ugly; maybe, at least, they would negotiate this ineluctable episode with tranquillity, even though it could only be a prelude to other episodes of the same kind.

Back in Copenhagen, we took a reading on what we had seen. In a quiet professional office situated in a converted flat, we interviewed the coordinator of professional services of the Child Welfare Authority. Yes, he said, it was a terrible place, and the government had had a hard time to decide what to do with it. Its evil reputation had been built up over many decades; its very name struck fear into the hearts of the young throughout Denmark. Finally, the budget makers had been persuaded to allow its demolition. A new institution in another part of the country would be built to replace it. Meanwhile the anomaly of placing the operation of an institution for the most difficult boys in the system in the hands of a pleasant but untutored policeman had been recognized. Next month he would be replaced by a clinical psychologist who had done excellent work at one of the youth prisons. He would have a difficult job and he would have to perform it in the old monstrosity.

We did not have to look far in any country except the Soviet Union to find survivals and remnants of the bad old times in the institutional care of delinquent youth. (In the Soviet Union the samples seen were hardly enough to assure adequate representation.) The dilapidated old horrors still stand; sometimes remodeled, sometimes crumbling into welcome deseutude. The staffs which occupy such buildings often match them. Sometimes they have seen a welcome light in the middle of an uninspired and obscure career; the light has changed their entire way of doing things. Sometimes they are grumbling their way into unlamented superannuation.

The fervor with which the welcome light is welcomed is matched by its lack of validation. The light is the conviction that whatever the route by which a child found his way to a juvenile institution, another route can be found for his social restoration. Such a route should begin in a small specialized institution in which a professional staff will diagnose, prescribe, and treat. Diagnostic categories may not be as yet well defined, and their implications for treatment are unsettled. Treatment itself will consist of friendly, individualized custody in relatively small units. Psychiatric treatment will be directly available to some and indirectly mediated through consultation. Social casework with children and their families will be on hand to build and maintain the essential route back to the community. For younger children in particular, and ordinarily for all children, a program of remedial education will be available. For older children a selection, often elaborately wide, of apprenticeship training courses will be offered. Finally the whole program should not last very long, perhaps six to nine months in some places, fifteen to eighteen in others.

The journals, the literature, the national and international conferences have done their work well. No one familiar with the noisome practices of the reformatories and borstals of forty years ago, and less, can deprecate the solid achievement before us now. In all civilized countries, planners like those in Copenhagen are devising new buildings and scheduling the demolition of the architectural atrocities of the not very distant past.

But here again the correctional apparatus balances on an irrational equilibrium. A standard practice of institutional care for juvenile offenders still rests heavily on borrowings from psychiatry and social casework administered to poorly differentiated delinquents by staff members who are undertrained, poorly paid, and often ill supervised and ill organized. Massive issues in theory, administrative organization, and public ethics must be solved before we can break through the present ineffectiveness. Most youth correctional systems are making the best accommodations they can of the present public philosophy to the immense caseloads they must assume. The little crises are solved from day to day; the large crises are somehow surmounted and sometimes they are even foreseen. But the great issues get small attention, for there is so little attention to spare.

What are these great issues? As we see it, there are four: (1) diagnosis and differentiation; (2) treatment and training policy; (3) the identification of objectives; (4) the recruitment, organization, and training of staff. All four of these issues confront the rest of the correctional apparatus. They seem to be most sharply defined in the juvenile training schools. We shall discuss them briefly here, remembering that each issue, translated into different dilemmas, bestrides the fields of probation and parole and the development of the adult prison.

First, as to diagnosis and differentiation we find the conventional training school relying on the psychiatrist and his particular set of pigeonholes for sorting out the caseload. This schematization still has its uses for the treatment of mentally disturbed patients by psychiatrists. It even has some use for the correctional administrator; after all, it is an infallible justification for the banishment of unsettling inmates who can be described as psychotic. But not many adolescents can be committed to mental hospitals on that basis. Most of them are described as "character disorders," "sociopaths," or "psychopathic personalities." None of these epithets carry any specific implications for treatment. Indeed, to most psychiatrists they still suggest a condition about which nothing can be done. Most clients of the correctional apparatus in general and the training school in particular are described in these terms. No guidance for differentiation can be expected from this source. Nor have we been able to discern any prevalent wisdom about differentiation other than the proposition that, if possible, recidivists should be kept apart from first offenders. Even here, the conventional wisdom is not quite sure of itself. How far apart should these two groups be kept? How important is it that they should be kept apart? And what on earth do you do with the hard-core, bottom-of-the-barrel, bloody-minded, and hard-headed recidivist? How can anyone run an institution consisting of a population so selected and at the same time hope to attain the enlightened goals of the system? The issue resounds through the correctional apparatus; differentiations must be made, they must be practical, they must be related to the goal of social restoration.

Second, the institution day has to be filled up, as constructively as possible. But how, and why are some programs to be considered applicable to some inmates? Now only must the day be filled, but months, and sometimes years must be planned for this or that inmate. What makes us think that any of the possible permutations of program will be well invested in bringing about the social restoration of some specific youngster? We do not lack successes in the juvenile institutions but we have the utmost difficulty in accounting for them. How did cause become translated into effect? All institutional practitioners know what they must not or should not do. The evils of corporal punishment have been well dinned into their ears. Where repression survives it is in a carefully rationalized form, or its administrators do not feel it necessary to conceal more primitive measures from the public. But if we know what not to do, and even why not, we are on much less firm ground on what we should do. Guidance is vague. Until we gain confidence in the precepts which establish treatment methods, we shall scarcely make headway in constructively differentiating our charges.

Third, we are not clear about the realistic objectives of the juvenile institution. Eloquent creeds abound, as for example this paragraph from an official text:

> Most people working in the field of juvenile delinquency believe that a training school should provide re-educative treatment, geared to the development of a happy and healthy personality and a successful adjustment to society. They believe that through a new experience in community living the delinquent child can be led to realize that life holds many recognitions and satisfactions for him which he can achieve by following socially accepted modes of behavior.[16]

Maybe this philosophy succeeds with those who come to the school and leave, never to return; maybe it succeeds in some unassessable way with those who in later years become able to apply what was learned at a stage when socially acceptable behavior was socially impossible. But the success of the present training school in applying this philosophy to conflict-ridden young gangsters from the monstrous slums of our new megalopoles is so slim as to open the question whether such a lofty goal is applicable. Can a happy and healthy personality be developed in a training school? Can a child whose whole life experience has been marked by rejection or indifference be prepared for a successful adjustment to that part of society from which he came: his disordered home and the violent, threatening street on which he lived? Can he be prepared for a successful adjustment to any other home on any other street? If we want happiness and adjustment for children in juvenile institutions, what must we do to make what we want a realistic objective? If this is not a realistic objective for a considerable number of the children who come our way, can we think of a reasonable alternative? Perhaps training schools must exist for several different objectives designed for several different kinds of children.

Finally, we found throughout our travels a pervasive concern over the personnel problem. Not only training schools and their superin-

---

[16] U.S. Children's Bureau, *Institutions Serving Delinquent Children; Guides and Goals* (Washington, D.C.: 1957), p. 1.

tendents agonized over the difficulty of finding and training adequate people. Correctional agencies and institutions were blocked by the blank spaces on manning tables and the accommodation of the unsuitable employee to the otherwise unfillable job. The origins of this crisis are obvious; the solution is not in sight. Institutions organized to repress might be adequately served by housefathers with ready fists and content with the lowest civil-service salary. Often their wives would pitch in on the cooking, and, outside of a few teachers and perhaps some work foremen, no more staff was required to accomplish what little the community expected. The basic organizational structure of the training school survives, even though the personnel policies have changed. Still at the bottom of the ladder is the houseparent, whose predicament is well described by Bloch and Flynn,[17] drawing from the authoritative statement on the training of houseparents by Schulze and Mayer:[18]

As Schulze and Mayer, in the outstanding statement of the problem that has thus far appeared, succinctly put it, the houseparent's job in an institution for delinquents is composed of five major parts, all of which are equally important: (1) consistent provision of protection and control; (2) purposeful organization of everyday living; (3) creating a "we" feeling in the group; (4) development of a relationship to the individual; (5) integration of the houseparent's job with the various other services of the institution. But in reality very few houseparents meet the standards of personality and maturity required by the functions described . . . large numbers are beyond the age of fifty before joining the staff of a training school; frequently they represent failures to a certain extent rather than successes; and, if personal observations are valid, the wife in the married couple team is the dominant, even aggressive one, and the husband is on the indolent side, carrying out his "outside" assignments such as supervising work details, or marching groups of children from place to place, in a perfunctory, listless, uninterested fashion. With the coming of the eight hour day for state employees, the married couple as cottage parents has become something of a luxury. Nevertheless, even the underpaid, poorly equipped cottage parents employed are required in relatively large numbers under present conditions.

---

[17] Herbert A. Bloch and Frank T. Flynn, *Delinquency: The Juvenile Offender in America Today* (New York: Random House, 1956), pp. 433–434.

[18] Susanne Schulze and Morris Fritz Mayer, "Training for House-Parents and Kindred Personnel in Institutions for Juvenile Delinquents," in *Training Personnel for Work with Juvenile Delinquents*, U.S. Children's Bureau (Washington: 1954).

It may be, as Bloch and Flynn suggest, that the contact personnel in the training school do not really have to play the roles of parents; they may be coaches, counselors, teachers, or even big brothers and sisters. But they have to be trained. What is expected of them in the job description specified by Schulze and Mayer is talent and skill which cannot be found on the open labor market at any price. At the wages which training schools are paying and with the virtually nonexistent career opportunity which training schools have historically offered, only good luck and the uncanny motivation to serve can account for the adequate cottage staff of so many schools.

Personnel recruitment and training afflict juvenile institutions at other levels. Professional groups attach neither status nor interest to institutional services. Opportunity for advancement or economic success is notoriously insignificant. Juvenile institutions are often situated in remote places, far from colleague stimulation or the cultural opportunities of metropolitan life. This is as true in Sweden or England as it is in the United States. Far out on a winding secondary road in Sweden, hours from Stockholm, we discovered the Boys' Residential Center of Lövstå, a well-equipped school designated for seriously disturbed delinquents. No psychiatrist was on the staff, and none available, though all thought it would be good if so difficult a caseload could be presided over by a specialist in psychopathy. With teachers, social workers, trainees, and an able clinical psychologist to lead, a presentable milieu program had been constructed. But as we had so often seen, it was an improvisation from the materials at hand, not the convincingly planned treatment institution which the texts and the apparent necessities of the caseload called for.

Everywhere, the juvenile institution faces an exacting future in which it could easily be overwhelmed by the force of disorderly numbers. It has managed to arrive at a consensus that humanitarian methods are basic to everything else to be undertaken. Until this generation, society seems to have been able to afford an unselective intake policy; the training schools could accommodate whatever boys and girls the courts chose to send them, for whatever cause. For some time it has been apparent that this could no longer be so. From the first, the California Youth Authority has had the power to reject as untrainable juvenile offenders not deemed capable of benefiting from its program. Empirically it has established a program which seemed to do whatever was thought effective for the types of children most frequently referred. But as its director told us, "there has to be a better way." Through a rigorous examination of the four issues we have tried to state here, that way may be found.

THE PRISON

The literature of the prison is abundant and puzzled. For generations it has poured from the experiences of men and women who have served as staff and as captives. It has satisfied the appetite of the public for the theme of the Augean stables. Reformers and wardens have recounted horrifying abuses corrected in the face of apathy, cynicism, and outright sadism. Articulate former prisoners from the time of Oscar Wilde have returned to the public in what measure they could the abuse, the misery, and the sense of waste which they experienced in confinement. Of late, an impressive volume of scientific studies of the prison as a social organization has accumulated. The works of Clemmer,[19] Sykes,[20] Cressey,[21] Ohlin,[22] Klare,[23] Fox,[24] Galtung,[25] and Morris,[26] have described, hypothesized, analyzed, and speculated upon the forces at work in the prison. Some have managed to be dogmatic and clear; some have raised questions which seemed to need answers, but which had never before been raised; some have confessed ignorance and proclaimed a need for a vast amount of more research.

But it is a puzzled literature. The puzzle is in the dilemma which the prison has posed to society ever since those days in the early nineteenth century when it replaced the absurd severity of the gallows and the no longer available solution of banishment. If the condemned criminal is to be resurrected, if the exile is to return, what

---

[19] Donald Clemmer, *The Prison Community* (New York: Rinehart & Co., 1958).

[20] Gresham Sykes, *The Society of Captives* (Princeton: Princeton University Press, 1958).

[21] Donald R. Cressey, *The Prison: Studies in Institutional Organization and Change* (New York: Holt, Rinehart and Winston, 1961).

[22] Lloyd Ohlin, *Sociology and the Field of Corrections* (New York: Russell Sage Foundation, 1956).

[23] Hugh Klare, *The Anatomy of Prison* (London: Hutchinson, 1960).

[24] Lionel Fox, *The English Prison and Borstal Systems* (London: Routledge & Kegan Paul, 1952).

[25] John Galtung, *Fengsels Samfunnet* (Oslo: Universitetsforlaget, 1959); summarized in: "The Social Functions of a Prison," *Social Problems*, 6 (1958), 127–140.

[26] Terence Morris, *Pentonville: A Sociological Study of an English Prison* (London: Routledge & Kegan Paul, 1963).

magic must be conjured up to transform the outcast into a neighbor? And if no magic is at hand, is not the entire process a dreary and dangerous exercise in futility? Sir Alexander Paterson, the innovator of British corrections, has said: "You cannot train men for freedom in conditions of captivity." Minimum costs of humane care are high, no matter how easily satisfied we are that the care is humane, and they are going higher. Only in very recent years have we had a reliable inkling of the consequences of prison care in statistical appraisal of recidivism. Whatever interpretations are made of success rates, which vary between the 55 per cent success found in California parole statistics,[27] or the 60 per cent claimed in England,[28] there seems to be an arithmetical constant of failure which loudly echoes Paterson's paradox, and a corollary of futility which follows from it. Nor can the penologist safely comfort himself with the 50–60 per cent of his charges who have gone forth from his gates to sin no more. Sol Rubin [29] has suggested that no one knows how many of these successes would have flourished as well and with immensely less waste if they had been placed on probation or gone scot-free. No one knows, it is true, but the uneasy question compromises the confidence of the prison administrators and clinicians that successful outcome can be attributed to anything they do.

Nevertheless, what must be done, must be done well. We must confine, and we must confine humanely. Penal reform has traversed a tortuous route to reach the present levels of standard practice. In the United Nations *Standard Minimum Rules for the Treatment of Prisoners* [30] and in the *Manual of Correctional Standards* published by the American Correctional Association [31] a level has been reached to which at least surface compliance is generally accorded. An investigator still would not have to look far to discover deviations from the spirit of these standards, some of them mocking unmistakably the idealism implicit in the very concept of standards. But we are not

---

[27] California Department of Corrections, *California Prisoners, 1958 and 1959* (Sacramento: 1960), pp. 80–81.

[28] Board of Prison Commissioners, *Report of the Commissioners of Prisons for the Year 1960* (London: HMSO, 1961, Commd. 1467), pp. 186–195.

[29] Sol Rubin, *Crime and Juvenile Delinquency* (New York: Oceana Publications, 1961), p. 222.

[30] United Nations, *Standard Minimum Rules for the Treatment of Prisoners and Related Recommendations* (New York: 1958).

[31] Cited in n. 1.

concerned here to denounce the substandard in correctional practice. Rather, we must examine the orientation of the present prison practice. There are many places in the world where prison administrators have applied the standards enjoined on them by the official wisdom of their profession. What does the fruit of their zeal look like? The differences are interesting; the similarities are significant.

A large number of administrators have managed to acquire expensive new structures. Most, of course, are still making the best of prisons intended for the rigorous confinement of the offenders placed in their charge. In coping with the obsolescence of the physical plant, some have even been heard to apologize to their inmates for the malodorous austerity of their premises. But new or old, well or ill planned, the prison structure must now house not only staff and inmates but also a program. Through the medium of the program, some kind of magic must safely restore the offender to a community which rejected him because of the menace he afforded to peace and good order. The history of prison programs and their development has been described in many other places, as, for example, in the *Manual of Correctional Standards*,[32] or in Sir Lionel Fox's definitive account of the development of English prisons and borstals.[33] The actuality is our concern. This turns out to be a regime whose formal components are education, vocational training, industry, various kinds of group and individual psychotherapy, the appearance at least of religious observance, and a modicum of physical conditioning, sometimes disguised as recreation.

In our wandering, we became accustomed to a standard tour accorded to all fellow professionals. The usual philosophical statement of objectives would be offered in the superintendent's almost always impressive office. Whether we wanted to or not, we would be invited, as soon as the philosophical statement was complete, to accompany him on the rounds of the institution. This would typically begin with a turn through a shop for vocational training, in which we would see a small group of inmates busy with lathes or saws or trowels. We would be likely to be taken through a number of such shops before arriving in a large and redolent kitchen. Often the inmates working on the vast tubs and stoves would be described as apprentice cooks.

---

[32] *Ibid.*

[33] Lionel W. Fox, *English Prisons and Borstals* (London: Routledge and Kegan Paul, 1952).

From the kitchen we would be taken to an industrial plant, likely making furniture for government offices, but sometimes weaving cloth, making uniforms, or, in the Soviet Union, fully integrated with the production schedule for some needed item of consumer merchandise. Sometimes, especially in the Soviet Union, the inmates would be obviously working very hard; sometimes, as in England or in some American prisons, they would be working as desultorily as perfunctory supervision would allow. And sometimes, but only in the United States, they would not be working at all; they would be totally idle.

From the industrial sheds we would be taken to the education buildings, often laid out with lavish equipment and sometimes with appropriately small classes, much smaller than would be found in schools in the community. Enthusiastic teachers would recount special achievements or unusual programs they were pioneering. We shall not soon forget the tutor-organizer (that was his challenging title) at Dartmoor Prison, remote on a Devon hill, who delightedly reported his success in reaching dull and intractable prisoners through instruction in italic calligraphy. He was typical of an unquenchably enthusiastic breed.

Finally there would be a psychiatrist, a social worker, or a clinical psychologist who was responsible for diagnosis and treatment and, perhaps, for the professionalization of the institution. Nearly all would have a special attack on the mysterious problem of motivating the unmotivated. Some would be engaged in group therapy, some would be consultants to an administration uneasily aware that any innovation in an institution of total control might have unforeseen consequences. Some had found a safe refuge in cynicism, epigrammatically summing up their work as a hopeless task of salvaging the hopeless.

We would return to the quiet elegance of the superintendent's office, there to be asked what we thought of what we had seen, and given answers to our many questions. Almost certainly a reflective moment would arrive when the superintendent would ruminate about his plans for the future. They might call for a specially staffed treatment unit, a new building embodying a radically different concept in prison design, the organization of a special plan for increasing the effectiveness of contact between personnel and the inmates. In the Soviet Union, the corrective-labor-colony director whom we interviewed happily foresaw a day, not far in the future, when correctional institutions would no longer be needed and he could retire to his trade as a machinist.

Industry, vocational training, academic and remedial education, and group and individual psychotherapy: these are the ostensible supports of the program in the modern prison. It is a long way from the Big House of the sensational literature of the days before World War II. The treatment prison has emerged in structure and concept. It is a more humane place, despite some doubts on the part of those who have neither seen nor considered the consequences of the old prison of repression and punishment.[34] Society, through the staff, is offering its prisoners the means for social restoration. But the impression which observers, investigators, and the staff themselves gain is that the program is received with indifference, apathy, or, at best, as something to manipulate. The present state of affairs between program and prisoner was well described to us by the governor of one of England's most progressive institutions, the prison at Wakefield:

Wakefield has reached a distinct point in its development as an instrument of rehabilitation. We've removed from our closed prison the more obvious examples of repressive treatment and we've thrown open to the prisoners a great choice of activities. This is not a full permissive regime, but it is permissive insofar as the prisoners are able to make a choice. Of course there are well-defined limits beyond which a prisoner may not go. . . . The interesting thing is that although the emphasis in English prisons for the past ten years or so, has been in the relaxation of repressive measures so that prisoners may profit from the social experience of community living, this is neither so simple nor so grand as the statement might suggest.

Prisoners when they are given the choice to express themselves or to do things on their own will do some things to please you, and a great many things to cause the staff a great deal of concern. The staff concentrate their efforts on the repressive measures of the prison — which is a simple, understandable thing — and the prisoners react, just as strongly, against the activities of the officers. They achieve their satisfactions within a framework opposed to the administration.

But if you destroy this simple structure, something very much more complicated emerges. The prisoners have an easily understandable process for dealing with their resentments. But the officers are left in an uncertain condition, trying to exercise discretion, deciding each incident on its merits. I

---

[34] Cf. Sykes, *op. cit.* Sykes' contention that the pains of imprisonment in the modern prison are worse than those of corporal punishment is a sensational speculation which cannot possibly be demonstrated. Such hostile absurdities do nothing to make the valuable contributions of sociology more accessible to the prison administrator.

think this produces a maximum complexity for the staff in dealing with prisoners.

Clearly this statement describes a transition, the condition which administration, staff, and prisoners must cope with while the correctional apparatus moves from repression to "the therapeutic community," the aspiration which seemed to be on everyone's lips. In this transitional state, the prisoner, reinforced by the traditional values of the inmate community, sees the program as a device to punish, to increase control, to exploit. Observers will be able to duplicate this analysis for prisons wherever an effort has been made to effect major changes in process and program. It is the survival of a tradition of self-interested resistance to repression, when repression was all that the inmate could possibly encounter in a prison. The resistance now works against the self-interest of the inmate in release and social restoration. It is an irrational resistance, an irrational component in the precarious equilibrium of the contemporary prison.

Beyond this opposition between staff and inmate, in which, to quote the same governor "(the prison officer) is, by definition, an expression of social worth, while the prisoner, by the same definition, is almost a complete social opposite," there is the inadequacy of staff, in numbers and in training, to do the jobs for which they have been hired. An institution which in respect to structure and personnel is as intelligently equipped as any — and better equipped than most — is the relatively new Haney Correctional Institution of British Columbia. An interview with the supervising counselor elicited:

All casework services are centered in the Classification and Counseling Section which I head up. Now, the original establishment for this section was to be four trained caseworkers, and by *trained*, I mean social work trained, with Master's or at least Bachelor's degrees in social work or criminology or sociology or psychology, but it was made plain from the beginning that we would prefer to have trained social workers though we would take alternatives.

Even from the beginning we did not meet this standard. The original idea was to have four such people, taking the population as four hundred in the institution, and each of the counselors would have approximately one hundred cases nominally in his jurisdiction. He would offer casework service to some, and we would work out a *lay* counseling program as we called it. We never did get the complement of trained people. We increased our establishment from four to seven — we now have seven caseworkers — but we've lowered the standard of acceptability. We will take people now with a straight B.A. degree — no other training, no other experience at all. We have one M.A., but he specialized in the study of fisheries.

The organizational structure for casework works out in this way: we have eight living units in the building and we have cases assigned to counselors for casework service according to the unit. The counselor will make a selection, among his caseload, of those that he works with more intensively, those that he works with on a supportive level only, and the group that he probably doesn't see at all. . . .

I think we're going to have to do something about maintaining the original level of qualifications. We've dropped them because we were unable to get what we wanted. There's a terrific scarcity of the trained people that we want, and when you can't get what you want, you drop your sights and take the next best, or the next best to that.

He was describing a situation in which a provident correctional leadership had organized an institution for young adults in which the central figure is a counselor with a caseload of fifty. As in field services, the issue of caseload size in the institutions is as unsettled as the role of the caseworker. But it would be difficult to find an adult institution with comparably favorable professional conditions for the correctional counselor. Indeed, the intended level of service is higher than can be found in any but some of the most advanced juvenile institutions. But the service cannot be provided as planned simply because trained people of the caliber intended cannot be found to carry it out. Most institutions have made much feebler gestures. Caseloads of three and four hundred are not uncommon. A bookkeeping rationale is accepted; a parole officer with eighty cases spends a great amount of time in travel and looking for his parolees — time which in a prison can be given to actual contact with inmates who can be readily enough found. The assumption that any human mind can encompass the personalities and predicaments of three hundred people is too ludicrous to retain professional personnel. Institutions quite as contemporary in physical structure as Haney, and with even more public funds invested in capital outlay, find themselves offering professional services which are not *credible* to inmates or to fellow staff members.

What is a credible professional service? For the correctional institution, the model would seem to be that provided by the medical officer. Unless he is demonstrably incompetent (and this happens), the inmate will be willing to regard the physician as prepared to furnish a reliable medical service. If the inmate breaks his leg, contracts pneumonia, or fancies a headache, he does not question that the medical services provided will effect a remedy. Inmates accept the physician's credentials, though often enough the canard will be heard that he would hardly be working in a prison if he could support himself in private practice.

Similarly, in most prisons the competence of educational services is seldom in question. Teachers have established credentials, they work with established curricula, and they are generally equipped with the paraphernalia of their profession. It is not uncommon to encounter resistive, antisocial inmates who have been able to make constructive use of an institutional school program, simply because the service was credible.

The physician sets out to cure, the teacher sets out to teach. The caseworker and his colleagues, the psychiatrist and the psychologist, set out to influence and modify behavior, a vague mission. Few have been professionally prepared for the application of their skills to this special caseload. Most caseloads are so large that even with skill the most that can be hoped for is diagnosis and evaluation of release readiness, neither of which activities is directly related to the mission of change. When the professional people who are to provide these services are without relevant training, the services to the inmate are not credible. And when untrained persons are assigned responsibilities for diagnosis and evaluation, the lack of credibility reinforces hostile resistance to the program. There are forces and interests which contain this resistance in an equilibrium, even though its irrational character is nowhere more evident than in its incapacity to acquire the professional tools to do the job which needs to be done.

It is not only in casework services that the prison program lacks credibility. Sentences to hard labor in institutions where even ordinary labor at the pace of civil employment is impossible have long been the object of ironical comment. The damage incurred cannot be measured, but neither idleness nor inflated work are defensible as measures of resocialization. General principles governing the employment of prisoners, the objectives to be gained, and the obstacles to be expected have been well described in a recent British report.[35] The difficulties in finding suitable industrial projects, the traditional prison schedules which conflict with industrial requirements, the lack of skills

---

[35] *Report of the Committee on Prison Labour* (London: HMSO, 1961).

in inmate populations, and the frequent failure to meet quality and deadline requirements combine to present formidable obstacles to the development of a literal program of hard labor. The British investigators found inmate work weeks in British prisons running as low as sixteen hours. It is doubtful that many correctional institutions could be found, outside of frankly exploitative situations, in which the work week was forty hours, except perhaps in the Soviet Union. Regardless of whether the purpose of correctional industry is intended to be preparation for economic production after release or constructive participation in the economy while in prison, the essential feature, without which little purpose is served, is realism. Few inmates can survive after release at the pace of work to which they must accommodate while confined.

All administrators we encountered assigned the highest importance to the question of labor. The demoralization of inmates in institutions in which underemployment prevailed was helplessly described and deplored. Many administrators had worked out local solutions such as land reclamation, fire-fighting, the transcription of books into Braille, reforestation, and public works. But few were satisfied that the problem was even on the way to solution. Generally they still are forced into expedients to keep inmates busy. Schools are loaded with uninterested pupils. Vocational training programs were organized frankly as work substitutes; though expensive and unproductive they could more easily be installed than to overcome the united opposition of employers and unions. And where education could not be made to serve, work would be inflated through the assignment of two or more inmates to do the work of one.

It would be pleasant to report that an impressive solution to this problem had been found in the United States or in a Western country. It was in the Soviet Union, however, that we saw prison labor most impressively used. At the corrective labor colony of Kryukovo, not far from Moscow, we saw large, poorly housed but well-equipped factories turning out such consumer goods as kitchen utensils, fire helmets, automobile engine parts, and metal tools. The pace looked fast, and it was explained to us that the production norms were the same as for civilian industry. We noted that great attention was given to each man's performance in relation to the norm assigned. Charts were on display on bulletin boards, and it was evident in the shops that there was a sense of urgency that group norms should be exceeded. The joys of socialist labor, by which the reclamation of the miscreant Soviet citizen is expected, were at least attainable. There was a great deal of labor to be done. What punitive sanctions spurred on the slacker and inspired the incompetent may not have been clear. Group ridicule of sloth and eulogy of outstanding production was everywhere evident. These measures may have been effective in the peculiar context of Soviet society. But a positive incentive in the form of full pay at regular rates would be enough to account for a considerable difference from the stagnant pace of prison industries in most Western countries.

During a period when Communist influence was strong in the Finnish prison system, the labor-colony organization of corrections was introduced in that small but heavily alcoholic country. Production colonies were established for short-term prisoners so that they could work on airports, roads, and in the forests. Full wages are paid with appropriate deductions for family care, institutional services, and restitution, as indicated. All prisoners leave with accrued savings, and some are released with the largest stake in society which they have yet accumulated. The Communist political influence on the prison system of Finland has long since evaporated, but the labor-colony organization survives. It solved a problem with too many benefits to the community to be threatened by special interests. Even though Finland's economy fluctuates from boom to recession in rapid cycles, there has been no serious attack on a system which makes possible substantial contributions to the national welfare from those who would otherwise be liabilities.

In Sweden public opinion has not yet accepted an economic wage for prisoners. But in a full-employment economy there is little resistance for the policy of the Director-General of Prisons with respect to industries. "First we build a factory; then we build a prison to house the men who will work in the factory." A credible system of industry has resulted, and production levels are not far below comparable outside industries.

Finally, in the Netherlands we visited the justly famous van der Hoeven Kliniek for psychopathic offenders. Good sense prevails in all plans of this institution. Though its inmates are mostly very disturbed and often highly institutionalized criminals, a productive industrial shop has been established through contracting with private enterprises for the manufacture of various items which can be efficiently pro-

duced by a small pool of semiskilled and unskilled labor. Inmate committees are allowed considerable control of the working conditions
and rates of pay. Workers are paid at economic rates, and the level
of activity is impressive.

We cite these examples as indications of what can be done in institutions where a credible program of industrial employment is established. We cannot provide data in rubles, kroner, or guilders which
will prove the point to an accountant, nor are there data on reduced
rates of recidivism which will convince the statistician. But a comparison of the Big Yard at a typical American prison with its idleness,
its domino players, its little knot of weight lifters, all day and every
day occupied with the chatter and the time-killing devices which are
incidental only to an orderly life, to the purposefulness of a well-organized shop in some European prisons is convincing enough. Some
of the most obvious benefits of life are the least susceptible to rigorous scientific analysis. People of good sense and generosity sometimes have to rely on their instincts.

The program of the standard Western prison consists of therapy,
education, vocational training and industry. It is an irrational program
in its execution, though reasonable in conception. Those who administer it are accustomed to accommodating to obstacles and adjusting
to faulty implementation. The achievements promised in the original
conception of such programs can hardly be accomplished until impatience takes the place of accommodation. Common sense and a concern for efficiency will some day bring the promise of the standard
prison closer to realization.

BUILDING FOR THE CENTURIES

Unreason prevails in the very structure of the prison. Most were
designed in the first place for punishment alone. The design of better
prisons is hampered by the inexperience of architects. The instructions
they receive from their clients are not often illuminated by the lessons of experience or by inferences from the social sciences. Instead,
the design is a compromise between tradition and good sense. A legacy of enormous structures such as Jackson, Joliet, Auburn, and San
Quentin has been left to the present generation of prison administrators by their insensitive predecessors. In England and other European
countries the sanctimonious barbarism of the Pennsylvania system of
silence and solitude has been built into the bricks. It is possible to
keep a semblance of orderly operations going in such places. The ex-

perience of running them confirms legislators, treasury officials, and architects in the feasibility of a compromise between a prison monster with two to six thousand inmates and an institution of reasonable size. The compromise is specific in the *Manual of Correctional Standards:*

It has been held that the maximum population for a prison for adults should not exceed 1,200, and some say should be as small as 500. Any institutional operating as a single unit becomes increasingly inefficient and unsafe as its population exceeds 1,200. No one has ever offered any serious disagreement with these figures, except that many complain that the 1,200 figure is, perhaps, too large. . . .

Ideally, from the standpoint of safety, segregation, and a rehabilitative program, it's probable that the best results could be obtained, other things being equal, if prisoners were handled in groups not exceeding four hundred. It seems rather obvious that the taxpayers are not going to authorize the scrapping of hundreds of millions of dollars worth of existing prison plants, and equally obvious that the high per capita cost of operating small units of four hundred would not be supported with adequate legislative appropriations.

Therefore, it would appear that the correctional administrator is faced with a dilemma. His only practical hope is in compromise. What form shall this compromise take? Shall he attempt to insist upon institutions of 1,000 to 1,200, knowing that inevitably the time will come when attempts will be made to enlarge them; and if not to enlarge them to overcrowd them? [36]

The key words in this rationale seem to be *inefficient* and *unsafe*. They come from the vocabulary of control. It is a relevant vocabulary for the prison, and the considerations which are embedded in it are essential to planning and operations. This is the language in which the accumulated wisdom of generations of wardens, turnkeys, and yard captains is expressed. To this wisdom the recent recruits from the professions have accommodated themselves, having no reasonable grounds for difference. But building goes on, with principles like those quoted providing the basis for vast public expenditures. The compromise on the critical figure of 1,200 is further compromised through an ingenious plan developed in California:

At the California State Prison at Soledad, a 1,200 inmate institution was built adjoining an existing facility of 1,500 capacity. The new 1,200 inmate institution is divided physically, functionally, and organizationally into two 600-man units. Each 600-man unit is split into two 300-man housing units,

---

[36] *Manual*, pp. 199–200.

further divided into six 50-man living units. The 50-man units are the basic treatment grounds around which the treatment program is planned.[37]

Neither the Manual nor other references provides us with a rationale other than expediency and the impressions accumulated from experience to support these extremely expensive decisions. Indeed, in the present state of our knowledge, it is hard to see what other decisions could have been made. Prisons, which are needed to accommodate prisoners who must be housed, cannot wait for an analysis of the problem of the relationship between size of unit, effectiveness of treatment, and degree of control. But the urgency of the problem does not discharge the correctional planner from the responsibility for an analysis of the problem. The warden of a very new and costly institution told us:

As far as the cost of construction goes, I think we made a mistake when we built an expensive, concrete institution. I don't see any reason why we can't use more temporary types of construction for living units. . . . If we want to experiment, we try something — we've had it for five years and we don't like it; well, we've got our use out of the initial investment, and let's go ahead and put up something a little different, something that is an improvement by experience. . . . We lose all our mobility by building these bastilles. The bastilles may no longer have actual bars — maybe they've got security sash, but nevertheless they're darned hard to get rid of, and we're stuck with them for years and years and years. I like to think that corrections is developing fast enough so that what we're satisfied with today, we won't be satisfied with ten years from now.

Not all countries are forced by economy and floods of commitments to resort to the expedients which American prison planners have had to adopt. Approaches to the problem in England and in Sweden have proceeded from task-oriented hypotheses, from which some compromises are allowed to propitiate the fiscal interests. Until American prisons proceed from such hypotheses to the compromises which inevitably will be made, hope for the rationalization of the penal system is not justified.

PUNISHMENTS TO FIT CRIMINALS

The indeterminate sentence was introduced as a feature of American and some Continental correctional systems as a device to relate

---

[37] *Ibid.*, p. 200.

the length of confinement to the problem to be solved. Somehow, we have been aware for many generations that punishments must fit criminals. This object has never been reached. The time served *is* the punishment. When practical penologists say that prisoners are sent to prison *as* punishment rather than *for* punishment, they are skirting the reality that the punishment occurs day by day and hour by hour; it does not cease with the clang of the reception door in the sallyport. It goes on with differing degrees of severity with differing inmates, but the passage of time punishes, and changes as it punishes. How long it goes on is of overwhelming importance. A system for rationally deciding the length of term in advance has never been devised. In England and some Continental countries it has been impossible to divest the sentencing function from the courts. Essentially the punishment is fitted to the crime by the judge, and minor adjustments, usually in favor of the criminal, are made by the prison administration through the remission of time for good behavior. Some judges are to some extent guided by presentence investigations, but these are never more than an optional source of information.

To a considerable extent, American courts have been removed from the complex and social considerations of sentencing. In the United States the parole boards and commissions have been assigned a share in the sentencing process which determines the punishment on the basis of an appraisal of the success of treatment adjusted to an impression of the tolerance of the community. Both considerations are subjective and based on assumptions which derive little from theory or principle. Generally the decisions are made by laymen, sometimes assisted by experts and staff. The net effect is to reduce the credibility of treatment. Gains from treatment are hard enough to assess without the interference of the prospect of release as a secondary gain. Where treatment achieves a gain, but no release, the confidence of both inmate and clinician will suffer. The situation is parallel to that described by Cloward [38] in his studies of military prisons in which the officially promised objective of restoration to duty is not honored. A climate of accommodation and resistance rather than of treatment prevails. If parole boards accord insufficient credit to treatment and do not base release decisions systematically on its results, the treatment

---

[38] Witmer and Kotinsky, *op. cit.*

process will lack credibility. Our concern here is to record the present situation as one of the most seriously irrational elements of American prison administration. Its consequences in the creation of tension, alienation, and manipulation of services for secondary gains have never been adequately studied. It is a reasonable hypothesis, however, that the indeterminate sentence as at present administered not only contributes to the great length of American sentences but also to the essentially antitherapeutic culture which prevails despite the increase of services.[39]

In the foregoing appraisal of adult confinement we have touched on only a few of the irrational elements which confound our objectives of change and control. Some of these elements are remediable with the knowledge and skills which we have. Leadership insisting on conditions of employment in which realistic work can be done by professional workers can make possible a credible treatment service. Prison industries can be installed if the public is led to an appreciation of their importance. For these improvements, at least, prisons can be made ready as soon as the public will agree to the cost and the implied changes in values. But no one really knows what the size of a housing unit or a living unit in this or that kind of prison should be. Until research and analysis produce answers to this insufficiently asked question, no one can possibly know. Similarly, no one is going to find out much more optimum terms until release policies are much more rigorously studied. Study of treatment method and its relationship to the realities of control and the effects of punishment is only beginning in such imperfect research designs as the Highfields Project[40] of the applications of the Mannheim-Wilkins prediction methods in England.[41] But until these and many more such designs have been applied and have produced operational results, our prison systems will rest on precariously irrational foundations.

---

[39] For an impressive analysis of the relationship between indeterminate sentence laws and length of terms served, see Sol Rubin, *op. cit.*, pp. 121–144.

[40] Herbert Ashley Weeks, *Youthful Offenders at Highfields* (Ann Arbor: University of Michigan Press, 1959); Lloyd W. McCorkle, Albert Elias, and F. Lovell Bixby, *The Highfields Story* (New York: Hoff, 1958).

[41] Hermann Mannheim and Leslie T. Wilkins, *Prediction Methods in Relation to Borstal Training* (London: HMSO, 1955).

CONCLUSIONS

It must be repeated that the word "irrationality" in describing the correctional apparatus is not used here in a maligning sense. Thousands of sincere and professional workers, including ourselves, are committed to careers in the discouraging work of corrections. We do what we can with the means at hand, hoping for the best and always fearing the worst. It is an equilibrium we maintain, whether in a probation office, a county jail, a training school, or a prison. Apathy surrounds us from the outside and the inside. What little change for the better occurs is almost invariably generated from the inside.

We accommodate to an equilibrium which balances an endless series of personal dilemmas presented by the offenders with whom we deal. These dilemmas can be traced back to the great internal conflicts of standard correctional practice reflecting in turn the conflicted values of the social order around it. This is the place in which these conflicts can be summarized; we hope that support for their existence is sufficiently explicit in this chapter.

The Conflict of Control and Change. — If the role of the prison staff is to control ultimately through force, how can the permissiveness and the individualization required for change be safely introduced? The resolution of standard practice is in favor of control — control through surveillance by the field agency, and control through the traditional limiting characteristics of the total institution in both juvenile and adult institutions.

The Conflict of Objectives and Capabilities — There is little disagreement on the official goals of correction, but the capabilities of the apparatus to reach them are restricted by ignorance. We do not know what we must know in order to perform the tasks which we have to do. Research is unevenly but with increased momentum pushing back the frontier. The practice of control is rooted in tradition and unexamined doctrine. It is only incidentally related to propositions developed from scientific method. Traditional methods of control cannot be supplanted until validated theory supports a change. Similarly, the methods of planned change and therapy are only moderately reliable in the field of conventional psychiatry. For the clients of the correctional apparatus we cannot yet point to a procedure which can be reliably applied to any group in any typology yet conceptualized.

The Conflict of Standard and Actual Practice. — We discussed the assumptions of standard practice as found in manuals and other official statements; and we examined the framework of the three elements of the correctional apparatus in some relatively advanced communities. The gap between assumptions and the means provided is so wide that the question arises whether assumptions are meant to be acted upon. They are assumptions which have been the sources of correctional goals for generations. The Declaration of Principles of the American Prison Association in 1870 only brought together postulates about humanity and human nature which had inspired reformers and enlightened penologists for many previous generations. As principles to affirm they are comforting to the social order in general and specially to those of us who must work within the field. As guides to action they are impeded by the same obstacles which block the practical application of any great ethical system. Money is lacking, and the lack is eloquently bewailed. Even more evident is the lack of goodwill and the irrationality which is born of ill-will. Concern and care for the thieving, violent, and mendacious men and women who are our clients is difficult to engender and even more difficult to sustain. It is much easier, much less bruising to construct and justify systems which will do justice and protect the public than to provide for change and to create systems and communities which facilitate change.

The Conflict of Tradition and Reason. — Resistance to organizational change in any field of group activity is always in part rooted in tradition and custom. Tradition and custom are particularly influential in correctional services. Methods and procedures are sometimes the fruits of hard-won resolutions of long forgotten crises; sometimes they are meaningless rites installed on a caprice. Whatever the reason, they are known and understood — they may not be very effective, but they fit into a system which holds together. Some methods and procedures have to do with the protection of staff, inmates, and the community at large from obvious hazards. It is no light matter to remove the baton from the prison officer or the gun tower from the wall. Equally and even more effective controls may be thought of but confidence in reason will be superseded by the weight of tradition until reason is overwhelmingly reinforced by experimental evidence. Under the circumstances, such evidence is rarely acquired in reinforcing volume.

With these conflicts pervading its structure, the correctional apparatus is in uneasy and irrational equilibrium. Where it is under the pressure of numbers, as in the Anglo-Saxon countries and as in Sweden, changes occur because they are required by circumstance. In the administrative and official climate of the times, organizational change tends to be guided by recourse to analysis and the rule of reason. The consequence has been a considerable amount of conceptualization, experimentation, and re-formulation of principles. The next chapter will examine these consequences as the basis for a rational organization of correctional services.

The present equilibrium *processes* its hapless clientele. A ponderous mechanism receives the offender, collects relevant and irrelevant information, tabulates data, maintains activity, and releases him. Some offenders are the better for the experience, some have at least suffered no harm, and some are incomparably the worse. To contain this motley segment of humanity is achievement enough for some; not to increase criminality is the goal of others. To achieve the favorable modification of the behavior of as many offenders as possible is the rational goal which emerges before us and which encompasses the lesser objectives.

III

MASTER CORRECTIONAL
PATTERNS

Although the correctional apparatus everywhere rests on a precarious balance of reason and unreason, the components differ widely. To sense these differences, we have only to compare the grimy walls and inimitable odors of an English prison with the brightly painted new pavilions in which Sweden confines its felons. Or, to cross the Iron Curtain, walk through the austere but busy factories in which Soviet offenders feverishly work to achieve their work norms and reflect ruefully on the contrast with the domino tables and the Big Yards of American prisons in which inmates doze their time away, occasionally interrupted for group therapy.

These contrasts reveal more than relative economic prosperity and labor shortages or surpluses. This chapter examines some of the basic national patterns affecting the development of correctional practice. It is no accident that the therapeutic-community idea, for example, has such great appeal in Anglo-Saxon correctional practice, even though its application is poorly formulated. The heavy stress on realistic work experience supported by peer-group controls in the Soviet corrective labor colonies is directly related to Communist life. Correctional practice is not entirely determined by the culture in which it takes form. Ideas cross national boundaries and flourish astonishingly well on alien soils. Nevertheless, national patterns in bureaucratic organization, in morality, in crime, and in many other aspects of community and individual life deeply affect the peculiar structures of the correctional apparatus.

UNITED STATES

It is not too harsh to describe the dominant correctional pattern in the United States as an impersonal monster. Its critics see the monster as fit only to intimidate, to humiliate, to maim, and to disable its hapless clients. Readers of the almost classic studies of the prison community written by Clemmer, Sykes, and Cressey can discern the core of the apparatus in the fearful outlines of the adult prison. From the structure described and its implications, the pattern for probation, parole, and the juvenile institutions can be inferred.

A bleak picture! The correctional client is plunged from court into a foggy realm in which no one knows what he is doing or why, in which corruption inevitably flourishes as a consequence of the natural order of events, and well-meant "treatment" is transformed into punishment more severe than the pains of flogging.[1] A seemingly rigorous sociological analysis leads, as from day to night, to a conclusion of futility and despair. The analyst allows few loopholes for the intrusion of hope or purpose.

To us, this analysis seems incomplete and premature. Its complement of validated propositions is meager and the territory left unexplored is vast: Empirical studies of the prevalent correctional systems are scanty. The data seldom are organized for comparison or replication. The apparently inevitable progression of futility is based on simple studies of strictly custodial institutions. The wide variety of mutations concocted by American ingenuity and muddle-headedness has not been described or accounted for. Within this range from purpose to aimlessness nothing has yet been shown to be inevitable, despite the prevalent sociological pessimism.

The development of the American correctional apparatus is the process of narrowing specialization of services. Obviously unsuited to all offenders, the prison's function has been narrowed down to the containment of adult felons. Probation, parole, and juvenile services have been improvised and refined to meet requirements more economically, more humanely, and more therapeutically than a congregate facility for the confinement of all offenders could possibly do. The intentions behind this continuing history of correctional specialization have been generally humanitarian. In the second chapter we have commented

---

[1] Gresham Sykes, *The Society of Captives* (Princeton: Princeton University Press, 1958).

on the gap between intention and practice. Here we must account for the gap.

In looking at the entire American system of corrections, some common factors stand out. From state to state and community to community similarities in the quality of practice recur. If these similarities are examined, we may infer some generalizations about the determinants of the prison scene.

We are conscious of the dangers of the task we now undertake. In discussing any feature of American culture, the similarities are easy to note. The range of regional adaptations of a common cultural theme is wide, hard to account for, and hard to describe significantly. Conformity is a national worry; whether or not it is desirable in the administration of criminal justice, it certainly has not been attained. Therefore, in listing the common patterns of American correctional practice, we must warn that we fully recognize that neither space nor method is available for all the shades of emphasis that exist. We are here only laying the groundwork for the description of correctional advance as we have seen it in this country.

RETRIBUTION

Basic to the operation of any correctional system is the expectation of the community which supports it. Essentially, this expectation is written into the penal law. American criminal law has acquired a reputation polemically described by Weihofen [2] as the "most ferocious" in the world. However true this may be, and certainly there are some European competitors for this superlative, it is essential to understand that the administration of criminal justice in the United States rests firmly on the principle of retribution, buttressed by compatible considerations of deterrence. Though the indeterminate sentence is at least partly justified by the intention to individualize the penalty in accordance with response to the correctional program, Cressey has rightly emphasized [3] that individualized treatment cannot be fully reconciled with equity in the administration of justice. The legislature, judges, juries, and parole boards still fix terms in accordance with an estimate of the relative magnitude of the crime. This concept rests on

---

[2] Henry Weihofen, *The Urge to Punish* (New York: Farrar, Straus, and Cudahy, 1956), p. 148.

[3] Donald R. Cressey, "The Nature and Effectiveness of Correctional Techniques," *Law and Contemporary Problems*, 23 (1958), 754–771.

the widely accepted, if irrational, notion that it is possible to establish a system by which the relative gravity of offenses can be scaled in money or in lengths of terms of confinement or probation.

We do not wish to add here to the literature of dispute about the ethics of retribution. Retribution exists; it is an essential determinant of correctional practice. Humanitarian reforms may temper its acerbities. Enlightenment from the social sciences constantly increases our knowledge of the possibilities of combining retribution with rehabilitative treatment. Eventually we may become so proficient in changing human behavior that we can confidently undertake a treatment-oriented overhaul of the structure of criminal justice. Such a revision of the terms of justice is not now possible, as witness the quality and constituent elements of the discourse about the Durham decision,[4] which takes only a few short steps in this direction. The ethical balance of American society is grounded on the expectation that wrongdoers must be treated as responsible. They must pay for the wrongs they do; the collector is the correctional apparatus.

If the consequence of conviction of crime is treatment, then control must be justified only as a means of facilitating exactly the right amount of treatment. But except for the defendant allowed to plead to diminished responsibility on account of mental disturbance, the duration of social control is not basically related to the requirements of any kind of treatment theory. Actually, there has been little or no overt movement away from the retributivist principle of justice for adults in Anglo-Saxon societies since the introduction of the M'Naghten rule. There has been an improvised accommodation of treatment to retribution for the subjects of retributivist justice.[5] Whatever patterns of treatment are provided for in correctional advance, they must be consistent with the socially prescribed requirements of retribution. Again and again we were told by correctional administrators that in projecting future improvement of the correctional system, they had to be careful that they did not "get too far ahead of the general public." They meant that treatment must be seen by the community as consistent with just retribution.

---

[4] *Durham* vs. *United States*, 214 F. 2d 862 (1959). See also Weihofen, *op. cit.*, pp. 132–135.

[5] For an excellent recent analysis of the issues of retribution and rehabilitation, see K. G. Armstrong, "The Retributivist Hits Back," *Mind*, LXX:280 (October 1961), 471–490. Though Armstrong is concerned to show the positive ethical value of retributivist justice, a rigorous analysis of the implications of deterrent and "reformatory" justice is included.

For juvenile offenders, the pattern is less clear. In most American communities correctional practice is supposed to be rehabilitative for juveniles. It is seldom so apprehended by the juvenile offenders themselves. This is small wonder, for though much specialization is attempted, neither the court procedures nor the consequences in confinement and control are significantly dissimilar from those used for adult offenders. It is also at least possible that for most juveniles as for most adults the drive for status as independent moral agents survives strongly enough to dictate a preference for the implications of retribution than for the dependency which ensues from a position as a patient under treatment. However this may be, though the intent of the whole system of criminal justice may be clear that control is for rehabilitation only, the operations of very few juvenile institutions in America exclude overtly retributive influences. A teenage ward of the California Youth Authority at its superbly staffed and equipped new Youth Training School at Ontario said:

My parole officer was very good to me. . . . I guess I kind of let him down. Just before I got picked up I was in his office talking to him and he felt sure I could make it now, that I was mature enough to know what I was doing. And when I got picked up my mother told me that he didn't even believe I was in jail until he came down to see me; didn't think this would happen any more. And I let him down and my family down on this, and, like I say, it was my own fault; I can't blame anyone. I wish they would have given me an opportunity instead of bringing me back to the Youth Authority.

A treatment relationship is sketched in for us here, but it is accommodated to the necessities of retribution which "they" impose and which the boy accepts, however regretfully. No judgment is possible on whether this is the way it should be; our point is that *this is how it is.*

CONTROL

If crime must be paid for, the payment must be assured and verified. Once identified as a correctional client, the offender must be controlled until officially restored as a participating member of society. A variety of reasons prescribe control. It is the prime consideration in institutions. Its equivalent significance as a dimension of probation and parole establish control as the common denominator of whatever else may happen in corrections. To reconcile humanitarian and rehabilitative activities to the requirements of control is the first order of business in any kind of correctional planning.

In no other country we visited is control so elaborately provided for as in the United States. Prison walls are guarded by officers armed with rifles. Not any other country, except the Soviet Union and West Germany carries the requirement of control to this extreme extent. Contact with a probation or parole officer is a limiting requirement reinforced by the penalty of confinement in jail or prison. The consequence is logical enough but avoided in other countries using probation. We must think of control as a constant in every correctional equation. Decision makers will first reckon the client's need for control before deciding what else to do with him.

In addition to meeting the basic requirement that retributive justice must be satisfied, control is demanded for the following reasons:

It incapacitates the offender. The offender has presented a verified hazard to the community. This hazard is diminished or eliminated to the degree and for the period that he is under official control.

It intimidates the offender. The experience of control contains unpleasant features in itself. It also contains implied consequences of additional unpleasantness if the offender does not meet requirements imposed. This is deterrence added to retribution.

It makes rehabilitation possible. A heavy-handed witticism familiar to all correctional workers in the present Age of Treatment is the insight that criminals cannot be rehabilitated by absent treatment. They must be present in person to receive the benefits of a correctional program. Unlike many penological aphorisms, this precept is completely true. Rehabilitation must depend on favorable processes going on within the individual, or upon some kind of systematic intervention designed to bring about change. We cannot rely on the chance occurrence of spontaneous change. If intervention is to be made possible, outside control must provide for it for the unwilling client of correctional service. The intervention may in the end by completely ineffective, but it cannot take place in the correctional context without accompanying control.

Retribution, incapacitation, intimidation, and rehabilitation — these four supports to correctional control must each be considered in planning change in correctional practice. The organization of control must in the end satisfy all four objectives. Because most American correctional administrators understand this, control is the essential business of the correctional apparatus. To the extent that the community at large feels secure about the effects of crime, control may be relaxed, but there are very few places in the United States today where it is.

JURISDICTION

A feature peculiar to American government is the four-level structure of administration: federal, state, county, and city authorities divide among them correctional as well as other governmental tasks. In nearly every other country, the correctional apparatus is national and monolithic. The gains to bureaucratic efficiency and uniformity of service are obvious.

But one source of innovations seems to be the number of jurisdictions autonomously operating correctional apparatuses. Small systems can risk changes more safely than large, explosive organizations. What can be ventured as a reasonable experiment in a county or a small state becomes an irresponsible hazard in the correctional system of a whole nation. Such American innovations as the indeterminate sentence, the Huber plan for local confinement, or the system of probation itself, arise from the flexibility afforded by a multiplicity of administrative authorities.

Nevertheless the dismal contrast between the scattered complement of professionally operated local jails and the rigorously inspected and maintained facilities of the United States Bureau of Prisons demonstrates a disparity inevitable in this division of labor. No system can retain autonomy under outside inspection. Autonomy implies the right to inaction as well as to innovation.

A paradox must be noted here. All organizational affairs in the United States as well as in other countries have been moving toward a centralization of authority and services. There is no good reason to suppose that this is a reversible trend. Nevertheless, correctional systems in the United States have been exempted from this trend. Few counties are proud of their jails, but none will willingly part with their control. Statewide probation systems are in a small minority, even in geographically small states where such systems might be especially appropriate. How long this local autonomy in corrections will persist is in doubt, but we must suppose that there will at least be pressure on local services to merge with statewide agencies or to accept inspection and standard-setting.

At the same time, correctional research consistently finds social restoration depends largely on attention to the social system from which the client came and to which he returns. The intimate relationship between the correctional institution or agency and the surrounding community has never seemed as important as it does now. Centralization of correctional service is occurring at a time when the need for its localization has for the first time become really apparent. In later sections we shall have more to say about this paradox.

There are few institutions or agencies in the United States in which horrifying tales of incompetence and brutality cannot be dredged up from the recent past. Neither bumbling nor barbarism have been exorcized from all correctional institutions yet, but their incidence is evidently becoming much less frequent. For the most part these evils of the past were tied to the operation of the political spoils system. The transformation of the conditions of public employment from the favoritism of the victor at the polls to the operation of the civil service is not complete. It is, however, far enough along to have had several prevalent effects.

First and most important is the increasing consensus among correctional workers that theirs is a public service. This was not true of the old-style correctional system, whether probation or prison. Then it was the conviction of the correctional employee that this was a self-enclosed system providing for the confinement or control of offenders and the employment of job holders. Public interest was neither expected nor desired. No one was trained to perform work specific to corrections, and cynicism pervaded the whole field. It was a cynicism about both ends and means, natural enough to anyone doing a job for which he is wholly unprepared.

This cynicism is disappearing. The American correctional worker may be as untrained as ever, but he is now uneasily aware that there is a general opinion that he should be an expert. He may resent this expectation, but it affects his attitude toward himself and his job in ways much different from his arrogance about his prerogatives in the system as it was in the old days.

The old days survive, however, in the correctional cadres blanketed in with the coming of civil service. They survive in patterns of relationship between offenders and staff. Expectations once established linger on long past the occasion of change. This is especially true where a new profession had to be created through reliance on the formally untrained survivors of the old regime.

Civil service had a beneficial effect on employment security. A complete turnover of personnel does not occur with every change of the party in office. By and large the correctional worker is no longer an opportunist flitting from job to job without ego-investment in any. He has become a career worker, well aware as tenure becomes assured that this is probably the only career he will ever have. He can no longer take risks, nor can he allow himself the idiosyncrasies of the employee who expects only short-term profit from the system. To him the stability of the system is an end in itself, sometimes the only end he can discern.

Finally, the civil servant tends to be specialized. A promotional scheme establishes requirements of knowledge for advancement. Examinations are administered. The person taking an examination is told that he should be an expert on crime and its correction and is informed of the specifics of the required expertise. A special influence on correctional expertise in America is the vertical mobility of the civil service. Americans are expected to start at the bottom and, through industry and merit to rise to the top. This is particularly true in the unusually hierarchical structure of corrections. What is learned by experience at the bottom becomes a necessary prerequisite to advancement to the top. The locking and unlocking of cells, the safe routines of the large probation caseload become the subject matter to be mastered for successive advancements. Omissions from the sequence of such learning experiences are deemed undesirable for promotion to the responsibilities of control, administration, and planning. From this progression of empirical learning there accumulates a central core of knowledge required as the essence of the correctional specialization.

This influence of civil service on the professionalization of corrections contrasts, as we shall see, with English and Continental correction systems. In these structures, definite barriers are established between classes of the civil service. Bottom-level experience is so little valued that administrative personnel rarely have it. Recruitment and training for correctional administration are designed to draw from a class educated and trained to accept administrative responsibilities from the first. American correctional experience relies on the accretion of specialized knowledge over the years of progression to the top. It is presumed that the successful migrant from bottom to top will have accumulated somehow not only the relevant requirements of his successive jobs, but also the ability to plan, decide, and implement. Evidence that this process is not producing the desired results we found everywhere in the widespread concern about the sources and training of personnel.

CLIENTELE

In volume this country exceeds both absolutely and relatively the criminality of any other civilized nation. Besides, our crime is notable for its violence, its fraudulence, and for its association with alcohol and narcotics. No other country compares with the United States in the incidence of crime involving firearms. Probably few other countries experience so high a rate of crimes of fraud, usually petty, and usually punished vigorously.

The specific correctional problem in this country is the control and change of a population of gangsters, brawlers, confidence men, armed robbers, alcoholics, and narcotics addicts, as well as the large complement of the housebreakers, thieves, and sex offenders which other countries produce primarily. If we are to organize our programs around the requirements presented by kinds of offender differing widely from each other, there will be important differences between our requirements for the kinds of criminals we get and the kinds which more fortunate nations cope with. The armed towers on our vast fortress-prisons remind us that many of the inmates inside are accustomed to the use of firearms and other weaponry in the commission of crime; they must be controlled at the point of a gun, or so it plausibly seems. This is an anxiety which does not influence prison planning anywhere else.

Our clientele is also significantly distinguished by its ethnic heterogeniety. The criminal classes of most countries are drawn from the lowest segments of the class structure. Our crime has the additional complication of racial diversity. Special problems of individual treatment, mass management, and realistic social restoration ensue from this mixture. Practical plans for a probationer in a disadvantaged minority group, the prevention and control of racial conflict in a juvenile training school, and the understanding of folkways and cultural influences in some of our ethnic ghettoes all present urgent professional problems to correctional staff. They may be only vaguely aware of many of these problems, but the reality and the importance of the issues is not thereby diminished. Racial and cultural pluralism conditions American society as no other country. The significance of this diversity for correctional practice has only begun to be examined. For the country as a whole, its ethnic diversity is a source of tremendous strength; for correctional practice it is a special complication not paralleled in any other country observed in our travels.

MONEY

Correctional administrators are ironically fond of rueful comments about their position at the end of the queue leading to the public coffers. It is a sardonic truism that prisons have no alumni associations nor are probationers given to public testimonials as to the worth of the services rendered them. Few elements in the electorate are even moderately interested in correctional service. Fewer still look at this service as deserving of more support than it gets.

Public apathy is relative and is impossible to quantify. Despite the undoubted disadvantages of the correctional administrators in competing for public funds, American budgeting for institutions and agencies has not been penurious. With the establishment of civil service in support of insistent leadership, with the obvious increase in crime, and with an increasingly clear idea of the task to be done, correctional leadership has not fared badly either as to capital investment for building or as to personnel augmentation. Especially in the juvenile field, where the public is concerned and willing to supply funds, the provision of facilities has been at least comparable in adequacy with other services in the public sector of the economy.

Nevertheless there are many unreasonable disparities. Most of them may be laid to the differing levels of responsible jurisdiction. The squalor of our country jails is more attributable to the inadequate yield of real-estate taxes than to a public demand for a noisome level of service. The relatively more abundant tax structure available to federal and state governments makes possible physical conditions and personnel practices which are feasible for few local governments. Short and poor shrift is given to first and petty offenders in America; it is only when they move to the standing of confirmed recidivists, when they are verified menaces to the community, that they can qualify for treatment beyond the simple requirements of control.

THE PATTERN

Most Americans are familiar with the operating model of the correctional system. It may wheeze, clank, or run with precision, but there is some version of it in every American community. Resemblances are so frequent as to give the impression that there is some inevitable sequence of events in the administration of criminal justice. Differences exist, but they are qualitative, having little to do with organization. In all countries, any governmental organization is limited to standard jurisdictional requirements, and this is particularly true in correctional organization. To change the organizational pattern of corrections in the United States would profoundly affect so many governmental and judicial arrangements that it is no wonder that the basic design seems immutable.

These are the elements of the American correctional apparatus:

JURISDICTIONAL CONTROL	ADULT	JUVENILE
Local supervision	County probation	County probation
Local detention	County jail	Juvenile halls and
	County work camps	detention homes
		County training schools
		County work camps
State supervision	Parole	Parole
State detention	Prison	Training schools
Federal supervision	Integrated probation and parole services	
Federal detention	Local jails	Local juvenile halls
	Prisons	Training schools

This apparently simple aggregation of public services contains an intricate system of power centers and autonomous entities which limits correctional effectiveness. The administrative career of the correctional client demonstrates the problem in one significant way. To see how the nature of the organization restricts its means of achieving its objective, we consider the administrative progress of the ordinary offender in broad outline.

Correctional clients randomly acquire experiences in one or more of the elements of the correctional apparatus. There are many who manage to cram experience of all into their careers. The quality of the experience is determined by accident. A term in an excellent training school may be followed by parole under an obtuse field agent and return to an idle and poorly organized prison in another state. The client cannot choose his treatment or even the agency in which he is to be treated.

As far as possible, decisions are removed from the hands of the correctional client. The allocation of clients is limited by criminal law, primarily an instrument of retributive justice, as interpreted by the courts. Within the law, the courts have considerable latitude as to allocation in accordance with objectives which may be purely retributive, purely deterrent, or even purely rehabilitative, or a mixture of all three. Courts may accept the advice of the district attorney, usually motivated by retribution, of the police, who may be more interested in deterrence, of probation officers who ordinarily are thinking of rehabilitation. Judges may disregard or accept the advice of any of these, or of anyone else, for that matter. Neither in the law nor in judicial interpretation is there a reliable principle governing the placement of the correctional client. From the outset of his experience of the consequences of criminal justice, the client is faced with inconsistency regarding intentions and objectives. What seems like retribution is intended for deterrence and explained as an opportunity for rehabilitation and self improvement. Hardly anywhere else in a citizen's relationship with government is this level of ambiguity encountered.

A somewhat different situation confronts the juvenile correctional client. Standard juvenile court laws are clear that their primary purpose is protection and rehabilitation. Still, few juvenile court judges are consistently able to exclude retribution and deterrence. If rehabilitation is substituted for retribution in the juvenile-court equation, the mixture of considerations and motives will resemble the ambiguities of the criminal law.

The administration of criminal justice in the United States increasingly begins with leniency and progresses through various treatment efforts to end with what is essentially preventive sequestration. Suspended sentences, probation, and local confinement are intended to solve criminal problems with shock effects and with personality or environmental manipulations. Sometimes a service is offered a client; usually it is imposed. Rough and ready differential diagnosis by the court, sometimes professionally advised, determines the type of service to be furnished. Many courts prefer to avoid confinement because of the cost to the community, the stigma to the client, and a lack of confidence in its results. Other courts, placing deterrence ahead of rehabilitation, will systematically impose confinement.

As criminal careers progress and criminal identities are confirmed, fewer alternatives to confinement remain. Probation, in so many contexts synonymous with leniency, becomes inappropriate. Local confinement is used only for temporary control. The established criminal needs containment by the state institution, adapted for long-term confinement. The fully identified correctional client spends most time under state or federal control. The prison contains him and may treat him. An ancillary parole system, superficially similar to probation in the early phase of the correctional sequence, becomes the means for maintaining a surveillance and developing a special opportunity structure for a clearly handicapped group, the felon convicts.

The expectation of the penal authorities is that their clients will be socially restored. No allowance is made for other than "normal" functioning. Though the client may be assisted by the apparatus through its treatment operations to some sheltered position in the opportunity structure, the assumption of the system is that each client is potentially capable of functioning within the normal limits of the tolerance of the community. Consequently the apparatus itself typically contains no intermediate levels of control between total, coercive power and the complete relinquishment of all power. Few correctional administrators are aware that the lack of an agency on which to depend becomes a cause of crime for some of their clients. The notion is increasingly accepted that the correctional apparatus exists to provide an individualized treatment program designed to help each client to normal functioning; yet this amounts to recognition of a principle by the responsible administrators rather than a program of action. Within the framework of the prison or the field agency, the client is largely left to his own devices. He may be prescribed work, education, or treatment, but so little of any of these goods are at the disposal of the staff that he need only go through the motions. Nevertheless, if he is to be discharged within a reasonable length of time after his minimum term, it is essential that he "make progress." The kind of progress which he must make depends on that element of the apparatus with which he is involved, but whether it is an initial experience in a probation department or a long sentence in a prison, his progress will be commended and the lack of it will be deplored.

Progress connotes change, and its reward is the logical justification for release. The principle of the indeterminate sentence lends itself to a system of rewards for rehabilitative effort by the offender. It also lends itself to differential scales of retribution, and few offenders are ever sure as to which system operates with regard to themselves or any others. As no absolute values are available in establishing either kind of scale, offenders are typically unsure as to whether they are passively submitting to retribution, actively responding to rehabilitative opportunities, or simultaneously doing both.

If the correctional client is confused as to what is expected of him, the correctional administrators are no less perplexed. Reliable statistics are not easily come by in criminology, and this is particularly true of corrections. Nevertheless, correctional administrators universally believe that their success may be partly gauged in terms of recidivism. In the United States, over-all recidivism estimates tend to be stated at 50 per cent success for institutional confinement and 60-70 per cent success for probation. Most correctional administrators feel uneasily that these figures are not good enough, but there is no consensus as to what would be a reasonable rate of success. Because the return of an offender to criminal behavior seems to be an easily measured item of information from which various comparative data analyses should be readily obtained, both the public and the system itself tend to rely on estimates and, sometimes, on reliable statistical compilations of recidivism incidence for evaluation. No other social service contains within itself so clear-cut a method of self-appraisal. Neither schools, nor mental hospitals, nor police departments are subject to such easily applied measures.

Here, then, is the American correctional apparatus, an intricate network of apparently autonomous governmental units. Levels of service intended and actually provided differ profoundly. Expectations are confused by sometimes conflicting, sometimes compatible philosophies of service, still oscillating among the three objectives of retribution, deterrence, and rehabilitation. A disarmingly simple method of evaluation is available, but no agreement is to be found to scale the system of evaluation against the expectations of society or of the various treatment doctrines in operation.

From this confusing situation advance in the direction of simplification, standardization, and professionalization is inevitable. The need for simpler organization of correctional agencies and their better coordination is obvious to professionals and lay observers. Enormous efforts have been made by the American Correctional Association and the National Council on Crime and Delinquency to develop standards of humane and professional practice.[6] Finally, from the concern over per-

---

[6] American Correctional Association, *Manual of Correctional Standards* (New York: 1959). See also Sherwood Norman, *Detention for the Juvenile Court* (New York: National Probation Association, 1946).

formance and from the increased body of applicable social science, the foundations are well laid for a specialized correctional profession. The ferment does not yet indicate the constituents and quality of the brew in the making. But the assurance of imaginative new advances is obvious. The correctional apparatus can scarcely be recast to the heart's desire, but the increased resources available and the growing experience of professionalization promise a more reliable service than can be expected from the present welter of cross-purposes.

UNITED KINGDOM

American correctional practice emphasizes local autonomy, but nevertheless produces similarities amounting to standardization in spite of jealously guarded independence. The English correctional apparatus is directly or indirectly controlled from Whitehall but astonishingly diverse from institution to institution and from system to system.

A long way out in the Oxfordshire countryside is an open borstal, presided over, until recently, by an ascetic baronet of ancient lineage. The visitor is met at the bus stop by a well scrubbed "lad" who conducts him down a lane to the barracks concealed from the road and also from the nearby stately home of an automobile manufacturer.

The baronet welcomes the researcher in a bare office decorated only by religious pictures. He disclaims special knowledge or skill. He never reads books, he says, and doesn't encourage staff to spend time on correctional literature. He probably means it, though there are a few unused-looking volumes and brochures in a glassed-in bookcase.

Institutional program is aimed at vocational training and residential care of about 130 dull normal boys of about the ages 17-19, mostly unsophisticated first offenders. The structure is entirely open, consisting of four large barracks. So far, there is nothing which could not be duplicated almost anywhere in the world — including the nonreading governor.

But the baronet is an eccentric even by English standards. Long before we arrived, we had been briefed by his colleagues on his unusual methods. One former assistant had told that when he reported for duty on a Saturday afternoon, he was informed that the governor was out in the field, picking up rocks with a boy on punishment. Another former staff member, now a principal officer, had told us of his sheer astonish-

ment when ordered to lock the governor up for overnight in a punishment cell next door to the cell occupied by a lad adjudged guilty of
some especially heinous infraction. Here was a governor who lived with
his charges, ate with them, and even spent his holidays on trips to visit
lads on after-care to see how they were getting on.

We asked the shy but friendly old man directly about his unusual
methods. Well, he said, a chap can get rather lonesome on a hot summer afternoon out in the field picking up rocks when all the other chaps
are playing cricket on another field. It's a good thing for him to have
someone around, and who would be a better companion then the governor himself? Good experience for the governor, too. Governors are all
too likely to forget how it feels to be all alone on a summer day. They
are also likely to forget how it feels to be locked up in a punishment
cell with no privacy. Not much we can give these lads, but we can sincerely share some of the hardships of borstal life as well as all the fun.
Likewise, one makes friends, one wants to keep them, and one looks up
lads, when one can, after they're back on civvy street.

Results? Back in London we asked the usual question about recidivism. Close to average for the system as a whole, with about a 50 per
cent rate of recidivism during the borstal after-care period. But we were
cautioned that it is hard to make comparisons fairly. This borstal took
in a large group of disadvantaged slum boys with poor capacities and
poor prospects. Who knows what the results *should* be with a population like that? Who knows what the effect on a boy may be when he can
remember a drowsy afternoon spent in a field clearing away rocks with
the help of an old man settled in his mind that his personal inconvenience is irrelevant to the serious business of helping unhappy boys?
There are few certainties in the social sciences, but one of them, surely,
is the value of disinterested good will in the influence of others.

Whatever we may think of the baronet and his methods, we must
concede to the system which contains his institution a degree of flexibility not attained by most correctional apparatus, or by other kinds of
governmental systems, either, for that matter. This is a system which
also contains a facility like the local prison at Leeds:

Armsley Road is lined with the disheveled old brick houses of the
very poor. Cheer and good heart seem unlikely on the best of days on
this street, and the weather in the West Riding tends to dirty rain and

smog. At the top of the road stand the blackened walls of Her Majesty's Prison at Leeds, grimly ornamented with gimcracks in masonry. A crisp but friendly principal officer carrying the fine North Country name of Sucksmith met us at the green-painted entry gate and conducted us through the somber interior.

Comparatively large as English prisons go, Leeds is designed to hold 559 male inmates. By the deplored expedient of cramming three men into cells intended for one, as many as 928 have been accommodated in recent years. This is an adaptation of the Pennsylvania System, and its influences are still to be seen here and there although the system itself has long since been discarded. Nothing so ambitious as behavioral change is intended here, not even in the pietistic sense of the old Pennsylvanians.

This is an exercise in control. Staff are concerned with feeding, housing, occupying, and moving a constant stream of all sorts of offenders. Here is a gloomy, windowless room in a battered shed in which sit several dozen surly looking inmates sewing with needle and thread at varying speeds on the mail bags which have kept English prisoners busy for so many generations. Some sew at a rate evidently agreed upon tacitly as the minimum to be tolerated; others, we noted with surprise, were sewing at speeds far in excess of the apparent group-supported norms. Whatever group dynamics were at work here, rate-busting is at least permissible in the English inmate groups. Blue-uniformed prison officers were stationed at the middle of each wall, and an instructor wandered about to check the work of his charges. Black looks met and followed Principal Officer Sucksmith and the American intruder.

In the administration building we were taken to the office of the assistant governor, a genially harassed prison service professional whose office seemed to engulf him in records, files, reports, and memoranda. In the middle of a distracted interview a rabbity looking inmate of indefinite age was brought in for final clearance for his "red-band," an insignia of trusty status. Indulgently paternal, the assistant governor switches from professional concerns to a medley of congratulation, admonition, sympathy, and words of trust. The inmate leaves, looking pleased with himself if not with the assistant governor.

On to the governor's office, dark and unlit except by a desk lamp and a bright coal fire. The governor is a tall, spare, retired brigadier said to have a distinguished military record and much experience in the management of German prisoners of war. The governor and the visitor sit;

subordinates stand at ease, awaiting the governor's pleasure. The governor ignores them and explains the administrative problems of Leeds Prison to visitor. The problems consist of maintenance, idleness, overcrowding. It is dangerous to be as overcrowded as this establishment is. Mail bags and gas-mask salvaging are poor work projects, but they must keep the men as busy as possible. Too much turn-over of short-term prisoners to accomplish anything. Leeds should have at least one wing for longer-term prisoners so that the staff can feel some sense of accomplishment. No professional staff is assigned, therefore one cannot expect that the program will include treatment. Nevertheless, there is much progress, discipline is good, and staff morale is better than might be expected. We noted that the governor has a sense of accomplishment.

The fortress on Armsley Road and the borstal in an Oxfordshire wood are both under the jurisdiction of the Board of Prison Commissioners. So too are about eighty other prisons (central, regional, and local), borstals (open and closed), and detention centers (senior and junior). It is a huge apparatus, controlling in 1961 about 26,000 inmates and employing a staff of about 5,700, including inspired borstal governors, diligent researchers, former military persons finding new feet in a deceptively similar service, clinicians (able and indolent), and hundreds of prison officers, some passing quickly in and out of a service offering little scope for advancement, some patiently and grimly waiting it out. It is an apparatus which has expanded enormously from its prewar nucleus of 10,000 inmates controlled by a staff of less than 2,000. Its small, almost intimate quality is recalled, especially by borstal staff, with nostalgic regret. The memory is cherished of the now legendary Sir Alexander Paterson who seems, in retrospect, to have single-handedly overturned the service, firing sadists and incompetents, ending barbarous practices, introducing common sense, and hiring bright young idealists from Oxford, settlement houses, public schools, and from among the sons of his friends. His lean intense profile is prominently displayed in most prisons and borstals of the country. Elites which he selected for borstal duty have moved up the ladder and across the border to the administration of the prisons as well as the youth facilities, and the policy-making offices of Whitehall as well as the solid comfort of a governor's office.

To replace the free-wheeling personnel recruitment that Paterson and his colleagues carried on in the 'twenties, a system of training based on minimum standards of selection for two levels of entry has been developed. With Paterson's own initiative, an Imperial Training School for Prison Officers and Staff was founded at Wakefield, across the road from an old but standard prison specialized for confinement and training of long-term prisoners. With the decline of empire and the expansion of the prison service, the old Imperial Training School has been divided into two units, the staff college for the training of assistant-governor candidates,[7] and the training school for prison officers. Under the leadership of Duncan Fairn, now chief director of Prison Administration, R. E. Owen, assistant commissioner for Training, and Mark Winston, principal, the entrance level training for assistant governors and beginning officers has been expanded to a pattern of continuous training for all staff members. What will happen to gifted eccentrics and youthful idealists remains to be seen. But a veteran chief officer of the staff, approaching the end of his service, told us in harsh reminiscence of his induction to the prison service three decades ago:

When I started work at Liverpool I was one of the few fortunates of eight hundred applicants. I hated to go to work every morning. I hated it. I hated my job, and if I could have found another job, I would have gone. . . . When the war broke out and I was called up, I was delighted. And when I came out of the army at the end of the war in 1946, if I could have found another job I would have taken it. The change between that time and the present day has been absolutely phenomenal. I wouldn't even entertain the idea of leaving the prison service . . . it's as interesting and satisfying a job as I can imagine myself having.

And an interview with the enthusiastic principal of the school brought forth the following account of the ferment at work in the correctional apparatus of England:

They used to have a feeling of being very low persons in the social scale as prison officers; they were subjected to constant criticism outside the service. They're now in a very much better position than they were, say, twenty-five years ago. I'm not talking about salaries and wages; I'm talking about their dignity. They sit on committees with the governors of their institutions. It isn't every prison officer that really adjusts to this. There are quite a few of the old school that say, "The governor is the man that ought to tell us what to do,

---

[7] For an account of this school, see John P. Conrad, "The Assistant Governor in the English Prison," *British Journal of Delinquency*, X:4 (June, 1961), 245–261.

you know. I do what he says, right or wrong." There is a real excitement for the newly joining prison officer in a borstal or a training prison to sit on a review board and so on. He has an opportunity to speak his piece about the people under his control. Now, in the old days, you'd have to be at least a principal officer before *anybody* would ask your opinion.

We asked what the future of officers in the English prisons and borstals would be, granted the persistence of the "excitement" of professional correctional practice. Our informant began:

This is a changing picture because the prisons themselves are changing. A few years back, there were no open prisons. That sort of thing was unheard of until 1936 in this country and in most other places. Now we accept that. What's the next thing? Well, we are accepting the idea of prisoners going out to work during the last stage of their sentences and earning normal money, making their own commitments and all the rest of it. We have to teach the officers of the future to accept when it comes, that a very large percentage of prisoners won't be in prison in the normal sense of the word. They won't be locked away from the moment the judge says three years — they will just be living a different sort of life. Some of them might be locked up for week ends only; some might be locked up for the first year or two and then go to almost completely open conditions. That's the sort of future you've got to look forward to for the prisoner, and the prison officer has to associate himself with this. If he doesn't we are not going to be able to put these changes over with the public or even with the prisoners.

He added:

I don't think it's true, really, as some people picture us, that we have the job of convincing a lot of wooden-headed officers who are perfectly happy to stay as they are, that it's to their benefit and to everyone else's benefit to move. One of the things which almost always comes out of our in-service training refresher courses is that in many respects they, the officers, are way ahead of us. They are urging *us* to go forward and saying, "You know, we can do this and the sooner you let us do it, the better. Why are things so slow in developing?" We pose problems to them, problems like providing work for prisoners or the use of group counseling as a technique. In almost all cases we've had officers wanting to know more about these things and wanting to know when this or that can be done at *their* establishment. I think we are bringing them progressive news of the future. But we find that in many of these things they are way ahead of us. For example, they seized on group counseling so eagerly in the last couple of years because they do have this feeling very strongly that they aren't doing very much, and of course this is true of a large majority of our institutions. Very much isn't being done for the prisoners, and I think the officers are really conscious of this and they are anxious to have something — like group counseling — that they can do.

From these excerpts from our notes emerges, we hope, a picture of the English Prison Service as a diversified apparatus containing some strategically placed elements eager to build in further improvements and innovations. There are also senior staff members who are so concerned with the pressures of day-to-day control in an almost uncontrollable situation that innovation is seen as an unwelcome threat to a precarious stability. As in the United States, an equilibrium accommodates a large element of the staff which is wearily coping with the unrelenting expansion of population to be humanely confined in facilities never intended for such numbers. This equilibrium must also accommodate a restless vanguard discontented with an assignment which asks only that aseptic social conditions be maintained in the country's penal institutions.

From all accounts, this is an equilibrium which is not significantly affected by outside interest groups. In a communication to us on the topic of public opinion and the Prison Commission of which he was the chairman for so long, the late Sir Lionel Fox wrote to us:

I suspect the two basic assumptions of public opinion are still the feeling that evil-doing should be met by retributive justice of an unpleasant character, and that the "principle of less eligibility" should prevail. But in this country, public opinion in this broad sense seems to be apathetic, and, in spite of every effort to create an informed opinion through all the media of public information, remarkably ignorant.

. . . there is no lack of Parliamentary interest. Pressure here is generally toward further and faster progress with penal reform, with very little pressure the other way. I say this without forgetting the strong and vocal pressures of recent years in favour of capital and corporal punishments, but this line of thought does not seem to have any reaction on the administration of prisons.

What I have said about Parliament is also, I think, broadly true of the press. For some years past the administration has taken great pains to co-operate with the press on a friendly basis. . . . Maybe for that reason, informed Press comment on what happens in prisons is usually fair and balanced, and, as in Parliament, comment is more often directed to pressing on penal reform than to holding it back.

Fox's appraisal of public interest in prison and borstal administration was borne out by his associates. One of them put it this way:

Society expects *nothing*. Society, as a whole, has no concern with the prison system. Its concern springs into action when some crisis arises, when somebody escapes and some scandal is unearthed. But I don't think it *expects* anything. . . . It's only a conscious minority that is interested, the active, progressive people who take care to inform themselves. . . . What the Prison Commission has done, over the years, has largely been due to the stimulus supplied by its members, helped, here and there, by the co-operation of an active Home Secretary.

The English correctional apparatus, then, is a system heavily engaged in keeping up with the demands made on it, not by a largely indifferent society, but rather by the volume of offenders. The stabilized apparatus of the years before World War II has had to accommodate change in deference to the numbers of its clients and in the light of staff initiative. Some organizational details will establish the direction which change is taking.

For adult offenders, the process began with diversification of service. Prisons of containment need only the modest specialization required by the essentials of control. Before World War II, prisons for adults could be largely divided between the local establishments for short-term commitments and the central prisons, such as Dartmoor and Wakefield, for those serving long sentences. The innovations since the Criminal Justice Act of 1948 provided for four types of prisons to which inmates might be assigned from the local prisons which still form the substructure of the system. These are:

OPEN PRISONS: Adapted from American practice, these rural centers for the training of adults draw on the availability of country mansions with large estates attached. All classes of offenders except those serving the longest and the shortest terms are eligible. For the most part, despite the advantages of economy and milieu, the prison commissioners have been cautious about their use. About 10 per cent of their adult charges have been assigned to open conditions, in spite of general agreement on the good effects of programs so conducted.

REGIONAL TRAINING PRISONS: Offenders serving first terms or considered to have good potential for training are assigned to these establishments, usually with sentences of less than four years but more than six months. Institutions like Wakefield and Maidstone are included under this heading, and a heavy emphasis on vocational training and remedial education has characterized their programs. Another 10 per cent of the population is confined in these establishments.

CENTRAL PRISONS: In these establishments are concentrated offenders serving long terms. Central prisons vary from grim fortresses like Dartmoor, a remote legend in the Devonshire fog and mist, but soon to be abandoned, to Eastchurch, an open prison established on a former RAF base in Kent. Two concepts of social control are represented in the central prisons of England. Conventional long terms awarded to especially dangerous offenders on a generally retributive basis are served at prisons like Dartmoor, Wakefield, or Wormwood Scrubs. But England also has a special system for the control of the persistent recidivist in which prevention rather than retribution is the purpose of the sentence. Under the system of preventive detention, about a thousand offenders are confined for terms ranging from five to fourteen years. Though the purpose is prevention rather than punishment, the differences between ordinary imprisonment and preventive detention as administered from day to day are not perceptible to the observer, nor, so we are told by those most affected, to the inmates themselves. However, because of the special purposes of the program, a system of phasing has been built into it which culminates in the possibility of placement in a prison hostel for especially favorable prospects. Because of the relative success of the preventive detention hostels in the employment of long-term prisoners in private industry, the central prisons have also been afforded this facility for selected inmates in the last year of their sentence. Both inmates and the staffs assigned to prison hostels are generally much impressed with the value of this program, but it has so far been carried out on too small a scale to be regarded as a major component of the apparatus. Very little has been done to adapt this system to a program for behavioral change; its design is consistent with the control orientation of the central prisons. Throughout this part of the service the primary concern is the maintenance of conditions which will keep deterioration of the prisoner to a minimum. The prospect of a placement in the hostel with a possible additional remission of the sentence serves not only to ease the resocialization of the fortunate few inmates affected but also is intended as an inducement to conform to the regime for inmates who would otherwise have little motivation to respond to any administrative action other than coercion.

CORRECTIVE TRAINING PRISONS: A special feature of the Criminal Justice Act of 1948 was the provision of corrective training sentences for young recidivists. Intended for recidivists ranging in age from 21 to 30, the central notion of the law was to provide remedial education and vocational training to young men whose legitimate opportunity was limited

by lack of employable skills. Such sentences are awarded without regard to the actual crime committed but rather on the evidence of need
as shown by repeated convictions and an appraisal of "suitability" by
the governor of the local prison in which the offender is confined pending sentence. A term of not less than two nor more than four years ensues. The confusions which also result from the necessity in many in-
stances of mixing trainees with prisoners seem hardly to be to the
advantage of the system. Here is an inmate at the expertly administered
prison at Wakefield:

This present system isn't working. There's this distrust of the habitual
criminal leading the first termer — the one who's made a genuine mistake —
on to crime. A rum bit of work, this mixing everyone together — though keeping men in cages didn't work either. . . . But judges say to offenders when
they sentence them: "I'm not going to send you to prison; I'm going to give
you a chance. I'm not going to give you two years of prison time but I'm going
to give you three years of corrective training!" Well, that person arrives at
Wakefield — and I arrive myself, also, after having been sentenced to imprisonment — and we meet! Which actually is which? If I'm not getting corrective training, what is it? I know quite a number of people who have tried
all the five vocational training courses which are available to all prisoners.
A corrective trainee is entitled to demand, as a right, one of those courses.
I've listened to quite a number of them and they say, "Well, they've sent me
here, but there's no use in trying to make me do anything."

Who can say how common this attitude toward this system may be?
Corrective training mixes motives, operates with the vaguest of criteria,
and produces results which support no confidence at all. Systematic
studies of the process are lacking, but in the Report of the Prison Commissioners for 1960 we find (p. 32):

Corrective training. — The difficulties inherent in the rehabilitation of
those selected by the courts as likely to benefit from this form of training are
illustrated by the fact that of the 2959 men released during the six years com-
mencing 1954, nearly two-thirds had been reconvicted by 31st December
1960. Even more regrettably, the failure of nearly two-thirds of those convicted had occurred during their period of supervision. Our associates testify
to the very great difficulty in establishing a relationship of confidence with
these men.

The persistence of this system despite results which suggest nearly
total failure must testify to a certain dogged quality in the culture. The
difficulties encountered in its administration are serious, as our inform-

ant at Wakefield clearly described. The application of vocational training to a class whose common factors are recidivism and a flat sentence
usually exceeding the processes of retributive justice can only be justified as a desperate compromise between retribution and reform. Once
such a system is embedded in Anglo-Saxon law its uprooting becomes a
matter of educating the legislators and the courts on not only its defects
but also on the advantages of a reasonable substitute. For this group of
offenders neither the administrators nor the social scientists can offer
with confidence an attractive alternative, even though almost *any* alternative would be more effective.[8]

Under this system of long-term confinement for adults there lies the
basic circuit of local prisons. Distributed rather irregularly around the
country, they are made to serve a large variety of control purposes, but
their common denominator is short-term confinement. Not much is expected. One administrative official told us:

At the moment, all the local prison staff can do is to receive, count, feed,
clothe, and release them. Until we can reduce the pressures in these places,
I think we do an enormous disservice to those who come to us. But over 60
per cent of our prisoners in any one year come to us for six months and under. . . . I see no good chance of doing much with those who are with us
for a few days only. I think all we can do is to clean them up, and sometimes
that takes a little doing! But with a term of four weeks or more I think our
experience in the open prisons has shown that something can be done.

Who knows what can be done? The 1960 Report of the Prison Commissioners contains, buried in an appendix, an accounting of the reconvictions of releases from the regional open, medium, and closed prisons.
Of the 569 released from open prisons in 1954, 91.7 per cent and of the
963 released in that year from closed prisons 80.7 per cent have kept out
of trouble. Such a statistic assures us that the Prison Commissioners
have sent their better risks to open prisons. It does not assure us that
the open-prison experience in any way contributed to their success.
Nor do we have a glimmering of what would be the consequence of
local, short-term confinement in the stately old homes of England rather
than the slum citadels in which most petty offenders serve their time.

Here, then, is a vast, hard-pressed, and physically dilapidated collec-

<hr>

[8] For a caustic account of the weaknesses of the system by a prejudiced but articulate former trainee, see Frank Norman, *Bang to Rights* (London: Secker and
Warburg, 1959).

tion of prisons whose managers are painfully attempting to accommodate a few concepts of change within a structure designed for control.
For generations, a stern circuit of local prisons has exacted the price for
crime. These consequences are sufficiently impressive to keep those
coming to prison for the first time from coming back again — perhaps
75 per cent of them. For the remaining 25 per cent the end is seldom in
sight. A preventive sentence poorly disguised as corrective training
merely demonstrates the inapplicability of logic to the irrationality of
offenders. This ineffectual device is followed by a harsh but appropriate system of preventive detention designed to incapacitate, if not deter,
the offender. Finally, as a concession to humanitarian initiatives, a modest investment has been made in open prisons. In a few inactivated
RAF bases and stately old homes the offender's capacity for social restoration is supported by trust, reasonable living conditions, and selection for success.

The British correctional apparatus has generally dealt with the offender as an independent moral agent. Built into its fabric is the notion
that criminals are capable of choice; and that a person who experienced
punishment would not in his right mind willingly go through it again.
Probably because of this reliance on the capability of the apparatus to
deter, the after-care facilities seem more like afterthoughts. Though the
organizations administering services to discharged prisoners have a century of service behind them, it has been a service consisting primarily
of the doling out of bounties to deserving cases. The National Association of Discharged Prisoners' Aid Societies (NADPAS) is a privately
controlled organization with public funds granted to it for the administration of after-care. Mostly relying on volunteer "associates" and the
guidance of local committees, it has provided the local prisons with
such casework services as it could. Gradually the need for professional
service has been accepted, and welfare officers with social-casework
training have been installed in the prisons. A training program for staff
is complementing this recruitment so as to bring about the rapid expansion of the service which is overdue.

A recent addition to the work of the Discharged Prisoners' Aid Societies is the Central After-Care Association. This association, founded
in 1910, provides compulsory after-care for borstal, corrective training
and preventive detention releases. Working through its own staff in
London and through probation officers in the counties, it has only recently been professionalized. Like its companion, the NADPAS, the

image of the Central After-Care Association with the people it is supposed to help has been compromised by a long tradition of inadequate resources hopelessly unrelated to the need they were supposed to fill. Interviewing prisoners throughout the country we were struck with the bitterly contemptuous references which we encountered whenever the subject of after-care came up. Summarizing a Home Office study of the NADPAS structure, Howard Jones reported:

> When prisoners are released they pass into the care of the DPA's, which means for most of them the end of any attempt at real treatment. This is borne out by an enquiry carried out by the Home Office research unit among a group of exprisoners who were outside the compulsory after-care scheme operated by the CACA. Over 80 percent visited their DPA and 71 percent received some help . . . but only 6 percent received subsequent help of any kind. This emphasis on a single interview is consistent with a picture of the service as more concerned with handing out small doles and a cautionary word to prisoners immediately on discharge then with support and reeducation." [9]

And in the 1960 Report of the Prison Commissioners we hear that

> considerably less than half of those eligible accepted our voluntary help in the first instance, and fewer still maintained contact for any long period. Even allowing for a proportion who have no intention of changing their ways, this evidence must stimulate enquiry into how our services can be more convincingly presented to our clients. The anticipated enforcement, on this category, of statutory supervision in no way lessens the need for inspiring confidence.[10]

The anticipation so soberly faced concerns the consequences of the Criminal Justice Act of 1961. This legislation makes a cautious step ahead in the implementation of after-care. Under its provisions, as soon as adequate staff is on hand in the Central After-Care Association, compulsory supervision will be required for prisoners in three new categories: prisoners serving sentences of four years or more; prisoners serving sentences of six months or more with previous sentences of corrective training, preventive detention, or borstal training; prisoners under the age of 26 at the commencement of a sentence of six months or more.

---

[9] H. Jones, *Prison Reform Now* (London: The Fabian Society, 1959), pp. 15–16.
[10] *Report of the Commissioners of Prisons for the Year 1960* (London: HMSO, 1961, Cmnd. 1467).

The scarcity of staff trained or trainable to perform the services required by the new law adds to the difficulty of creating a new tradition for a well-meaning but ineffectual service. Nobody disputes the need for major changes in after-care, but England is not alone in the lack of people who wish to fill this gap in the social services.

For two reasons, mention should be made of the large organization of prison visitors which carries on the magnanimous tradition of Elizabeth Fry in the English cell blocks. Institutionalized with a National Association, standardized procedures, and official approvals the visitors nonetheless continue to represent a precarious bridge to the community over which some contact between cell and home can be kept up. Further, from the prison visitors have sprung a number of innovations, most notable of which is the Norman House movement, of which we shall have more to say in the next chapter.

The objectives of prison-visiting have been discussed by Fox:

> The normal fate of an Ordinary Class prisoner is to be locked in his cell by 5 p.m., and unless it is his night for a class he may not see anybody to speak to again till he is unlocked next morning. This is a bleak and lonely period . . . and it is at this time that a visit from someone from the outside world, quite unconnected with the prison staff . . . may not only prevent the prisoner from solitary brooding over real or fancied grievances, but may actively direct this thought in profitable directions.[11]

Though the value of this kind of service, directed not to counseling or uplift, but rather to the maintenance of contact with a world which otherwise exists only in the imagination, cannot be disputed, the need may be diminishing. Merfyn Turner, in whose prodigious experience of prison-visiting the Norman House movement is rooted, appraises this adjunct of the prison service as follows:

> There was a time when all men in prison spent more than three-quarters of their sentence in solitary confinement. It was reputed then that a donkey dressed in prison visitor's clothes would have been welcomed by the men, for any diversion from the grinding monotony of the prison regime was something to be welcomed. . . .
>
> But the situation has changed. . . . Attitudes towards the prisoner and his imprisonment have slowly changed. Solitary confinement is no longer general, partly because the prison population is greater than the number of

---

[11] Lionel W. Fox, *The English Prison and Borstal Systems* (London: Routledge and Kegan Paul, 1952), pp. 205–208.

cells to accommodate it, but chiefly because it is no longer penal policy to isolate a prisoner either from the world of people outside or his fellow-prisoners inside. . . .

Prison visitors are thus faced with competition for the first time in their history. . . . A prisoner is now able to choose his diversions, and the visitor whose visits intrude on other activities is rarely popular. . . . He is no longer a window through which the prisoner was meant to catch a glimpse of the good and honest world outside. . . . Slowly, but inevitably, prison visiting is being changed from a pleasant diversion into a service which is becoming involved in the prisoners' after-care.[12]

Nevertheless, the structure which the system has been able to tolerate for the voluntary service of interested citizens is a major source of strength for the prison service. Few prison visitors are inspired to such creativity as brought about the development of Norman House, but an understanding of the problem and the need is brought back to the community by many. Even the least effectual of them serve as pledges to the prison community of concern about them in the community at large.

CORRECTIONAL SERVICES FOR YOUTH IN ENGLAND:

In the correction of adults the organizational development has tended to provide opportunity and occasion for change to the subjects of a system intended for retribution and deterrence. It is not likely that the orientation to change will soon offset the traditional emphases.

In the correction of youths the insistence has long been on bringing about change in the still pliable humans involved in transgressions. The insistence of Sir Alexander Paterson that "you cannot train men for freedom in conditions of captivity" implicitly designates the task of the borstal. No matter how appropriate captivity might be for older offenders, it is for the borstal to train men for freedom, whatever the risks may be. A half-century has passed since a special Home Department Committee recognized the responsibilities of the system for the treatment of the youthful offender. These responsibilities were put into words and action by Sir Evelyn Ruggles-Brise, the founder of the borstal system:

. . . up to a certain age, every criminal may be regarded as potentially a good citizen. . . . His relapse into crime may be due either to a physical degeneracy, or to bad social environment . . . it is the duty of the State at least to try and effect a cure.[13]

---

[12] Merfyn Turner, *Safe Lodging* (London: Hutchinson, 1961), pp. 101–102.
[13] Fox, *op. cit.*, pp. 331–332, quoting Sir Evelyn Ruggles-Brise.

It is not our purpose to trace the course of borstal history to its present complexity of services. It is important here to describe a structure and a philosophy which have influenced services for youthful offenders throughout the English-speaking world and beyond. Because this structure and philosophy have aroused such dedication in its practitioners, they have heavily influenced the practice of corrections in the English adult prisons, too.

Ruggles-Brise defined the problem. The age group in question, from sixteen to twenty-one, has given correctional practice its most difficult subjects both before and since his time. Segregation of these subjects was as far as Sir Evelyn could be expected to go, once recognition had been achieved for the responsibility and the need. It was left to Sir Alexander Paterson to produce a method to make the segregation of the young offender serve a purpose beyond social antisepsis. Summoning up the experience of the English public schools in moral training, Paterson adapted the structure intended for the training of England's elite to the training of the country's least hopeful youths. In the *Principles of the Borstal System*, the "little gray book" which became the manual of the borstal staff, Paterson set down the essence of both structure and philosophy:

In the moral training of an Institution the individual virtue is discovered and developed, while the discipline of the Institution is founded on the *ésprit de corps* it has evoked. Two great weapons are here in daily use. One is the personal influence of the members of the Staff upon the boys. Governor and his Deputy, Housemaster and Matron, Chief and Principal, Instructor and Officer, keen optimists with a care for others, by word and example set a standard before each lad. The second weapon, forged only in the course of time, wielded only by the apt, is the public opinion of the lads themselves. This is perhaps the more potent influence of the two, but its use is far more difficult. Only the man with a genius for sympathy can gauge the tone of a set of lads, only one with a rare gift of leadership can slowly raise it to a point at which it shall lift up every member of the group.[14]

Borstal training is long and indeterminate. Originally the commitment was for four years to be divided between institution and after-care, but though a division of the time between confinement and community supervision has been maintained, the Criminal Justice Act of 1961 reduced the commitment to two years. Compulsory after-care is provided

---

[14] The Prison Commission, *The Principles of the Borstal System* (London, 1932).

by the Borstal Division of the Central After-Care Association. Most of this service is performed by local probation officers outside the Metropolitan District. Originally borstal community supervision was mainly a voluntary operation conducted by "associates." It is now entirely in professional hands, the volunteer associates having been preëmpted for other services with the onset of World War II.

With the development of the Mannheim-Wilkins prediction system,[15] classification has become an instrument to facilitate the specialization of borstals. Perhaps to a greater extent than any other correctional system in the world the English borstals are homogeneous as to the expectations of all concerned. Some receive youths whose prospects are certain "success" — or at least the avoidance of reconviction. Some receive virtually sure prospects for failure. But neither social science nor statistical method have yet sufficed to refine predictions into real assurance for the greater part of the population. Of the 2958 receptions in 1958, 6 per cent were "A risks," or probably successes, whereas 11 per cent were "D risks" or probable failures. This contrasts with the situation in 1947, when 19 per cent were "A risks" and 3 per cent were "D risks." [16] Other criteria, such as age, intelligence, physical maturity, and mental stability distribute the remainder of the population.

But in spite of the great variation in the kinds of correctional communities established by these classification methods, the same program goes on in each borstal. Working parties march out to the fields or to the shops in the mornings, arms swinging and feet stamping like so many aspiring guardsmen. School and vocational training take up some of the time of nearly all borstal youths. Staff will see to it that each youth is exposed to exercise — football, cricket, or physical training. Whatever he makes of it, a borstal boy is going to see the inside of a church every Sunday, and many may occasionally have an interview with a "padre."

Finally, and most important of all, there is the house system. Adapted from the organization of the English public school, the borstal house is centered on the influence of a house staff on a residential dormitory. The anonymous "little gray book" ascribed to Sir Alexander Paterson sets forth the basic notion:

Having . . . done their best to arouse the right forces in the lad, the Staff will rally to their aid the corporate spirit of the other lads. To facilitate the

---

[15] Hermann Mannheim and Leslie T. Wilkins, *Prediction Methods in Relation to Borstal Training* (London: HMSO, 1955).
[16] *Report of the Commissioners of Prisons* . . . , p. 46.

use of this weapon, the House system has been introduced into the Institutions. Lads are susceptible to the personal influence of a strong man, but probably for many the spirit of the community, to which they belong for the time being, has an even greater effect on them. The spirit of a good House catches hold of what is best in the worst of lads, and he will do for the group of his comrades what he would never do for a master imposed upon him. This common opinion can only be of benefit if it is sound and healthy. If it is rotten and diseased, the lad will be almost certainly better in solitary confinement. . . . The Housemaster and his colleagues must therefore ensure that the spirit of the House is good. They will do so by the careful selection of leaders, by training them and standing very close to them, by being always in and out of the House, by thinking of it as their family, by being there for meals and recreation because they do not want to leave it. It is they who make the spirit of the House, and it is that spirit, in addition to their own efforts, which will bring out the good in a lad and help him to save himself.[17]

Does this system, rooted in the pedagogical style of the nineteenth century, with its appeal to *noblesse oblige* and the loyalties common to adolescence, cope adequately with the delinquent of today? There is considerable evidence that it is less and less relevant to the rapidly changing English social order. Whether the system is beyond modifications appropriate to rootless youths we cannot yet tell. But the statistical trends are not reassuring.

These data do not compare favorably with the prewar rates of success. Fox, citing comparable data from the Prison Commissioners' An-

TABLE 1

RECONVICTIONS OF PERSONS DISCHARGED FROM SENTENCES OF BORSTAL TRAINING,
1954–1959, AS REPORTED TO DECEMBER 31, 1960.[18]

Year dis- charged	Period at risk	Number dis- charged	Not reconvicted		Reconvicted not recommitted		Recommitted	
			Number	Per cent	Number	Per cent	Number	Per cent
1954	6	1741	717	41.2	216	12.4	808	46.4
1955	5	1667	706	42.4	227	13.6	734	44.0
1956	4	1484	556	37.5	189	12.7	739	49.8
1957	3	1703	590	34.6	259	15.2	854	50.2
1958	2	2178	868	39.8	322	14.8	988	45.4
1959	1	3115	1568	50.3	452	14.5	1095	35.2

SOURCE: *Report of the Commissioners of Prisons for the Year 1960* (London: HMSO, 1961, Cmnd. 1467), p. 190.

---

[17] Cited in n. 14.

nual Report for 1949, found that of 1741 boys discharged from borstal training in 1937-1938, 1039 (59.5 per cent) had not been reconvicted seven years later, with an additional 340 (19.5 per cent) who had been reconvicted only once. From these data, Fox concluded, with some justice, that "borstals at their best were achieving complete success with about six boys out of every ten discharged, and if we include those who after one reconviction settled down, with nearly eight out of every ten. . . . In most examinations, a mark of 75 per cent achieves distinction." [18]

What do the staff members and inmates in the borstals think of the system? From numerous interviews at all levels we gained an impression of pride mixed with uneasiness. It was at Lowdham Grange that some of the issues became most sharply defined for us. This is the famous institution built brick by brick by a working party of borstal boys in the early thirties. Its governor, at the time of our survey interviews, stoutly maintained that while borstal boys should be builders, they should not build borstals:

When it was a project it was doing a far better job than when it became Lowdham Grange Borstal Institution. It was much more alive than it is now in this dangerous phase. I think it's dangerous because it's settled into an institutional routine. Inevitably the boys have become institutionalized. I have the task of developing a whole mechanism for de-institutionalizing just before release. Now we spend three months just moulding a boy into a sort of a thing, and then we have to spend the last three months extracting him from this institutional thing that he's become.

The governor's subordinates shared his concern over the pertinence of borstal training to a world out of joint. After telling us at some length of the satisfactions of borstal service, of the favorable contrast to service in the harrowing prisons, one officer told us:

We do lots of things here. The great thing is to instill in these lads a will to a different type of living, to better standards and so forth. But for the dull kind of boy we're getting it must be jolly difficult once they get back. They're not leaders by any means; they're the boys that will be led. . . .

This borstal thing is changing all the time. Who's to say what's right and what's wrong? I, personally, think that a boy responds better to severe, rigid discipline, rather than having things too easily laid on. Here every lad has TV, constant hot and cold water laid on for him — things he never has in his own house. But as we say in borstal, where's the carry-over value? You teach

---

[18] Fox, *op. cit.*, pp. 399–400.

a lad to play rugby, and he may be a very fine rugby player, and you say, "Well, where is the carry-over value here?" Because this lad couldn't hold a conversation with people in an outside club. And after a game in an outside club, what's going to happen when the chaps say, "Let's all meet in the club-house and talk about the game?"

We do everything we can think of here. We take them canoeing; we're building additions to the institution. We take them up into the mountains and do light-weight camping with the house officers. There's a tremendous variety of stuff which these chaps have never even *seen* before, never entertained doing before. And where is the carry-over value?

What we heard from the governor and his staff is seen in about the same light but heard in a different language by Alan Little, an intensive observer of the system. After citing the results shown in the table on p. 90 Little asks:

Why has the Borstal system failed? Two broad types of answers to this question can be given: the first suggests that the system has failed because the reforms have not gone far enough. This argument implies that there is nothing radically wrong with existing principles or practice that further reform of the same type will not change. A second set of arguments suggests that present practice contains major weaknesses that only radical rethinking and reformulation of Borstal practice can solve.

After dismissing as improbable the idea that the existing structure can be sufficiently modified to obtain better results than ordinary imprisonment, Little indicates the lines on which radical rethinking will be needed:

To change offenders into non-offenders two things are desirable: an adequate theory of crime and efficient antidotes to its causes. Experience of the past decades suggests that the "antidotes" used in the Borstal institutions are unsuccessful in reforming offenders, probably because they are based upon an inadequate theory of human behaviour in general and crime in particular. . . . [The] common problem in Borstal training [is] the failure of the inmate to identify himself with the system and its aims. This failure has a variety of causes. One is the failure to make Borstal experience relevant to the offender, and another is the failure of Borstal practice to be relevant to the cause of crime.[19]

---

[19] Alan Little, "The Borstal Boys," *The Twentieth Century*, CLXX:1012 (Winter 1962), 35–42.

Little proposes no solutions to the problems he sets forth except the need for a massive investment in research. Pending this distant prospect, it can be expected that staff will strive to maintain and improve the inherited structure.

Parallel to the borstal system is another substructure of the prison system, set aside for a class of inmates under the age of twenty-one and committed for crimes either too minor or too major for borstal commitment. Until the Criminal Justice Act of 1961, these youths were segregated into special sections of local prisons if they were minor offenders, or, if substantial terms had to be served, special institutions were set aside for them. Of considerable concern in the evaluation of the borstal system is the statistical trend which indicates a favorable differential for young prisoners as against borstal boys.[20] While the two groups are comparable in only the crudest dimensions, there is some evidence that when common factors are controlled, there is no significant difference in recidivism between borstal and young-prisoner releases.[21] The questions which this anomaly raises have not yet been answered, but from the thought which is given to it we may expect innovation to emerge.

THE APPROVED SCHOOL

The long and confusing history of the English approved school is fortunately irrelevant to an understanding of the complete correctional system of the United Kingdom. Like the borstal, it represents an accretion of improvisations, in this instance aimed at the younger offender. Unlike the borstal, it is administered by a separate agency of the Home Office, and its leadership is essentially pedagogical rather than correctional. Again, the long English experience of residential schools for the young is brought to bear on the problem of delinquency, just as in the evolution of the borstal.

The approved school derives its designation from the official approval of the Home Secretary for the residential treatment of delinquent children. Approved schools vary widely in origin and in character. Some came into being more than a century ago as industrial schools for destitute children; some began as reformatories for delinquents. Some are managed by religious bodies or philanthropic organizations concerned

---

[20] *Report of the Commissioners of Prisons . . . , op. cit.*, p. 191.

[21] Sir George Benson, "Prediction Methods and Young Prisoners," *British Journal of Delinquency*, IX:3 (January, 1959), 192.

with the welfare of children. Others are under the direct control of local authorities. There are now 117 approved schools in England and Wales, caring for about 8,000 children. Eighty-two schools are provided for boys; thirty-five are for girls.

All these schools are maintained by public funds, the principal costs being shared by the Home Office and the local authorities. Inspectors from the Home Office Children's Department are responsible for the maintenance of minimum standards, but details of the program and its conduct at each school are under the control of the headmaster, with the general supervision of a board of managers. Because of the great variety of auspices under which approved schools operate, specialization of service is wide, and many schools have taken initiatives in the development of innovations. Some schools, such as Aycliff, have pushed ahead imaginative systems of incentives to induce the apathetic, failure-oriented children of metropolitan slums to adopt achievement patterns in spite of themselves. In the next chapter, we shall report more on this school, and on the ideas of its headmaster, John Gittins.

Park House, situated in a stately old home an hour or so south of London, is pushing ahead under its headmaster, Leslie Crew, with a social-service program designed to bring parents as close as possible to the life of the school. With a social worker stationed in London, contact is maintained with families for the twenty months or more during which boys committed to this institution usually remain in its custody. At Park House the bridge to the community from the school's isolation in the countryside is open to considerable traffic. Its good-natured, optimistic staff provide a milieu reminiscent of a private boarding school rather than the correctional institution.

At the other end of the scale is such an institution as Carlton School, remote in Bedfordshire, assigned to the task of caring for nearly a hundred senior boys. Increasingly disturbed boys in recent years had been assigned to this school, despite the lack of psychiatric consultation and mental-health staffing. The strain of improvising adjustments in traditional and successful methods so as to accommodate a population for which these methods were never intended culminated in a series of disturbances in August, 1959. The disturbances ended in a mass escape from the school, which brought on a full-scale investigation. From the report [22] can be clearly seen the enormous difficulty in providing staff

---

[22] Victor Durand, *Disturbances at the Carlton Approved School on 29th and 30th August, 1929: Report of Inquiry* (London: HMSO, 1960, Cmnd. 937).

and devising method merely to contain the most disturbed and recalcitrant in the range of delinquency with which approved schools must deal. Fresh country air, cricket on the green, and football on the playing fields seem to have little relevance for the discontents and defeats of youth from the less hopeful boroughs of London. The housemasters who form the characters of England's elite in the public schools are not nearly so available for service with young thugs. Finally, as Durand pointed out in his analysis of the problems of Carlton School, the very idea of a *school* has only negative associations for the defeated youth which an approved school inevitably revive.[23] Like so many ideas in the correctional armory, the basic approved school approaches obsolescence as the goals of society, the standards of conduct, and the sources of power shift rapidly — more rapidly perhaps in England than in any country of the West. What worked well for the youngster who needed discipline, a chance at a trade, and perhaps removal from a noxious home, will not do for the problems of *anomie* ("the dissociation from norms") in the council houses of England. Just as the borstal begins to learn that it must make training relevant to the community to which its youngsters must return, the approved school begins to shift from its mostly pedagogical emphasis to the conscious use of the school community as an instrument of change and control. Some approved schools have always been aware of the normative uses of their living groups; others, like the unfortunate Carlton School, seem to have been so preoccupied with the attempt to do what they were not fitted to do that efforts at change, of whatever kind, were merely nominal.

Expansion of the numbers for which the approved schools must provide has been of at least the same order as in the other correctional institutions of the country. Whatever the causes of this increase in youthful criminality, the need for change is painfully evident. In the modification of program in the approved schools some of the stresses will be met. Other stresses will require innovation, and English correctional thought has already been resourceful enough to bring several into being.

THE DETENTION CENTERS

To us, the most interesting innovations in the English correctional system are the detention centers. Their implications as new departures

---

[23] *Ibid.*, p. 54.

in the management of delinquents will be discussed in the next chapter, but a brief account of their origins and their place in the penal structure is needed at this point.

Launched in the Criminal Justice Act of 1948, the detention centers responded to the feeling throughout the country that the gap between probation and residential treatment was broad and unreasonable. This feeling seems to have found its most popular expression in the notion, borrowed ironically from the ambiguous social commentary of *The Mikado*, that what was wanted for the teddy-boy was a "short sharp shock." [24] The phrase has haunted detention-center staffs ever since. The original model, as quoted by Sir Lionel Fox, was set forth by John Watson, a magistrate concerned with juvenile justice, as follows:

". . . this provision meets the case where no long period of training is called for, and all that is necessary is a short, sharp punishment to bring the offender to his senses and act as a deterrent. There is a very definite demand for some form of treatment of this kind, which would be of short duration but thorougly unpleasant, and available as a penalty for minor offences, including minor breaches of probation. What is needed is a small local establishment in which the discipline is of the sternest, the food of the plainest, where everything is done 'at the double,' and where there is the maximum of hard work and the minimum of amusement; the kind of establishment a young offender would not want to visit twice, and of which he would paint a vivid picture on his return home." [25]

This was the model adopted by the Criminal Justice Act of 1948. A public which had become thoroughly impatient with the appearance and antics of the postwar "teddy-boys" expected that the process of "de-teddification" would ensue from shocks that would be as short and as sharp as retributive imagination could devise. From their inception, the detention centers have been berated from two sides. There has been no way to satisfy some critics that they were sufficiently severe, while others have been disturbed with the implications of a regime which is arduous and demanding. In an interview with an experienced detention-center warden whom we found in the turmoil of transforming a

---

[24] The relevant passage by W. S. Gilbert runs as follows: "To set in solemn silence in a dull, dark dock, / In a pestilential prison with a life-long lock, / Awaiting the sensation of a short, sharp shock, / From a chippy, chippy chopper on a big, black block."

[25] Fox, *op cit.*, p. 340.

decommissioned girls' borstal into a new senior detention center, the dilemmas were fluently and thoughtfully recounted:

[The "short sharp shock"] disturbingly suggests that somewhere in a dim background there is carried on a system of semilegalized physical torment. Nothing, it need scarcely be said, is further from the truth.

The consequence has been the emergence of two principal bodies of criticism. There are those who unthinkingly welcome the sort of regime which the phrase suggested without considering how it was to be carried out and who, having since visited a center, have been disappointed that no short, sharp shock was readily perceptible. There are also those who condemned the idea of detention from its first inception, who seized upon the words as exactly expressing their worst fears, and who have since made no attempt to visit any center to reëxamine its methods.

It should, therefore, be said at once that however pleasing the short, sharp shock theory may be to those not actually called upon to undergo it, it does not stand up to serious examination. Intelligent persons have suggested that detention center inmates should not have beds; that they should never be allowed to wash in hot water; that they should not have books; should not play games; and so on. These suggestions are no doubt made so that detention may be suitably hard; though what is meant by "hard" in this context is something which has never been satisfactorily established. This is one of the dilemmas of penal reform and is particularly the dilemma of detention. It is not easy to decide what, in detention, is a luxury, and what is essential to it. It is even less easy to know how hard or how soft the regime should be. One thing, however, seems clear. To follow this sort of thinking very far is likely to result in detention centers becoming very much what prisons were some hundred years or so ago. . . .

In spite of this danger, it will probably be agreed that the young men sent to detention do require pulling up — and somewhat sharply. What detention has to do therefore is to provide a regime that will not reproduce all that was worst of the dirt and desolation of the old-time prison . . . and yet will provide the tonic shock suggested by those who inarticulately require that detention shall be *hard*.

There seems to be only one way to do this. This is to insist that whatever is done shall be done as well as the boy is able to do it and that no other standard shall be accepted. To be kept at a high standard of performance in everything all day and every day will, it is suggested, together with the paraphenalia of security and the atmosphere of discipline, provide all the short sharp shock that is necessary or practicable. And it has these added advantages: that when the shock wears off, as inevitably it must, and a feeling of familiarity takes its place, a natural inclination to do things well may possibly remain; and the method may be used to train as many boys as necessary throughout the whole of their sentences without undue strain.

Two kinds of detention center were established. Senior detention centers receive youths aged 17 to 21. Because this group has for the most part tried conventional education and found it wanting, little attempt is made to provide remedial education. Detention-center proponents are inclined to think that English and arithmetic are wasted on this group in the three months that most of them spend in the center. For the most part, detention-center youths are kept busy in working parties at agricultural labor or in mat-making — the British government is an enormous supplier and consumer of the common door mat. To fill out the rest of the regime, an active program of physical training is provided. One detention-center warden insists that no youth shall leave *his* detention center until he has run the mile in six minutes or less.

Junior detention centers are established for boys aged 14 to 16. In these centers, remedial education to some extent takes the place of work, and the atmosphere is faintly more paternal; indeed, one center actually provides a woman social worker. Nevertheless, the regime is severe, and its reputation in the communities from which the youngsters come causes dread. At Kidlington, a few miles out in the Oxfordshire countryside from the industrial bustle and academic cloisters of Oxford, we were allowed to talk to some homesick but throughtful youngsters from London. We asked one, a fourteen-year-old shop lifter, what he thought of the place. He was not sure that he was lucky:

Well, sir, instead of sending you to an approved school where y' get it all cushy-like, y' go to a detention center. They'll laugh at you when y' get back t' school, they'll laugh about all that marching up and down. But the PT [physical training] will be good for me, it's good to keep fit.

[What are they trying to do to you here?] They're trying to turn me into a self-respecting lad; I'm not that because nuffink much ever happened to me. . . . It's not what I thought it would be. I thought you was kept in cells all locked up like, and they'd be wearing truncheons and kick you abaht. . . . I could've been all right on probation, but it's better that I came here."

Somehow, the boys we talked to had absorbed the notion that though it was not as bad as they had thought it would be, that was just as well, because, "if it was better it wouldn't do us much good."

The capacity of the detention center is kept to a maximum of eighty. Commitments are for fixed terms; more than three-quarters of them are for three months; six months is the exceptionally imposed maximum. One warden, reflecting on his service in this rugged enterprise, thinks that a period of three or four months is about right:

Since we have been opened, 82 percent have been sentenced to three months, and this, we feel, is just about right; it is not too short for a man to look on it as easy, and it is too long for him to become completely acclimatised.

What are the results? Once again, in a situation where intuition takes the place of reasoning, it is difficult to know what should be expected. The decisions of lay magistrates are not likely to be governed by a judgment as to the effect of the detention-center program on the personality type of this or that unpromising youth before them. Whether guided by probation officers, police, or even a psychiatrist, there will be one basic demand, once the finding of guilt is made. Get him off the streets, get him away from the shops, the coffee lounges, or the cheap cinemas; maybe when he comes back after his stint in the detention center his mates will have regrouped — or perhaps he will have lost his taste for them.

Not many negative guide lines help the court in making this decision. The word is out that approved-school graduates are unwelcome; a youth who has been through that gamut for two or three years is not likely to be impressed by a few months of austerity at the double. Likewise, borstal boys should not be and are not committed. Generally, it is thought that detention centers should be reserved for first offenders. In fact, they accommodate nearly the full range of delinquent youth.

Under the circumstances, it is hardly possible to lay out the capabilities of the system. The prison commissioners, looking back at a confused experience of the detention centers, present a statistical summation which is suggestive of much but conclusive of nothing. In 1957, 498 boys were released from the senior detention centers. Of these, 88 were first offenders, 360 were recidivists, 44 had approved-school experience, and 6 had previously been confined in junior detention centers. Of the total, 272, or 54.6 per cent had been reconvicted during the three following years. Of the reconvictions, 36.4 per cent of the first offenders had failed; 55.8 per cent of the recidivists and 81.8 per cent of the former approved-school boys had been involved in further delinquency. As to the junior detention centers, the class of 1957 had 529 releases, of whom 87 were first offenders, 402 were recidivists, and 40 were former approved-school boys. Reconvictions for the total group in the ensuing three years were 294, or 55.6 per cent. Of the first offenders, 36.8 per cent were reconvicted; the corresponding percentages for recidivists and former approved-school boys were 56.7 per cent and 85.0 per cent. But whereas the failure rates for release classes which had been at risk for three years were fairly consistent at these levels, the class of 1958, at risk only two years, had a significantly lower failure rate for all classes except former approved-school boys released from junior centers.[26]

The success of the detention centers, then, is considerably greater than that of the borstal system for the same years. The comparability of the populations can be argued but both are so heterogeneous that experimental studies would be feasible. With the effects of contamination so incalculable, it would be desirable to examine the possible gains of specialization of detention centers as to maturity level, experience in crime, and other variables. At present, the detention center is an inexpensive, not very selective way of getting disorderly youths off the city streets. Already its positive potentialities are discernible in a cloudy set of uncertainties. With controlled evaluation systematically applied, it should be possible to decide whether the detention center will eventually displace the borstal entirely, as its enthusiastic advocates contend, or whether radical changes will have to be made to make them justifiable. In the meantime additional detention centers are being put into action without evaluation.

ATTENDANCE CENTERS

We did not have enough time or opportunity to study the attendance centers thoroughly. Authorized in the Criminal Justice Act of 1948, they are intended for the 12-21 age group. With a view to presenting the merely thoughtless child with a minimum consequence to his delinquency, the law empowers the courts to require a boy to present himself for Saturday-afternoon duty to some authority, nearly always the police. One attendance center is conducted in Manchester by the prison commissioners. It is subjected to an experimental design; the results are not yet available.

Our path crossed that of Inspector Bullen, of the Leeds police. A police inspector up from the ranks and a believer in the discipline that molded him, he is an infectious exponent of the attendance center

---

[26] *Report of the Commissioners of Prisons* . . . , p. 192.

which he has for many years conducted every Saturday afternoon. Indeed, so sure is he of the success of his methods that he leaves his enquirer wondering what social problem would not respond to the adoption of his simple expedient.

His center includes youths aged 12 to 17. From them the stern but engaging Mr. Bullen demands one hour on each of twelve consecutive Saturday afternoons. The regime is simple; floors in the police headquarters are scrubbed to perfection; windows are washed, and various other tasks requiring energetic application of muscles to dirt are provided. The model of an old-fashioned English police officer, brass and shoes blindingly polished, Inspector Bullen gave us his considered views:

I work on a syllabus, the main heading being *discipline*. I then proceed to the following essentials: One — punctuality; two — general appearance; three — manners and respect; four — individuality; five — responsibility. These essentials are lacking in England today. I insist on them. One-fifth of a second late, and a boy's attendance is not accepted. He goes home, and he will be on time the next Saturday. I insist on his respect for me; if he has respect for other people, then perhaps he will have respect for their property. I inspect them minutely as soon as they report. If I find dirt or slovenly appearance, I send them home. Next Saturday they'll be clean.

I allow no differentiation. For six attendances a boy scrubs the floor on his bended knees. After six weeks he progresses on his own initiative. It would be wrong for me to grind them down, not to allow them to show initiative. As he shows initiative in completing a simple task well, he is given other tasks without supervision. I never give a boy a job that doesn't want doing.

My most difficult job is to get *inside* them. My duty is not merely to punish but also to rehabilitate. You've got to hit a boy somewhere, and my idea is to hit him inside. Promising boys are allowed during their last four attendances to make something for somebody, for example, an old couple, a blind lady, or some children in the hospital. I've started a hobby club for boys who haven't finished their articles. It meets voluntarily once a week.

I've kept rigid accounts. Since 1952 there have been over 600 boys in the Leeds Attendance Center, with a bulge at the age of fourteen, and 65 to 70 per cent have never been back to court. About 60 of the 180 failures are boys whom I've taken back for nonattendance. Half the boys are thieves; the rest are committed for everything from house-breaking to indecent assault. I allow three infractions. On the fourth the boy goes back to the magistrates.

There's a nucleus of juvenile offenders that only a miracle can keep from further trouble — no attendance center can touch them. You can tell them by their empty outlook, and by their hostility to civilization and authority. I get some of them, but I'm not allowed to take any that have ever been confined before.

Despite his enthusiasm and his confidence in his methods, Mr. Bullen reflected that probably the police are not the best people to be running attendance centers. "We arrest, we prosecute; perhaps it's too much when we punish, too."

How well Mr. Bullen's account represents the forty other attendance centers we cannot say. The flavor of local improvisation, so typical of English corrections, suggests that other methods find expression in other attendance centers. The correspondence between Mr. Bullen's austere but paternal approach and the official intentions may be judged from the following description given by the Ingleby Committee's Report on Children and Young Persons:

> The aim of the treatment at attendance centers is to vindicate the law by imposing loss of leisure, a punishment that is generally understood by children: to bring the offender for a period under discipline and, by teaching him something of the constructive use of leisure, to guide him on leaving the center to continue organized recreational activity. . . . A period of physical training is usually followed by a lecture, employment in handicrafts, or other instruction.[27]

Whatever the details on the prescribed program may be, the general idea tests the value of a scheme of minimum retribution for juvenile offenders. The plan has been under study by the Cambridge Institute of Criminology. An unpublished report, cited by the Ingleby Committee, concludes from research covering nine centers

> that attendance center orders are quite effective when applied to a young offender with little or no previous experience of crime, coming from a fairly normal background. But, when applied to the recidivists with two or more previous offences, especially one who has already failed to respond to probation, the results are not at all encouraging.[28]

The attendance center represents the minimum correctional experience which we found anywhere. Its theoretical usefulness is as uncertain as any, but if the claims of 80 to 90 per cent success for first offenders in the juvenile range can be substantiated, we shall no doubt hear

---

[27] *Report of the Committee on Children and Young Persons* (London: HMSO, Cmnd. 1191), p. 90.
[28] *Ibid.*, p. 90.

more of them. Success with the adult offender has yet to be established. The randomly chosen limit of twelve hours filled so scrupulously by Inspector Bullen has evidently been extended to twenty-four to judge from the committee hearings on the Criminal Justice Bill, on the notion that if twelve is good, twenty-four must be twice as good. Attention to the content of the attendance-center programs has been slight, and the possible value of coördination with social services has been disregarded. Nevertheless, as a device to deal with the early offender before the development of delinquent identities, the attendance center has valid claims to further attention.

THE PROBATION SERVICE

A recent autobiography of an English criminal deals summarily with probation contacts:

We had long talks and arguments about politics, books, the world situation, things like that. But never about my after-care. He had a habit, this bloke, of putting on an air of familiarity, of being "one of the chaps," who knew it all and was just like you himself. This is a common way of trying to win confidence, and it gets nowhere. . . .

I've met a few others at other times in my life . . . and they usually fall into some recognizable type. There are hearty back-slapping ones who use words like "bloody" and "bugger" to show they've got the common touch. There are very earnest ones who've got a vocation for it, whom you hurt much more than you hurt yourself — they imply — when you let them down. There are the real tough guys who've heard all these tales before and won't have the wool pulled over their eyes — they're all right with kids, perhaps, who might take them at their own valuation. There are the very deep ones, who think hard as they pull at their pipes but say nothing, usually to cover up the fact that they can't think what to say. There are the frighteners who tell you how much bird you'll do the next time, threateners who say how much trouble they can get you into, pleaders who complain you're messing up the way they run their office.[29]

The writer, an unrepentant recidivist, was unlikely to discover positive aspects to a service which obviously touched him not at all. Yet implicit in his account is the heterogeneity of English probation which includes the dedicated and the time-server, the thoughtful and highly trained professional, and the untrained and case-hardened hack, all

---

[29] Tony Parker and Robert Allerton, *The Courage of His Convictions* (London: Hutchinson, 1962), pp. 132–133.

working at an occupation in which both standards and expectations
are ill-defined. Little is done to train them after they finally emerge
from their basic indoctrination. A division of the Home Office looks after recruitment, initial training and the maintenance of minimum standards of service. A National Association of Probation Officers concerns
itself with the development of professional ethics and identifications
as well as with the questions of economic security which are austerely
insistent for a new, underpaid, and state-employed profession. But
the character of probation is still locally determined. A principal probation officer in a busy city in the south of England described for
us the seemingly formal and unproductive machinery of the Probation
Committee of the local bench of magistrates. Recommendations are
submitted to be almost invariably approved; quarterly reports are filed
for review without special action. Yet,

I wouldn't want to change this structure. Locally controlled administrative
agencies in this country are more rigorous than those which are centrally controlled. As a matter of fact, I would like to see even more autonomy. As
matters stand at present, there is no strong sense of professional identity
among probation officers. Therefore there must be for a long time to come
some centralized control to maintain standards. But until we can as a profession attract people who will set their own exacting standards we should keep
the present central authority. But in this emphasis on standards I think we're
in danger of throwing out the baby with the bath. We underestimate the
value of the simple, relatively unskilled approach of warm-hearted people.
We are losing the element of *concern*. Perhaps the authority of the local
magistrates to whom we also submit keep us reminded.

What do probation officers do? To an American observer, accustomed
to considerable specialization in probation practice, the wide range of
interests of an English probation office is bewildering. It also bewilders
some conscientious English probation officers. A woman probation officer, contending with a caseload produced by the slums of the industrial north told us:

I think that one can't adapt adequately to everything, the load you are
expected to care for, to the hundreds of different little problems as well. For
instance, the child who is brought to us on a voluntary capacity because of
difficult behavior at home.

But everything is very nearly what the English probation officer sets
out to do in spite of himself. The entire spectrum of crime and delinquency falls into his hands. From advice to the harried mother, uncer-

tain of her course with a defiant child, the probation service takes on a gamut which extends to the after-care of old lags released from preventive detention for a look at an unfamiliar and hostile world. On the notion that the mending of breaking homes will prevent delinquency, courts refer to the probation office a steady caseload of matrimonial reconciliation cases. Homes whose fitness for children's care has been called into question, truants from school referred by education authorities, and cases of neglect provide the "hundreds of little problems" which complicate the task of coping with the continuum of crime and delinquency.

Since World War II there has been no official doubt about the primary role of the probation officer as a social worker. Although the enforcement of the conditions of probation is an inevitable concern, the training required by the Home Office heavily stresses social casework and contains virtually nothing of the curriculum appropriate to law enforcement. Recognition is given to the dual nature of the probation officer's functions, but the essential principles are reformative:

The following principles underlie modern probation practice. Firstly, it is recognized that most probationers are persons in conflict not only with society but also with themselves; consequently in order to befriend the probationer effectively the officer must both study his behavior and also acquire a sound knowledge of his environment and especially of his family. Secondly, the help offered should be sufficient in amount, and should be given in such a way as not to undermine his self respect. . . . Thirdly, there has been in recent years a growing recognition of the importance of helping the client to understand his own problems, to the end that he should make good by his own efforts and in his own way, rather than that he should be induced to conformity to alien ways which he cannot maintain when the probation officer's support is withdrawn. Finally . . . this relationship demands of the client the will to self-determination, and of the caseworker the insight and poise which will enable him to understand the client.[30]

Nevertheless, an opposing opinion persists and was described to us by a supervising probation officer in terms familiar to most American correctional workers:

The minority view is vociferous, and it holds that the probation officer has a specialized function in which casework plays a very small part, if any at all. His authority is derived from the court and his task is mainly to tell people

---

what they can or can't do and to see that action is taken if they do the wrong thing. This simplified system lends itself to the relatively untrained and un-skilled probation officers working in areas where only untrained probation officers can be found.

Like the rest of the British correctional apparatus, the probation service works with tools whose effectiveness is still uncertain. Expecta-tions are scarcely defined, and the means to achieve them are princi-pally borrowed from the allied field of social casework. From the top down to the recruit in training there is more than a conventional acknowledgement of the need for research. For the present the urgent need is for operational studies to help the officer in the field orga-nize his job so that his commitments can be realistically made. That task is being undertaken by the Home Office Research Unit.

But in the middle distance is a greater and eventually more urgent need. This is to bring into some order a base for decision-making which will not depend entirely on the combined intuitions of judges, magistrates, and the probation officers themselves to determine opti-mum circumstances for the grant of probation. English social scien-tists have pioneered the administrative application of behavioral pre-diction systems through the concept of base expectancies, one of the country's most important correctional exports. Applied to borstal pop-ulations, significant classification advances have already been made. Once the practice of probation has been adequately described and the discrepancies brought on by administrative muddle have been cor-rected it should be possible to proceed to define those offender groups which can profit most from the award of probation. Beyond that point, optimum judgments can be made about the division of labor between the field agencies and the institutional establishments. A gigantic en-terprise for which probation officers are not yet ready, for which the courts are probably even less ready, but which can get under way as soon as the present study of probation methods has been completed by the Home Office.

Huge though the task ahead may be, the English probation serv-ices seem in many ways to have established themselves as instruments of effective social concern. There is much to worry about in the rapid shifts of strength and weakness in the English social structure. The impact of these shifts on fragile individuals results not only in crime, but in the full range of social deviation. Because of the reputation of probation officers for effectiveness, national television programs showing their methods and achievements have gained great popularity. Sympathetic references to the social value of their ill-rewarded contributions to the welfare of the community are common in the press. Most significant is the rueful recognition of the probation officer himself that he is often credited with a greater capability for social problem solving than is convenient for him to accept. In Leeds we were told by an experienced hand:

> Our greatest problem is the number of cases placed under our supervision because the welfare service provided by other departments is found to be inadequate. Before the court their offenses are seen to be merely symptoms of serious maladjustment. The bench is under a dilemma; they know that such people need some help and are obviously not getting it from any other department. The only remedy is to place them on probation in the hope that something can be done.

As with many another profession, the stereotypes obstruct the work to be done. The probation officer, as seen by us, was neither the altruist described by the press nor the bungler described by his clients, but usually a cheerful, hard-pressed young professional, painfully aware of his lack of training, yet interested in and hopeful about his calling. With the excellent leadership he has developed in his own association, with the large amounts of research resources being allocated for the improvement of his practice, and with some evidence of public appreciation for his efforts, he has good reasons to be hopeful. But the best reason for hope seems to be the kinds of people attached to the enterprise. Nowhere else in the English correctional world did the word *vocation* in its older sense appear to be so frequently applicable. In the 'twenties and 'thirties the borstals were the hope of English corrections. These hopes have since found expression in the humanization of prisons and the transformation of English correctional practice. We think it is not unreasonable to expect that the hopes now held out for the probation services will be realized throughout the structure of the social services.

The prospects are good if British governments will match the hopes for probation with the means to make them good.

To sum up: We have discussed the variegated English correctional structure in detail because it is an apparatus which we can reliably examine. We cannot account for all irregularities and idiosyncrasies — from some of which, at least, much vitality is drawn — but some common features can be readily exposed. The important prod-

uct of such a survey is a pattern of relationships between community
and apparatus; between apparatus and staff; between apparatus and
client; between staff and client. From this pattern of patterns can be
found the sources of correctional advance through adjustment to the
demands of the times. More and more in the administrative climate
of England these adjustments are rational steps taken to maintain the
irrational equilibrium, outlined in Chapter II. In the next chapter,
we shall deal with three significant adjustments made in the patterns
of correctional practice in England. Here we are concerned to complete our review of the constituent parts of the apparatus by stating
some tentative generalizations about its external and internal relationships.

BETWEEN COMMUNITY AND APPARATUS

The demands of the community upon the correctional apparatus
are expressed through Parliament and the courts. Both have been articulate about expectations. Parliamentary consensus is that the correctional systems should deter people from committing crime, or, having committed crimes, from committing more. The frequent references
to training in parliamentary debates on criminal justice imply an expectation that something positive shall happen to fit the correctional
client to lead a good and useful life. Finally, even the most outspoken
advocates of corporal and capital punishment are outspoken that humanitarian standards of practice should be maintained throughout the
various correctional operations.

The courts insist on their prerogatives in the assessment of retribution. Determination of the length of sentences rests exclusively with
the courts with respect to adults. Though the various options for
penal disposition of juvenile offenders can be administered with some
latitude for the requirements of treatment and the needs to be met
for individual offenders, the choice of disposition remains with the
court. We encountered no informed observer who thought that the
indeterminate sentence was likely to be introduced into the structure
of criminal justice. Despite the advocacy of "treatment tribunals" by
such authorities as Dr. Hermann Mannheim,[31] despite some interest
in such an innovation on the part of the Howard League, this issue

---

[31] Hermann Mannheim, *Criminal Justice and Social Reconstruction* (London: Routledge and Kegan Paul, 1946), p. 227.

has not even been dignified to the level of debate. High Court justices openly prefer severe sentences; several have expressed their regret that corporal punishment is not available for crimes of violence. Because the courts hold so tight a rein on the prescription of treatment through the exercise of sentencing powers, correctional advance in England must consist in adapting the requirements of treatment to the retributive structure of punishment. Most of the individualization of the offender's treatment is determined by the court when a flat sentence is imposed. The court rarely considers staff opinion on the offender's need for more attention than can be given in the time allotted before he is ready for release. No one can definitely say whether this is the way it should be. Too little is yet known of the potentialities of clinical process, and the most optimistic advocate of reformative justice does not maintain that we are yet ready to prescribe or evaluate the exact amount of treatment which will make a safe return to the community possible for an offender. Further, the means are not yet available to determine what kind of balance should be struck between retribution, deterrence, and reform in assessing punishment.

Corrections in England must adjust to a sentencing structure over which the influence of experience is slight. Much can be done within such well-defined limits.

BETWEEN APPARATUS AND STAFF

Essentially there are three staff services in the English correctional apparatus: those attached to the Prison Department, to the approved schools, and to the nationwide probation and after-care services. All three are national services; for all levels there is much geographical mobility. This aspect seems to account for an isolation of institutional practice from much of the life of the community. To a lesser degree insularity is also true of the probation services. The conditions of work limit the scope of interpersonal interaction for staff to other staff members and to inmates. Communities of correctional interest, preoccupied at all levels with the events taking place inside rather than outside, have always existed in England under the prevailing conditions of employment. Only in recent years have administrators learned that the quality of experience within these communities can be adjusted through attention to the elements of staff leadership, training, and organizational forms. One result of this realization is the increased attention being given to the therapeutic community philosophy pro-

pounded by Dr. Maxwell Jones at the Social Rehabilitation Unit of
Belmont Hospital. Another consequence of the concern for environment is the development through service-wide training academies of
systems of training and seminars in which communications and organization in correctional establishments are studied. This trend toward increased self-study by staff has not yet transformed the face of
English correctional practice, but the recognition of a need to make
goal-directed correctional communities out of haphazardly coercive
institutions indicates a will to capitalize on the patterns of relationship established between the apparatus and the staff.

This self-study process may also achieve a closer relationship between the administration of the apparatus and the staff. No outsider
can fail to notice the paternal deprecation of staff by central administration and the irritated submission of the staff to Horseferry House,
far off and ill-informed in London. This reciprocation of hostility and
misunderstanding is not likely soon to be bridged, particularly when
the long tradition of autocratic domination from Whitehall has only in
recent years been attenuated. Participation by local staffs in the formulation of policy will probably lead to more positive involvement with
the total apparatus than in the past.

BETWEEN APPARATUS AND CLIENT

For the correctional apparatus of any country, the client is above
all a person to be controlled. Increasingly the English systems are
called on to control the client not only during the term for which
he is sentenced but also somehow to extend that control past the
time when the client is under obligation. Whether this end is to be
accomplished as a consequence of the unpleasantness of the experience or as the result of reformative treatment is left to the apparatus
to decide. In either case the client is an object of coercion. His alienation may be a matter of indifference, as in most prisons, or a matter
of concern as in most probation services, most approved schools and
borstals, and even in some prisons. The investment of resources for
the adult prisons is generally for adequate control devices to maintain
a necessary level of coercion. Staff in the large local prisons are
charged with the maintenance of order and the prevention of escapes.
Such clinical personnel as are assigned devote most of their efforts to
diagnostic trouble-shooting and have relatively few treatment responsibilities. Most of them would like to treat but regard themselves as

much too overwhelmed with the volume of their caseloads. It does not seem that the apparatus expects treatment or serious reformative efforts from them. To keep the inmates busy is enough.

Concern over alienation as the consequence of coercion is greatest among probation officers and borstal staff. By providing an adequate staff and facilities strenuous efforts are made to disguise coercion and to facilitate treatment relationships. But like most correctional administrators, those in England have no model of treatment related to the various problems. A long history of response to demands for humanitarian reforms has led to a certain confusion between humane management of the offender and the differential solution of special problems presented by offenders. To attempt a "friendly relationship with the chaps" may modify the roles of the coercers and the coerced. It will only accidentally achieve significant change. But in only a very few segments of the apparatus is any more purposeful activity made possible. Always it is the individual staff leadership in a probation office, in an approved school, or in a prison which provides the lead toward specialization of treatment.

BETWEEN STAFF AND CLIENT

English correctional staff are provided by their administrators with various bags of mixed tricks. Once they receive their clients, the tricks will be executed as conscientiously as possible. Some clients respond favorably and are never seen again. Others respond unfavorably and assume a lifelong relationship to both apparatus and to staff. Not much is done to select particular tricks for their effectiveness for any particular offender, nor do staffs from different elements of the apparatus ordinarily take steps to coördinate efforts. Most correctional staffs seem to regard themselves responsible for the effectiveness of the system. The lack of clinical staff in most places, the inadequacy of consultative services, and the absence of specialized training is seldom bewailed and then usually by persons who have been exceptionally exposed to opportunities for special clinical experience. This is not to disregard the concern which many staff members feel at all levels for the improvement of service. But most feel that improvement is a local responsibility of staff groups working together.

With this background of independent insularity and the use of humane administration of service as the treatment afforded the client, most staffs feel little need for basic changes in the apparatus. Clients who respond well to service are credited to the service given. Clients who do not are considered to be inaccessible to any imaginable kind of service. Much attention is given to improved methods of sorting, such as the Mannheim-Wilkins prediction tables. The use made of such devices is primarily to prevent contamination of the good by the bad. No special attention is given to the development of more effective ways of dealing with either the good, or the bad, or the indifferent.

THE STRAINS IN THE PATTERN

We have been concerned here to identify some of the trends from which advance in practice may be reasonably expected. It is the strains in a bureaucratic system that produce change. What advances can be expected from the strains in the English system? We think the present strains will produce clues to future advance.

Most important of all the strains is the increasing volume of intake. The resources of the system are hard pressed to accommodate this volume within present sentencing policies. Both resources and policies have had to accommodate to this strain, but the policies have changed much less than the resources have been augmented.

Second is the strain of expectations on staff capacities. A change in basic staff structure is unlikely in view of the shortages in most professions which might be used to reinforce services. Community expectations of improvement must be met by improvement of the technical capacities of existing staff to modify the behavior of offenders.

Third is the strain toward rational management. So long as the effects of coercion were regarded as no concern of the apparatus, it made little difference how the courts or the apparatus itself disposed of its clients. The walls of Dartmoor and the heavy hands of its warders could be applied indiscriminately to both tractable and intractable. Once humanitarian objectives had been introduced and differentiation became the logically required method of control, no backward steps could be taken. Within an intricate system of small institutions, the process of differentiation has gone very far. For those institutions which are blessed with the best clients, the pleasant results are peace, good order, and a very low rate of recidivism. For those which receive the worst clients, success seems to occur by accident, if at all. Sooner or later, correctional administrators in England must devise methods to expedite the social restoration of the best clients and to improve the effectiveness of control of the worst.

Similarly, rational management will require a better allocation of the probation caseload. At present, probationers vary from minimal offenders who do not need it to old lags who cannot use it. Differential management is the rational answer, and the strain in this direction can hardly be met by merely increasing the number of probation officers. The service must have a more precise directive covering the optimum use of its resources.

Other strains exist. We have emphasized these three because they relate directly to the English correctional advances discussed in the next chapter. Because the entire correctional profession in England is under such enormous strains at the present time we can confidently expect innovation and improvement. Impatient English criminologists regard the future with less assurance, but this is perhaps because neither the opportunities nor the threats in the future they see can possibly be met with present resources. An outside observer can argue from experience with inertia and indifference in static correctional systems that without the present strains neither the opportunities offered by the social science nor the threats of an accelerating crime rate could possibly be met. It is for Parliament, the courts, and the administration of the correctional apparatus itself to capitalize fully on the strains in the system.

THE NETHERLANDS:

The prosperous, but cramped, society of the Dutch can allow little tolerance for crime. Careful organization of a welfare culture has allowed as little as possible of the element of chance in the ordering of human affairs. With nearly twelve million inhabitants crowded into 12,850 square miles, a population density has been achieved in which people must be in their proper places. Effective measures must be taken to keep social deviation to a minimum and to maintain everyone's contribution to the common welfare at a high level.

Social planning has achieved irrefutable success in crime and delinquency. In the whole country, only 1800 men and women – including some surviving collaborators from World War II – are in correctional custody; 18,000 are serving terms of probation. Compared with other industrialized countries, crime is not a major problem in the Netherlands. Perhaps in the attention which the Dutch social sciences give to improving the nation's normative institutions lies the explanation of the success in driving crime rates down to a minimum.

The Dutch correctional apparatus has much of interest to the observer of advance. Two institutions, described in the next chapter, attracted our attention as among the most significant for the future. As a backdrop for their description, a brief examination of the apparatus of which they are a part is needed here.

In the South Holland city of Breda stands one of the country's few maximum security prisons. An immense umbrella-shaped structure, it follows the prescription of Jeremy Bentham for the "panopticon," in which observation of the entire interior of the prison is possible from the center. Surrounded with masonry walls which are armed with four of the few gun towers in northern Europe, its security is beyond question. A total staff of 86 employees maintains control of a capacity of 120 inmates. Long terms are served here; concern for security and order predominate. Inmates are housed, fed, and worked; there is little concern for what may happen to them, whether for good or ill, so long as none make their way out of the massive provisions for their secure detention. So far as we could find out, none do.

The prison at Breda serves as a model of Dutch correctional tradition. Security and order are assured by an essentially custodial service. All prisoners are assumed to be dangerous (though the governor of Breda told us that he thought only thirteen of his charges were properly so described), but through a system of massive deterrence and retribution, scaled arbitrarily by the courts, the greatest effort would be made to reform the criminal. For generations, the Dutch Ministry of Justice has provided, in varying degrees of austerity, for the confinement and employment of the country's criminals. During the postwar years the trend toward change became clearer. A young lawyer who was about to change his employment from prison governor to criminal court judge told us:

Our difficulty is that when we talk about these ideas of rehabilitation we ourselves have no proof at all that these ideas are effective. Everything is in the experimental state, really, and we don't know whether any of these methods will be beneficial to all the prisoners or only to part of them. But the development of our field is to be compared with the development of the whole field of social work or of mental health, not only in the Netherlands but in all the other countries. I have a feeling that the time is right for change. I mean we won't accept anything else. We don't know what we want yet, but we don't want it to continue in the lines that we have been working. I think this change came about just after the last war. We had been going on and on and we never asked ourselves why we were doing it.

Through training, the inauguration of a new and massive research program under the guidance of a professional sociologist, Dr. George Veringa, and the leadership of the director-general, Dr. Ernest Lamers, Dutch prisons are beginning to move toward new levels of service. Ideas and examples from closely allied fields abound in the country; it is reasonable to expect major advances from the present conservative correctional practice.

Juvenile institutions are under the auspices of the Department of Social Welfare. Much like English approved schools, they are integrated with a complex child-welfare system which reaches into every hamlet and neighborhood in the land. Unlike many other cultures which have been subjected to the twin strains of rapid urbanization and industrialization, the Dutch have been zealous to maintain the values of village and neighborhood communities. Supporting these values and in turn supported by the evident attachment of the people for communal, mutual-aid values, the child-welfare system includes volunteer advisers, often attached to local churches, to whom parents in distress about the problems of their children can turn. Professional help is never far off; volunteer advisers know to whom they can turn when problems are beyond their resources. Local child-welfare boards deal not only with the problems of delinquency but also with other social problems of child rearing, making use of both volunteer and professional assistance as needed. When institutional care is needed, the institutions under the jurisdiction of the Ministry of Social Welfare are available for a wide range of childhood problems, from serious emotional disturbance to the need for special opportunities for vocational training.

Much emphasis is given to early case finding and appropriate action when cases are found. The apparent strength of local community life in the Netherlands should keep the occasion of delinquency down to its present minimal level for a long time. By the development of a system of neighborhood help, institutionalized by the official supports of provincial and national governments, few children are allowed to drift into delinquency. The few who do are provided with appropriate residential training-school experience. As a result, juvenile delinquency seems to be generally regarded as a relatively well-controlled social problem.

Finally, a few references to the intricate system of probation in the Netherlands. Dutch probation is involved with the three principal religious groups, Catholic, Calvinist, and Lutheran. Schools, universities, and philanthropic institutions are tied to one of the three denominations. With probation the situation is even more complex. Six probation societies administer supervision and after-care of wards of the court, prison releases, and others under official or unofficial guidance after conviction of an offense. In addition to societies attached to the three major denominations, a fourth society was established by the Salvation Army; a fifth for the supervision of alcoholics; and a sixth, the Meijers Society, for the probation supervision of offenders for mentally disturbed delinquents. Except for the two specialized societies, a prospective client can elect assignment to whichever denominational supervision he likes.

Standards are set by the Ministry of Justice, which pays 90 per cent of all salaries, and the entire amount of all other expenses. Minimum eligibility for employment, training, research, and public relations are also determined by the central government. All administrative management of the central government's part in the program is in the hands of the upper-level civil service, the qualifications for which primarily stress legal training. Actual probation operations are conducted by personnel trained in social casework. This requirement is met with difficulty; although there are twenty schools of social work in the country, each with a three or four-year post-gymnasium curriculum, and each enrolling between two and three hundred students, most case workers are women, and turnover due to marriage is very high. Usually, Dutch women do not accept employment after marriage.

The small size of the country makes possible an intensive and coördinated training program which offsets some of the recruitment and organizational handicaps. Frequent all-day training programs are conducted with arrangements for all personnel in the entire service to attend simultaneously. Content of the programs is prescribed by the national director of probation with the assistance of the Federation of Probation Societies.

Review of the present position of the service with Dr. M. E. Tjaden, director of probation, elicited a sense of pride in the accomplishments of Dutch probation since World War II. Before that time, probation services were entirely in the hands of lay ordinarily voluntary personnel, with neither supervision nor professional consultation provided. The Netherlands has not entirely professionalized the service, with qualification in social case work a required standard. The interest and experience of lay volunteers has been retained. Their friendly interest in probationers, where an interest is needed, extends to job-finding, helping individuals to regain community respect, and general activities of sponsorship. Their understanding of the service is particularly important in building a strong public-relations position, an aspect of probation administration which greatly interests Dr. Tjaden.

Caseload standards reveal something about expectations. The basic caseload in probation service is one hundred probationers in supervision or one hundred presentence investigations, or any agreed combination of the two types of service. Caseloads in the Bureau of Alcoholic Rehabilitation are set at seventy-five; the psychiatric caseloads in the Meijers Society are still in a process of experimental adjustment. The country's expectations of the probation services, Dr. Tjaden thought, are still primarily oriented to control. Tactful control, and control reinforced by behavior modification where possible, but control must be maintained. The criterion for success, as almost anywhere else, is recidivism. In this endeavor the Netherlands probation societies have been conspicuously successful, or so it would seem from the not very abundant statistics available.

Dr. Tjaden estimated that the national rate of success on probation has been more than 90 per cent since the war. This figure is arrived at by the number of failures occurring in the standard three-year sentence. Success with after-care cases fluctuates markedly, with no clear evidence on what influences produce the changes from year to year. During the period 1948-1955 parole violation rates varied from 16.3 per cent of those released in 1949, to 25.5 per cent of those released in 1954.

Research in probation service has hardly begun. In 1960 a part-time sociologist was employed, with an enormous backlog of problems. The increased interest of the Ministry of Justice in criminological and correctional research makes probable a major program in the coming years.

To get closer to the actual practice of probation, we left the comfortable administrative offices in The Hague and went to the headquarters of the Dr. F. S. Meijers Society in Utrecht. Under the direction of Dr. W. A. Vaandrager, this agency has been built up during the past few years to a caseload of about 1,500 probationer-patients under the supervision of 25 probation officers. Each of the eleven provinces in the country has at least one Meijers probation officer assigned to its court. The caseloads vary: Dr. Vaandrager is sure that the average of 60 is much too high for the defective or disturbed delinquents with whom the officer must deal. Adjustments are made; some officers carry caseloads of 100, others, with especially difficult cases, may handle as few as 20. For each 50 cases at least three hours of psychiatric consultation is provided. There is no conventional psychotherapy, but psychiatrists see probationers for suggestions concerning special problems.

As might be expected, the Meijers Society has the highest rate of recidivism; Dr. Vaandrager thought it must be at least 50 percent. With better personnel, some reduction in the rate of failure is hoped for. At this point, neither the psychiatric staff nor the probation officers are all that could be wished. Nevertheless, certain canons of practice have been tentatively established. Their effective implementation, Dr. Vaandrager recognizes, depends on the recruitment and training of adequate staff. Basic to all Meijers Society patient contact are the following requirements:

Before any contact is made, the entire dossier must be thoroughly studied – a formidable undertaking in itself in view of the Dutch standards of exhaustive record keeping.

First contact must be before sentence in the case of an individual placed directly on probation, or at the institution in the case of after-care.

Probation officers from the first are expected to face patients with the necessity of thinking about their problems of personal adaptation. As soon as rapport is reasonably established, patients must be asked to think about the possible causes of a future breakdown. The theme of the whole relationship is starkly stated by Dr. Vaandrager as: "We think you will succeed, but it will be a narrow escape."

Many contacts will have to be made several times a week, and all contacts at least once a week, in the first months of probation.

There must be a heavy emphasis on training, much of it done by Dr. Vaandrager. Weekly consultations with psychiatrists are stressed, and some caseloads are also provided with sociological consultation.

There must be treatment for the probationer-patient's entire family. The patient must at all events see that the agency is on his side, but the family must also see why the agency does whatever it does.

Looking at the task ahead, Dr. Vaandrager sees his work as hardly begun. Because it operates within the framework of conventional probation, most of its clients, as well as the general public are inclined to think that its function is merely to find work for difficult probationers and to take care of their pressing material requirements. This extends even to the institutions, which tend to believe that it is enough for the Society to be friendly — with the hardly encouraging reservation that despite anything anyone can do, "we believe he will come back." This belief, not without justification in the results, can only change with great improvements in practice. At the heart of the improvements to be made, Dr. Vaandrager believes, is the development of methods by which truly stable relationships can be built with the hostile, fearful, and suspicious people with whom he is concerned.

With the problem seen so clearly, it is reasonable to expect that the Meijers Society will arrive at some significant advances in general probation practice and in the specialized care of disturbed delinquents.

With a rate of criminality almost insignificant in comparison to most other countries, the Netherlands has nevertheless achieved, by its professional establishment and the Dutch social conscience, a correctional apparatus to be envied by countries more afflicted with social deviation. On the basis of its enlightened practice, two impressive examples of advanced practice will be described in the next chapter.

SCANDINAVIA

Our attention now turns to the four Scandinavian nations, Denmark, Norway, Sweden, and Finland. History, geography, and language have produced many common features in the Nordic cultures, particularly in their governmental structures. Economic and political understandings have accentuated and to some extent institutionalized the similarities. The Scandinavian countries largely use the same organizational forms; such differences as exist are of no great moment except in Finland, where some adaptations of Russian correctional practice have been superimposed upon a basically Scandinavian structure.

Nevertheless, in considering Scandinavian corrections cultural differences affecting practice must not be overlooked. Denmark, with a low rate of property offenses, has given much attention to crimes against the person. Special institutions for psychopaths have been established under psychiatric auspices for the control and treatment of violent and sexual offenders. One of these institutions, Herstedvester, has gained world-wide renown under the clinical and administrative leadership of Dr. G. K. Stürup; it will be discussed in the next chapter.

Norway, with a low crime rate and a system of small, isolated institutions, has only recently begun to adapt its traditional penology toward correctional advance. Perhaps because many leading citizens had prison experience during the resistance period of World War II, there has been an exceptional amount of public interest and scholarly attention to criminological problems. Under the distinguished leadership of Professor Johs. Andenaes a group of imaginative and productive criminologists have managed to make the University of Oslo a leading center for crime studies, despite the paucity of crime to study. Their investigations have done much to move the ministries of justice and of social welfare to consider major changes in institutional program and design. Our visit to Norway coincided with the inception of these considerations. A program is currently under way which will incorporate milieu treatment and small-group control currently prevailing in advanced correctional thought throughout Europe.

In contrast with Denmark and Norway, the crime rate in Sweden is comparatively high. A prosperous country with a well-established tradition of spending money on social welfare, Sweden has embarked under the forceful leadership of Director-General Torsten Eriksson of the Royal Prison Administration upon an elaborate program of institutional construction, partly to meet a greatly increased need for capacity and partly to replace buildings now considered obsolete. Perhaps because the greatest social rewards have for several decades gone to service in business and industry, Sweden has not had the personnel to match its facilities. It is not likely that Eriksson's impatient administration will allow this discrepancy to continue for long. In the meantime, Swedish prisons and welfare schools are manned by traditionally trained correctional workers, prepared for moderate control rather than for the effective use of the handsome new buildings for the treatment programs to which they are so well adapted.

Finland's long and complex relationship with its eastern neighbor is reflected in the correctional emphasis on the therapeutic value of work. Finnish corrective labor colonies, designed for prisoners serving two years or less, are largely drawn from a Soviet model. In the late 'forties, a Communist Minister of Justice briefly in office brought the labor colonies into being. When a non-Communist minister took over, it was decided that this particular Marxist-Leninist innovation was working so well that it should be retained. Labor colonies are well suited to cope with the alcoholic traffic offender, of which Finland has an abundant supply.

But despite these variations of correctional problems and solutions in the Scandinavian countries, the basic pattern rests on similar legislation and structure. A look at the resulting forms will enable us to understand the advances to be expected from Scandinavian corrections. In many ways they are the most significant of all for the creation of a rational correctional structure in the future. Seemingly moved by a concern that the necessity for punishment of the criminal be reconciled with his need for help toward a normal life in the community, even the standard practice of correction in Scandinavia tends toward benign conventions and generous policies. Perhaps because the welfare state has been planned so well and has met so many needs in these countries, the public has been more inclined than elsewhere to make of the correctional apparatus an adaptive resource for the delinquent fringe in addition to its natural function as an instrument of control. Planning comes naturally to Scandinavians confronted with social problems. So does moderation in control measures.

CARE OF DELINQUENT CHILDREN

Throughout Scandinavia, concern for children in trouble is brought into focus by district child-welfare boards, sometimes elective, sometimes appointive, but always locally situated. Cases of childhood maladaptation of any kind, particualrly including delinquency, come before these boards for corrective intervention. Their first line of resources is local, as in municipal "social bureaus" in some Danish cities, or in "children's villages" available near some large cities in Sweden. Foster homes, volunteer probation officers, and local organizations are pressed into service to rectify neglect, family conflicts, or delinquency. Usually a member of the child-welfare board assumes a personal interest in a case in which the board has taken a hand. Probably most cases of

juvenile troubles demanding attention outside the home are handled
in this way.

If the problem exceeds the resources of the local community the
boards may turn to the state apparatus to deal with juvenile deviations. A comprehensive network of children's institutions is available
throughout each Scandinavian country. Most of them are specialized
for a particular kind of childhood problem. Commitment to such
residential institutions tends to be long-term, just as in the English
approved schools. Such establishments are usually small, with capacities ranging from thirty to seventy. Staffing is ordinarily rich; it is not
uncommon to find an institution with as many staff as children.

Throughout Scandinavia we encountered a uniform determination
by administrators and staff of the child-welfare boards and schools
that the boards themselves are intended to express the concern of society and that their decisions are so based rather than on specialized
professional considerations. Commitment to a residential school is not
intended to be punishment and is supposed rather to put into effect
a plan for needed care. Decisions are made without bench or bar.
Board procedures emphasize analysis of problems rather than findings
of guilt. Dissatisfied parents may appeal to the Ministry of Social
Welfare or to the courts if there is a question of inconsistency with
the law.

We could not elicit any idea on how the children themselves see
this procedure. Lawyers suspected that children committed under
such proceedings to institutional care or to other official intervention
felt punished, and unfairly punished, too, simply because punishment
is so zealously disavowed. Further, the lawyers thought that the indeterminate nature of the commitment kept the child in a state of
suspense often disproportionate to the gravity of the delinquent act
itself. Legal safeguards in disputed cases are not well provided for,
and the chance of real inequity is great enough so that children might
feel that everything is stacked against them.

On the other hand, child-welfare and ministry-school staffs uniform-
ly thought that these objections were more theoretical than significant.
Though some children might feel punished when being sent to a
school after having committed a delinquent act, they should soon find
that they are treated considerately and in consistence with present
behavior rather than with past records. Even boys confined in a
school for refractory recidivists in Denmark knew that any depriva-

tions were caused by their behavior in school rather than by the seriousness of their particular offense.

In the light of world-wide concern about the optimal organization for juvenile justice, it is to be hoped that studies will eventually be made of the perception of child-welfare-board procedures by both delinquent children and their parents. The issue is currently in much doubt, but there seems to be no question of supplanting the system with either the modified criminal procedure of England or with the equity procedure of the American juvenile courts. The view that social restoration takes place most surely outside the framework of retributive justice and deterrent theories of crime prevention is consistent with generalized concern in Scandinavia to provide each social deviant as much chance as possible to live a constructive life. This priority may not be met any more successfully than in countries where punitive theories of justice hold sway, but it seems certain that Scandinavian criminal justice will continue to place social restoration first among its objectives.

We visited many schools in Scandinavia. On an island in Oslosfjord, in an old country home in central Finland, and in elegantly designed quarters built for the purpose in Jutland we found substantially the same warm, friendly, and unsophisticated small institutions trying to provide a tranquil and stabilizing experience to boys who in their whole lives had never known tranquillity or stability. There was very little professional personnel. Usually the organization consisted of a school teacher, a social worker, or perhaps a psychologist directing a small staff of house parents, who might be almost anybody recruited from the local countryside, and a few people to teach school. Sometimes a psychiatric consultant would come in for evaluative interviews or in-service training; more often the staff hoped that eventually this kind of service could be brought in from a fairly distant metropolis.

Typical of such schools is Lövstå, far down a rather unimproved road about two hours from Stockholm. Situated like most Swedish institutions beside a lake, Lövstå gives an initial impression of complete seclusion from a naughty world. A small administration building and infirmary have been made from what was once a farm house. Scattered out over a considerable rolling acreage are school buildings and four or five cottages, each resembling an unpretentious Swedish home.

This fairly remote institution is set aside for Sweden's most disturbed delinquents. With a capacity of thirty-two and a staff of about twenty, the school sets out to do what can be done in a reassuring atmosphere. Everyone agrees, including the director, Dr. Dick Blomberg, a psychologist, that the school should be under psychiatric auspices because of the difficult boys to be dealt with. But psychiatrists are hard to come by in Swedish corrections, and none have yet been persuaded to move to such distant locations as Lövstå. School teachers have had to adapt their profession to their unpredictable charges. Social-work students are occasionally recruited for field-work experience in the cottages. But most of the continuity in the institution is provided by house parents trained in psychology and group dynamics by Dr. Blomberg.

Boys are sent to the school by the central administration in the Department of Social Welfare, after an appraisal of information and records submitted by the local child-welfare board. Some have been tried in other schools and found too disturbed to get along. Not many are transferred to other institutions from Lövstå.

The year is divided into three terms, with furlough privileges provided at the end of each. Boys come as young as nine and may return as late as eighteen. They are released to a special probation service attached to the welfare school system, and are allowed as many paroles as they can use, up to the upper age limit. All releases are realistically regarded as trials in the community, with the school ready to accept the boy's return whenever it becomes necessary. Each boy before release has seen other boys come back and has seen that no punitive action is taken. Though boys have been known to commit crimes to ensure their return, an effort is made to impress on all that no such drastic step is needed if life is not going well at home. Nothing is done to discourage dependency on the school; it is recognized that most of the boys sent there will have no one else on whom to rely safely. Even after boys are far too old for return as inmates, they return for visits to house parents and friends.

The success of the school is hard to evaluate. Dr. Blomberg is hampered by the inadequate state of Swedish criminal statistics. He has made follow-up studies which suggest that about 70 per cent of Lövstå boys have some contact with the courts within the first five years after their final release. With boys so difficult such a record does not seem discouraging. As we have so frequently had cause to mention, no one really knows what should be expected of a school like this: That it keeps boys under control with no disturbance to neighboring communities, that it manages to retain their loyalties long past release, and that it seems to do all this with highly disturbed delinquents suggests that much more can be done than is generally realized with a small program conducted by a sensitive staff under competent professional leadership. Certainly Dr. Blomberg would not contend that his is more than a zealous improvisation with the materials at hand. His use of these resources has been a rational effort to make the best of them.

In Stockholm we discussed with the chief of the welfare school system, Dr. Lars Bolin, the strains placed on the system by the increasing rates of delinquency in Sweden. Here, it seemed to us, was an essentially pedagogical method of dealing with delinquents which seemed to be adequate to the problem in most of Scandinavia. Even in Sweden, where the pressure during the past two or three years had become unprecedentedly severe, the small size of the schools and the experience of the staffs had kept operations running smoothly.

Dr. Bolin was by no means satisfied. The dimensions of the problem alarmed him. Within three years he had had to add to the capacity of the system to raise the number of beds from 750 to more than 1,000. Waiting lists for admission to the schools had been established; for a school like Lövstå, intended for disturbed boys, the delay between commitment and admission might be as much as three months. Still more building was obviously needed.

Even more difficult was the lack of staff:

You see, Sweden is an underdeveloped country when you are talking about psychology. Our training of psychologists in the universities is backward; it is essentially philosophical and statistical. There is no clinical training. We are at scratch when we try to place psychologists in our institutions. They come to me and ask: "What shall I do in this institution?" I must tell them that the first step is to try to understand what must be done by the institution.

We have small institutions made up of small cottages. They should only start treatment, to be fulfilled outside the institution in the after-care system. In our new Child Welfare Act we talk about care inside institutions and outside institutions. We no longer talk about after-care.

Even with the limited professional resources available, some steps ahead have been possible. At Eknäs, a welfare school for younger girls, a program of "controlled family care" has been initiated. Twen-

ty-five families have been enlisted to take girls into their homes from
the institution. Through foster-home care, the girls are removed from
collective influences in living groups but are returned to the school
for psychological treatment, remedial education, and vocational training. So far as possible, Dr. Bolin hopes, patterns such as this will pervade the system. The walls between residential training and the community will vanish, thereby increasing the correctional repertory.
Individual treatment will be really available for those children who must
have it, and group treatment will be provided for only those who need
it for the solution of their problems. Much remains to be done, particularly the establishment of guide lines for the determination of what
combinations of individual and collective management are most suited
to what delinquency problems. But Dr. Bolin has no doubt about the
need for better integration of institutional programs with the real life of
the community.

Along with the strain of new ideas in need of personnel able to
put them into practice is the strain of new forms of delinquency. One
fact apparently established for the present Scandinavian culture is the
high incidence of delinquency in the age group thirteen to fifteen.[32]
To Bolin, the problem presented by the typical delinquent of this
group is sharply different from the problems which the welfare school
was established to solve. The major problem for welfare schools is still
the child with a long record of delinquency and poor prospect for
resocialization in his own family and neighborhood. But in recent
years the country has been increasingly plagued with the *raggare*,
teen-age vandals, joy riders, and brawlers; usually members of gangs
with a tendency to riot. Though their records may be brief or nonexistent when they appear before the welfare boards, the tolerance of
the community for their behavior is so low that their removal is frequently necessary. Bolin sees this group as scarcely in need of the
long-term "inside-outside" care which he has been devising for the
more traditional caseload. Like his colleagues in England, he faces the
demand for the "short, sharp shock," for boys whose outlandish attire,
loutish conduct, and potential for damage overtax the community's
patience. His solution has been the new institution at Hammargården,
where in two or three months a vigorous program of physical train-

---

[32] Knut Sveri, "Criminality Among Children," *Nordisk Tidsskrift for Kriminal-
videnskab*, 47 (1959), 132–147.

ing and rehabilitation is carried out. The intention is to interrupt the aimless and destructive activities of the boys and to prepare them for an active year in a forestry camp, the Army, or other disciplined outdoor activity. No serious psychological treatment is attempted; the idea is to bring about such insight as can be furnished by relating general patterns of behavior to the delinquency which brought the boys to the institution. "We can only open their eyes," we were told by the superintendent. Whether this purposely superficial kind of program is enough to make self-controlled young Swedes out of leather-jacketed *raggare* remains to be seen. Dr. Bolin supposes that Hammarsgården will have to be an experiment for some time. At this stage of its development, neither he nor his staff are sure enough of its program to attempt a control-group evaluation.

Real innovation seems as yet to be beyond the capacity of the Scandinavian welfare schools. Except, in Sweden, where the strains are increasingly severe, major changes are probably unnecessary to cope with the kinds of delinquency problems which these schools must solve. Our brief review of their scope suggests that their stability, based on a cadre of experienced leadership, offers impressive opportunities for the resocialization of a troubled generation. As a laboratory for the study of small-group influences upon delinquent children, the welfare school as developed in all Scandinavian countries can scarcely be surpassed. It lacks only the clinicians and researchers to put it to effective use.

THE TREATMENT OF ADULT OFFENDERS

The patterns for the treatment of adult offenders, as of juveniles, do not substantially vary throughout Scandinavia. Probation is available in all four countries, dealing not only with offenders committed directly from the courts but also with releases from prison. As described in Chapter II, there is much use of volunteers, especially in rural areas. In Norway, Denmark, and Finland, probation is primarily in the hands of private societies which receive subventions from the government. In Sweden, probation has come under official auspices; it seems probable that a pattern of probation much along the lines developed in England will eventually be adopted. Professional probation officers are social workers with formal training in casework, though without much specialized background in correctional problems. Their caseloads range from forty to seventy, with some allowance made in some places — especially in such metropolitan areas as Oslo and Helsinki — for difficult supervision cases. Except in Finland, where special attention has been given to creating opportunities for probationers as socially handicapped persons, we were impressed with an earnest but unsophisticated approach to the profession which seemed to prevail throughout Scandinavia.

The structural model for Scandinavian prisons of the future is being built in Sweden. The traditional structure is straight out of Pennsylvania; to this day, one of the finest surviving examples of Pennsylvania prison design is the Vestrefaengsel in Copenhagen, where, until very recently, chapel seats were still boxed off in vertical coffin-shaped compartments so that privacy of the prisoner would be maintained and his contamination prevented. Obsolete, dilapidated, and irrelevant to this age and its problems, the metropolitan prisons of Scandinavia are shown to the visitor with reluctance and apologies. For the most part they are used for detention pending disposition or for sentences of very short terms. Not much happens to them, though an experiment conducted in Copenhagen by Karen Berntsen suggested inconclusively that even under the unfavorable conditions provided by Vestrefaengsel programs of casework and integration with probation services could produce a reduction in recidivism as compared with a group not afforded such service.[33]

In addition to the ancient Pennsylvanian bastilles, there are long-term institutions in which Scandinavian thought has found its own expression; these use small-group organization, full employment, and a supportive, relaxed atmosphere which stresses the inmate's predicament as a problem to be solved rather than guilt to be expiated. Coercive measures are limited to withdrawal of privileges and isolated confinement; there are no armed perimeters. The use of staff and program toward the creation of a benign climate has gone farthest in Denmark where, under Inspektór Rafael at Kragskovhede in the north of Jutland or under Inspektór Tolstrup at Norre Snede excellent conventional prison programs under open conditions are established. At Kragskovhede, California classification methods have been adapted to a 400-capacity institution. The familiar elements of vocational training, industrial employment, and remedial education are combined with so-

---

[33] Karen Berntsen and Karl O. Christiansen, "The Resocialization of Short Term Offenders," *United Nations International Review of Criminal Policy*, No. 6 (1954).

licitous efforts to keep in close staff contact with each inmate. Staff seem constantly to be pooling knowledge about each man, even to the extent that everyone has managed to memorize the register numbers by which inmates are known in Danish institutions. The staff assumes considerable responsibility for after-care. Periodic visits to Copenhagen, where most of the caseload comes from, are made so that the staff can acquaint themselves with families, assist with economic and social problems resulting from the breadwinner's confinement, and coördinate after-care supervision with the staff of the probation agency which has the primary responsibility. For men released to the Jutland cities, the staff often takes full responsibility for after-care. Well-equipped with adequately trained social workers, the Kragskovhede staff is hampered only by geography in achieving a complete integration of the institution with the community at large.

Norre Snede, a much smaller institution, was established for the confinement of young prisoners. With an average length of stay of about six months, and a maximum term of two years, the program is a combination of agriculture and education, relying on the cohesion and norms which can be established in small groups. The capacity of the institution is limited to seventy, and a staff of forty-three is prepared to maintain a culture of mutual concern and self-respect. Family visits are encouraged. Staff interviews with visiting family members are a firm rule. Family group treatment has not been attempted, however, in the belief that the undesirable relationships and identifications which might thus be established would outweigh in value any good effects.

Recidivism for Kragskovhede and Norre Snede is approximately 35 per cent for an exposure period of five years. At Kragskovhede, the staff makes a point of keeping the inmates informed of the standing of the prison with respect to success and failure after release. Like all Danish prisons, both institutions are far from capacity. Kragskovhede has had difficulty in maintaining all its program; a promising land reclamation project has had to be suspended for lack of inmates to carry it out. With such depleted populations, there is much staff speculation about the optimum length of confinement. The general opinion is that sentences are probably not long enough to achieve the required objectives. In particular, there is a feeling that the short term of less than six months can hardly be expected to accomplish anything worth while for an offender who needs confinement at all.

The consensus holds that the rates of recidivism would probably improve if sentences were kept to a minimum of about a year.

We discussed with a few English-speaking prisoners what they themselves thought of their experiences in prisons so generously intended, so thoughtfully organized. We were startled with the almost vituperative deprecation of staff which we encountered. The zeal for classification is seen as a paternalism which robs the man of free choice and individuality. The endless case discussions impress the inmate with a sense of vagueness and uncertainty; definite answers are seldom heard, and the notion gets about that staff are more interested in careers than in inmates. Our sample, restricted by language, was hardly representative. But, as nearly everywhere, communications in correctional institutions enable the staff to form only modestly informed speculations about the climate of opinion in the communities in which they are immersed. Though the need for such information is vital, the techniques for getting it are clumsy, expensive, and uncertain. Recent attempts to make such studies in Scandinavian prisons with methods developed by Stanton Wheeler [34] have not yet been completed. When available they will constitute a major contribution to the understanding of the influence of program intentions on institutional morale.

Our review of Scandinavian institutions must include a description of the system of preventive detention. Here the humane intentions of Scandinavian correctional leadership are most apparent. Most societies show concern for the juvenile delinquent, the first offender, or the disturbed criminal. It is much more exceptional to discover a sympathetic concern for the persistent adult recidivist. In most countries such people are consigned to survival on the minimum conditions which society will allow, often only as exasperated concessions to the resistance of the most unworthy prisoners of all. It is a measure of Scandinavian civilization that the confirmed criminal is dealt with on the basis of his psychological and social needs rather than grudgingly allowed to live.

Because Sweden can most easily afford to be generous it is to the Swedish system of preventive detention that we should look for models of Scandinavian care for this class of prisoners. To appreciate its

---

[34] Stanton A. Wheeler, "A Preliminary Report on a Scandinavian Prison Study," unpublished manuscript, 1962, in the author's possession.

operation, the Swedish law on prevention detention must be understood. Detention is defined as a protective sanction rather than as a penalty. Its duration is for a minimum of one year and a maximum of twelve years. An offender can be placed in preventive detention if twice previously sentenced to prison and guilty of committing an offense while in prison or within five years of release. The sentence is indeterminate, but the court must fix a minimum period before which parole may not be granted. Parole supervision must be fixed for a minimum period of three years, and is determined by a special board which supervises the entire preventive detention system.

There are about five hundred such detainees distributed among eight institutions with capacities from twenty-five to two hundred. The system is administratively sealed off from the rest of the Swedish prisons; transfers in and out of the circuit are not allowed.

So much for the structure. How does it work?

We visited Hall, the central and largest establishment. Situated about twenty miles from Stockholm in a forested area, it houses two hundred inmates in a closed facility and is the headquarters of the director of the preventive detention system, Dr. Gunnar Marnell.

At Hall, we were first introduced to Frank D——, an embezzler who spoke English fluently. His enthusiasm for Swedish correctional methods was hardly shared by many of this fellow inmates. With some insight into group psychology, he pointed out to us that although Hall housed some extremely recalcitrant recidivists, there is little trouble because Dr. Marnell and staff understand that in prisons pressure from above is balanced by pressure from below. He analyzed Hall's relatively peaceful atmosphere as follows:

> In the system in force here, we are treated fairly, and we really have a sort of freedom and responsibility. In this way, there aren't any specific groups which try to be in command of the other guys. . . . I, or any other inmate, have the right to be treated like a human being. In larger, harder prisons the inmates are herded together, and they are always looking for the easiest way to resist. That is why you in America have prison riots. Because the harder they treat us, the harder we will be, and the fairer they treat us, the fairer *we* will be.

In Dr. Marnell's office we inquired into the validity of Frank's interpretation of institutional policy. Dr. Marnell is a scholarly looking administrator with several technical papers for learned journals and congresses to his credit. Except when quoting himself as saying firm things firmly to recalcitrant inmates, he has a tentative, pacific manner. His kind is often found in borstals, approved schools and open prisons; we don't seem to have run into his reflective air and phlegmatic calm elsewhere in the top management of maximum security prisons.

What about coercion at Hall? we asked. "I should say," Dr. Marnell replied, "that nothing except the sentence is compulsory. We don't use group therapy by compulsion, nor do we have services that they have to attend or lectures they have to listen to."

But surely the inmates have to work?

They have to work, but you see, if a man doesn't go to the workshop for a day, he isn't under solitary confinement. He's still in the corridor. Our job is through talking with him to find out what is behind his refusal to work. In a *big* institution like Hall you have one or two problems like this every day. As a matter of fact, this kind of problem is one of the basic obstacles to their adjustment outside. They haven't been able to form a relationship with other persons so that they can get along in a factory.

Here a person who doesn't work doesn't get paid. Our inmates have leaves to plan for and they need money, like other people.

There are also group incentives to work:

Our best system is in the laundry, where fifteen inmates work. It's not a big laundry. Their income is divided among all of them, you see. So they keep each other working; if one stays in his room all day, the fourteen left have to do all the work for the fifteen in the group.

Inmates are paid from 3.5 to 5 Swedish crowns a day, the equivalent of seventy cents to a dollar. Dr. Marnell believes that their work is competitive with private industry; the institution accepts some contracts with private firms. However, there are many inmates who cannot adjust to the industrial situation:

A lot of them are all right as workers, but they can't stand the situation in a factory with the *noise* around them, with several persons looking on when they are working. They get nervous. A great many of them *need* to work in the fresh air. We have enough forest, garden, and agricultural work so that we can keep that type of inmate occupied.

We wondered how the institution compensated for the effect on the individual of being consigned to a system which expressed society's rejection of them.

As a matter of fact, we try to help them realize that they get much more of a personal approach to their problems than in an ordinary prison. If you compare our routine with those of other institutions in Sweden you will see that our way of meeting them and our attitudes toward them are rather different. We try to use something of a therapeutic community approach. If you took a hundred of our inmates and transferred them to an ordinary prison with a traditional prison system, with guards behind the inmates step for step, I think you would have a riot in a few hours.

What methods have brought the therapeutic community into being in such an unlikely place as Hall?

We haven't any special methods. We have just tried to meet the inmates as man to man, in a common way, as ordinary people outside deal with ordinary people of their own kind. We speak frankly to them, and they speak very frankly to us. We have discussion meetings to which we invite journalists, psychiatrists, Alcoholics Anonymous members, and so forth. We have sports clubs, discussion clubs, chess clubs, and bridge clubs. We do our best to break down official limits between groups. We break down the limits between staff groups, too. As I learn to know staff members I invite them to call me by my first name.

It seemed to us as we reviewed what we saw of the Hall operation that there were three methods rather than one at work in the building of a therapeutic community. First, an inmate was forced to make as many decisions for himself as possible, including the decision whether he felt like working. Second, a determined effort was made to break down communications barriers so that channels would flow without obstruction from top to bottom and back again. Third, a basis for building up associations among inmates was found so that no one could isolate himself from the rest of the community.

Dr. Marnell agreed, and added:

We also try to activate friendly relations, to collaborate with inmates in order to promote rehabilitation. So we very often invite their wives or fiancees, for instance, to sit down with us and discuss with the inmate, *together* with him, his main rehabilitation problems. I refuse to take separate interviews with family members. If I should speak with the wife of an inmate, he might think, "What have they really talked about? She told me what they said but I'm not convinced it wasn't other things, too." You ought not to talk with family members about other things than you could speak about with the inmate himself. It's most important to take up the most serious things during these joint interviews.

As Dr. Marnell was not only director of Hall but also of eight other preventive detention prisons, we inquired into the classification system by which inmates were dispersed.

I should like to stress that it is a nonsystem. We don't find classification in the traditional sense useful in treatment. We find it better to work with less homogeneous groups. You ought not to have a bottom group and an elite bloc. If you do, you have as a basic principle for the classification of inmates the behavior you expect them to fulfill in the institution. In traditional classification you have expectations and demands which the inmates know pretty well. Through their conduct they give an answer to you, but that answer isn't the true answer — it's merely opportune.

Dr. Marnell emphasized that his "nonsystem" could only work in small institutions:

If you have a small institution you can individualize the treatment. In a big prison you must have schedules and orders which you must press on them. You speak of training and instructing inmates. But real treatment must start the other way, from the inner side of the person. We must first try to give him a chance of expressing his inner drives and his real abilities. We must give him treatment appropriate to his abilities.

Disciplinary problems should be dealt with as symptoms of personal conflict. In a traditional prison, we just judge the symptoms — you give them fourteen days or thirty days of solitary confinement and say goodbye to him. The problem is locked in. . . . We haven't had solitary confinement for disciplinary disturbances for twenty years. . . . We do have a special, secure block, where they can be managed in a controlled group. But not as punishment, but rather because their own conduct requires it.

I say to them: "You haven't behaved according to our necessary control (for example, they may have overstayed a furlough, or they may have been drunk in the institution), and so you have to prove now, for a time, that you are quite suitable for this institution. You have made the decision yourself to be kept here; I haven't asked for it. You have now to prove that I can safely take a new chance in trusting you."

But transfer can always be used if there is no proof forthcoming:

When it's a very severe situation you just have to tell him: "Goodbye, Mr. Andersson. I think you had better be moved to so-and-so." "And why?" he asks, of course. "You see," I say, "I just think it would be more convenient to you, for a time." I never go into details. I never play the attorney general against them. If I discuss the details I always run the risk of being wrong on one point. For the rest of his life, the inmate will take for his defense, "I was right, because Governor Marnell was wrong on that point, wasn't he?" He will forget that *he* was wrong on all other points.

Life at Hall is kept as normal as conditions will allow. We asked our inmate informant, Frank, about the sexual problem incident to the long confinement which, though not vile, seemed certainly monastic. He said: "There is no sexual problem at Hall, anyhow, because we have free visits every Sunday. Our wives can come and see us in our rooms from nine in the morning to six in the evening. Absolutely private — you can lock your door. There is no ground for homosexuality."

In addition to conjugal visits, inmates are also allowed seventy-two hour furloughs, as a matter of right, each quarter. This system is not without abuses. Inmates fail to get back on time, arrive drunk and disorderly, and sometimes commit crimes while enjoying their brief respite. Of 3,085 furloughs granted in 1954, there were 442 which included such unfavorable incidents. For Swedish prison administrators the price seems not reasonable to pay for peace and respect in the prison.[35]

We have dwelt at such length on Governor Marnell, Frank, Hall and the preventive detention system not because it represents an easily translated model for other countries to copy, but because in it can be found a careful and realistic design of a correctional community related to a specific correctional purpose: the control of the inveterate recidivist. Its success, we are told, will neither shake the skeptical nor hearten the faithful, if expressed in terms of recidivism. More than three-quarters, we are told, of the men released from the preventive detention system find their way back into prison. But what can be expected from men whose lives have been conditioned to the remorseless cycle of crime and imprisonment?

The Swedish expectation is clear. The penal reform law of 1945 provides: "The inmate shall be treated with firmness and earnestness and with the consideration due him as a human being."

Of the Scandinavian correctional apparatus it can be reasonably said that if good intentions and community support of humane objectives will resociate offenders, then the outcome of Scandinavian correction should be impressively reasonable. Nowhere among either

---

[35] Hardy Göransson, *Some Aspects of the Swedish Prison System* (Stockholm: Regent Bocktryckeri, 1955).

staff or laymen did we encounter doubt that the generous, almost lavish, program was consistent with community feeling about the treatment of offenders. We heard nothing about the "just deserts" of prisoners or probationers; nowhere did we hear the familiar opinion that what they got was too good for them. A Norwegian criminologist pointed out to us that throughout Scandinavia it is difficult to get into prison, and for those who do, the courts and administration make every effort to get them out as soon as possible.[36] And in Sweden, a distinguished professor of law advanced to us the proposition that in corrections the rule should be that until we know what good correctional institutions can do the fewer people confined in them for the least possible time, the better off both public and offenders will be. There is a limit to what kindness can accomplish in correctional practice, but whatever that limit may be the best place to look for it is in Scandinavia.

FRANCE

Professor Leon Radzinowicz, in his survey of the status of criminology as an academic discipline, found that the condition of the science in France was deplorable. After discovering that France supported no less than eleven institutes of criminal science at various universities, he proceeded to study the capability of the Institute maintained by the fountainhead of French learning, the University of Paris. The level of study is summed up in an incisive paragraph:

As the Institute does not include on its full-time staff a single instructor with proper criminological qualifications, it is not surprising to find that in the criminological section seminars, which should properly be regarded as of vital importance, are seldom, if ever, held. Without the guidance of specially selected reading lists, without the exercise of more thorough discussion, and with no practical or research work, the student has nothing to stimulate him apart from the inadequately related series of lectures, delivered by visiting staff, who cannot take a due share in the life of the Institute.[37]

The reasons assigned for this unpromising condition of criminology are the relative lack of interest in criminal law and insufficient appropriations of funds for the support of research in criminal science. Al-

---

[36] Nils Christie, "Scandinavian Criminology," *Sociological Inquiry*, 31 (1961), 93–104.

[37] Leon Radzinowicz, *In Search of Criminology* (London: Heinemann, 1961), 75.

though the foundation of so many institutes surely signifies a rebirth of interest in a subject in which France at one time led the world, the results are not yet apparent in either the organization of its apparatus or in research aimed at its improvement. French correctional work seems to be distinguished by its remorseless application of unexamined mechanics. In the hands of effective practitioners the machinery produces a purposeful and optimistic social structure. Judging from a major disturbance encountered during our visit at one adult institution, the equilibrium can be exceedingly precarious. Because the machinery is identical in design for the whole country, we can neatly present its general operation. To begin with the institutional branches of the apparatus, we were able to identify ten different kinds of adult correctional facility. These are:

The *maison d'arrêt*, in which accused persons awaiting trial are confined in complete isolation, following the Pennsylvania system.

The *maison de correction*, for minor offenders serving short terms.

The *maison centrale*, for refractory prisoners undergoing sentences of hard labor in solitary confinement. These prisoners are confined in isolation at night under the Auburn system.

The *prison ordinaire*, for offenders not considered suitable for a program of reëducation.

Minimum security farms and colonies for prisoners suitable for a program of trust and responsibility.

The *régime progressif*, for prisoners classified for reëducation.

The *prison école*, for special intensive training for offenders below the age of twenty-eight.

Special prisons for offenders suffering from mental disturbance or senility.

Prisons for women.

Preventive detention, for habitual criminals, carried out in a special section of a *maison d'arrêt*.

Classification. — Distribution of intake is divided between local confinement in a *maison d'arrêt* for offenders with less than two years to serve, and centralized classification for those with longer terms. The process begins in a classification center, of which there are two; one at Fresnes for adults, and one at Toul for youths. We observed the process at Fresnes. Throughout, we were impressed with the determination of an efficient bureaucracy to meet administrative requirements for the production of a complete dossier on each inmate re-

ceived, at the cost of whatever inconvenience might be caused the
staff or the inmates themselves. Inmates are received in groups of
one hundred and twenty and held for six weeks so that work can be
completed on each man. The process always includes social histories
and psychological and medical examinations, all done in considerable
detail and formally presented at the conclusion of the classification period to a *commission de classement*. Nothing else happens. Inmates
not being interviewed or tested are doing nothing at all.

The *commission de classement* is presided over by a *juge d'application des peines* (judge for the supervision of the execution of penalties). He is a member of the judiciary assigned by the ministry of
justice to preside over all classification committees and to control the
treatment plan for each prisoner received. This function, new to the
French correctional scene since World War II, seems to be the focus of a considerable controversy. When interviewed by us, Jean Pinatel, secretary-general of the International Society of Criminology,
thought that this development was most auspicious:

> Immense new possibilities are thus opened for criminology and penal re-
> form in France, for we now have a framework which will enable the treat-
> ment outlined by the sentence of the court to be carried out continuously but
> flexibly under the orders of a judge. The period when criminology was de-
> manding a better method of dealing with criminals may be said to have
> ended. The new system makes the development of clinical criminology pos-
> sible. We are at the beginning of a period when clinical criminology will have
> to specify its methods and affirm its results. This will not happen without set-
> backs and difficulties. What is important is that it is now possible.

Other informants did not share Pinatel's enthusiasm. Prison officials
thought that the introduction of a decision maker without experience
in the operation of facilities reduced the status and the responsibility
of the operational staff. In view of the fact that the *juge d'application des peines* is charged with intervention in quite simple decisions,
his role amounts to a transfer of power from administrator to the judiciary. Considering Professor Radzinowicz' pessimistic appraisal of
the level of education in the criminal sciences available to lawyers, it
may well be questioned whether these judges are sufficiently prepared to assume their responsibilities within this highly complex structure.

Régime Progressif. — Of all the correctional facilities we heard about

in France, the system embodied by *le régime progressif* best exempli-
fies the range and quality of French correctional thought. It is simple
to describe what we saw, but we never were able to find a rationale
for the arbitrary and mechanical operation of a system which never
individualizes except for the purposes of control. Perhaps, after more
experience is under the belts of the *juges d'application des peines* the
kind of flexibility which M. Pinatel hoped for will be evident. This is
not now the case.

The system works in five phases. We observed its operation in adult
prisons at Melun and Mulhouse and at the *prison ecoles* of Oermingen
and Escroures.

Phase I: During this phase, the prisoner is confined for nine months
in a single cell under maximum custody. He eats, sleeps, works and
exercises alone. From time to time he will be interviewed by an *éducateur* (a specialized correctional counselor), or by a psychologist
with a view to evaluating his progress and preparing recommendations for later adjustment. How the accommodation of an offender
to the experience of protracted isolation can possibly be related to
subsequent experience either in prison or after release was never made
clear to us by correctional theorists in any of the several continental
countries in which this practice prevails. Whatever the rationale, a
report of adjustment is made to the *commission de classement* at the
end of nine months at which time three options are available:

a) Inmate may be advanced to Phase II.

b) Inmate may be transferred to another facility because inappropriate for the progressive regime.

c) Inmate may be continued in Phase I for further study.

Phase II: At this point the inmate is moved from the Phase I cell-
block and placed in quarters in which he will still eat and sleep alone
but will be placed on a group work assignment. Studies continue and
twice a year there will be reports to the *commission de classement*.
After six months he might be advanced to Phase III, but it is more
likely that caution will prevail and he will be retained for about a year.

Phase III: In an undeniably logical progression, the inmate is moved
from his isolation to a group situation in which he continues to sleep in
his own cell but carries out all other activities in a group, including, at
last, some recreational program. This phase usually lasts for at least a
year.

Phase IV: This is *liberté surveillée*, in which the inmate continues to reside at the prison but works at employment secured for him on a farm or in private industry. This phase may last for as long as six years.

Phase V: The final step in the *régime progressif* is conditional release. The inmate is allowed to go home without supervision but with the understanding that he may be returned to prison without further proceedings in the event he gets into further difficulty. Such paroles may last from one to three years, at the end of which the offender may be completely discharged.

The logic of this regime for an offender for whom life-long dependence on the system is intended can be understood. As the only determinant of progression from one phase to the next is the passage of time without unfavorable incident, it can be expected that this system will produce at best only a sort of resigned dependency. In that it is obviously intended for the better and more hopeful class of offenders, it is better testimony to French logic than to the common sense and practical experience of policy makers. Even at that, it transpired at Mulhouse that the system exists more in principle than in fact. A large proportion of the inmates of that institution do not progress beyond the second phase, serving out their sentences in a routine of labor and the routine observation of institutional rules.

Oermingen. — This is an adaptation of the progressive regime for the youthful offender. Intended for the 18-25 year old age group, it accepts men up to the age of 28. With a capacity of 125, it is located in an old cantonment of the Maginot line. In general, the institution does not accept prisoners with terms of more than ten years to serve. The program is primarily one of vocational education. Generally, the expectation is that release will coincide with the completion of apprenticeship, although this is not always the case. Usually inmates are paroled after about two years; almost everybody gets out by the end of six years. Sometimes the *commission de classement* does not see its way clear to release a youth when he has completed training; this often results in an offender learning two trades. His morale is not improved in the process.

In spite of a well-equipped, well-staffed facility, the *régime progressif* is carried out in principle, though with modifications. Phase I, the period of isolation and "observation," may last only 45 days, as contrasted with nine months for the adult prisoner at Melun or Mulhouse. He is, however, allowed to attend classes during this period, but this is the only group activity allowed. His overall assignment is to collaborate with the *éducateur* to whom he is assigned in developing a program for his future. This program is presented to the *commission de classement* at the end of Phase I. If all goes well, it will be accepted and the lad will progress to Phase II.

From this point on he will be involved in group living. He will be assigned to a group of eighteen inmates each with his own bedroom. An *éducateur* is assigned to each group, responsible for the constructive use of each inmate's time. There is both individual and group counseling, but the core of the program is vocational training. Eight trades are taught in some of the best workshops seen in Europe. The aim is to pass the rigorous journeyman examinations conducted by the Ministry of Labor. From all appearances, the youths assigned to this institution managed somehow to achieve a real pride of workmanship.

After six months in Phase II, the offender may be moved to Phase III, which does not change his training program but which affords him housing in the *pavillon de confiance*, or "honor cottage," and a somewhat more relaxed environment. It is intended that as a result of his experience in the Phase II the inmate will have internalized enough sense of responsibility to manage his program without the momentum provided by the *éducateur* and the group. We thought that the atmosphere in Oermingen *pavillion de confiance* was surprisingly cheerful and optimistic, particularly in contrast to the *pavillon* for adult trusties at Melun, which was a sanctuary for old lags.

The Oermingen regime continues with *liberté surveillée*, in which inmates are placed in a hostel-like arrangement in the nearby city of Nancy. The *foyer* contains twenty inmates and is presided over by an *éducateur* and his wife. A family atmosphere is provided, and the residents are subjected to few rules. This phase is usually quite short, no more than two or three months, and is followed by Phase V or conditional release. This does not provide for casework supervision or any structured contacts with the apparatus. It is a status preliminary to discharge rather than an active treatment experience.

Field agency programs in France. — Since 1891 France has had a system of *surcis* or suspended sentence. The sentence is suspended at the discretion of the court for a period of five years. No supervision is provided, but the sentence can be invoked at the initiative of the police and the *Procureur de la Republique*, an official roughly comparable to an American district attorney.

After World War II, a statute was added for the innovation of *surcis avec mise à l'épreuve.* The *surcis* so ordered are conditional and may be granted only to offenders meeting the following criteria:

The offender must not have a record of imprisonment for six months or more.

The sentence which is conditionally suspended must be one of imprisonment for breach of the *droit commun.*

Sentences to solitary confinement or hard labor cannot be modified. Fines cannot be modified.

Offenders meeting these requirements may be awarded *surcis avec mise à l'épreuve*, which suspends the sentence for a minimum of three and a maximum of five years. Rules are established by the court and are applied by the *juge d'application des peines*, with whom we have already become acquainted. If the conditions ordered by the sentencing court are violated, the judge may order his detention in prison or may apply in court for the implementation of the suspended sentence. He may also, if the conditions of *surcis* are met, apply in court to have the original conviction set aside.

Neither social workers nor other personnel are available to make either form of *surcis* anything more than summary probation. Under the circumstances, it is available only to a relatively few offenders. As experience accumulates and as a professionally trained cadre of personnel is created, it may be expected that *surcis* will develop into something comparable with probation. There is hardly even a superficial resemblance to probation as it is known in England and the United States.

Éducation Surveillée. — Under the leadership of Paul Lutz, deputy director for *Éducation Surveillée* of the Ministry of Justice, a much more impressive system has been developed for juvenile offenders than we have described for the adult apparatus. We visited the institution for girls at Brécourt. Somewhat like an English approved school, it is intended for girls aged fourteen to twenty-one. The average length of stay is between two and three years; the program is remedial education work and group-living. The institution is situated in a handsome castle confiscated by the French government from a collaborationist. At one time it had the distinction of being the residence of Hermann Goering when in France.

The capacity of the school is seventy-two, distributed among nine living groups of eight girls. Each group has its own *éducatrice*, its own "flat," and so far as possible its own separate identity. There are three pavilions, each with three groups. Each pavilion has its own kitchen; on a rotation basis each girl in the pavilion will have complete responsibility for preparation of meals for an entire week. It is intended that the experience will resemble as closely as possible the role as mother and housewife for which each girl is being prepared. Girls assigned to kitchen duty are not excused from ordinary duties. They are expected to organize their time and plan their work so the other twenty-three girls in the pavilion will be satisfied with her work. So far as possible the atmosphere in the "flat" is kept at a home-like, comfortable level; furniture is not institutional and as much as possible like what would be found in an ordinary French home. Similarly, work conditions in the shops are businesslike. Girls are paid monthly but are required to contribute a share of their wages to a fund which belongs to the living group. The group itself decides how this fund should be spent. The money can go for almost any purpose the group would like from redecoration of the "flat" to the purchase of pastries for a party.

The program consists of vocational training work, remedial education, and the life in the living group. In each of these areas a different *éducatrice* works with the girl. Each contributes weekly reports to the girl's dossier. The emphasis is on observation and the development of relationships. Little use is made of formal testing devices at Brécourt or elsewhere in the system. Mr. Lutz told us that there is sufficient time for the staff to learn all about the girl without formal tests. Peculiarities need not be ferreted out with special tests or dealt with by psychotherapy. Where experience indicates that there are behavior problems beyond the capacity of this kind of program to contain or change, a referral to special services is made. But throughout this system the effort is made to deal with the problem at hand with the resources at hand.

As noted above, the size of living groups has been given considerable attention. Mr. Lutz is convinced that eight is the correct group size. He believes that the correct approach to the problem of institutional size is through a determination of the number of *éducateurs* a chief administrator can know and supervise. Mr. Lutz thinks that this figure is nine. Each *éducateur* should be able to manage a group of no more than eight with this kind of program. Mr. Lutz was definite about his reasons:

In group living the children must be able to do some of the things they want. When they come together for lunch or dinner they must be happy to be together. But if it is as we find it in many institutions with a dining room with twenty or thirty children, it is extremely disagreeable. Twenty or thirty children are very noisy, particularly when they are difficult children in the first place. In my opinion, the living group should be a place where children who have worked hard in school can have time in a spot where life is easier. But if there are twenty-five children there, the *éducatrice* can only bring order and discipline. She cannot be occupied with the problem of this child or that child. In the little group the atmosphere is quite different. The *éducatrice* still has a hard job. She must be forever observing, seeing what is happening in the group. She must be with the group, leading conversations and discussions. If the groups are large, nobody will even hear what she is saying.

Small groups also make possible considerably more freedom of movement. Accompanied by a member of the staff, girls can go to the village for shopping or even make excursions to Paris.

Along with small living groups, Lutz believes in continuity of relationships. So far as can be arranged, the same *éducatrice* works with the girl during and after the institutional period. He reasons as follows:

With these difficult girls care and after-care are exactly the same thing. You cannot separate them. There's not one time when a girl is confined in an institution and another when she is out in normal life. I think the *éducatrice* can manage perhaps six girls in the institution and ten outside. The girl must be always with the same person; she cannot change relations and keep the same meaning.

Look at the way we do things usually. A child comes to an observation center — there is his first relationship with an *éducateur*. Then he goes to an institution — there's a new relationship to make. Three months later, a transfer to a new group and a new *éducateur*. Then after-care, and a new relationship. It's exactly what's needed to train children to instability.

After all, look at the same story they always bring to us. Before they come to us, they were three months with a grandmother, three months with an aunt, three months with a person who took in children on his farm, then perhaps six months with the mother. No stability. Then they come to us and they get more instability.

And here comes the juvenile judge and the *éducateur*. They play a sort of tennis with the child, lobbing him back and forth. The child never feels secure with anyone. It's an enormous problem. Everyone wants to have a good relation with the child. The judge says, "You see, you are my friend — you can come and see me when you want." The probation officer says, "Oh, *I* am a real father. I am your friend," and so on. Then the observation center staff and the *éducateurs* say the same. Finally, the after-care officer comes along and says, "*Now* you have the man before you on whom you can count."

Naturally the boy will say, "You are the twentieth man who said the same thing. None of you are serious."

In these samples of the French correctional apparatus two principal themes of the culture can be discerned. The famous national passion for logic stands out in the *régime progressif*. It is a logic of punishment, the application of strict rules of orderly procedure to the business of deterrence and retribution. These rules do not provide for feedback; there seems to be no interest in the extent to which the system succeeds or even in its relevance to the problem of crime. What matters is that once established the machinery should continue its operation as smoothly as possible without regard to the economic, social, or individual costs.

Logic in itself is not an evil in human institutions. The Anglo-Saxon disdain for its application to governmental and social organization is neither admirable nor likely to be forever feasible. What is required in any logical system is a firm relationship to the facts and a clear anchor line to an objective. When a system lacks means of self-correction through the examination of experience it will not remain logical. The lack of self-correction is evident in the French system of criminal justice for adults.

In the juvenile training schools a second theme of French culture is evident: the concern for community. What reciprocities must be established in order to create such a concern among unrelated delinquent girls and miscellaneous staff members? What should be the life of such a community if it is to be a fruitful experience for its members? Much attention has been given to making the life of a girl at Brécourt a comfortable, constructive, and nurturing experience. Current investigations at Vaucresson, the national center for training and research for juvenile schools, strongly emphasize the need for studying the delinquents and the staff, with a view to understanding both as well as possible. This kind of understanding will lead to building into a system of *éducation surveillée* the qualities of a therapeutic community, a condition which seems close to attainment in what we have seen. It is to be hoped that in France the same process of interaction between juvenile and adult correction which has strengthened correctional practice in the United States and in England will have a revitalizing effect on adult institutions. The world has much to learn from French juvenile institutions. The first to be learning should be the judges and lawyers who run the harsh modern bastilles in which French adult offenders are confined. It may be that the eleven institutes of criminology listed by Professor

Radzinowicz will eventually accomplish this end. Their task is formidable but their opportunities are great.

GERMANY

Concern, research, and curiosity bring visitors to prisons in every country. Perhaps it is only in Germany that prisons are memorials to martyrs of a savage recent past. These reflections were prompted by the sight of a bus load of school children dismounting at Tegel prison, near West Berlin. They had come to view a monument erected to the memory of a warden and his staff who were massacred during the Nazi regime because of their refusal to execute a group of their prisoners. How long their memory will remain fresh is yet to be seen, but the homage paid to them symbolizes a national concern about prisons which, in this form, we encountered only in Germany.

What we saw in this country haunted by the recollection of penal abominations was a highly conventional correctional apparatus administered by kindly but unimaginative men. Many of them had suffered themselves under the barbarous abuses of the Nazis. It was easy for them to understand the vicissitudes of their inmates. Understanding that much, they were gentle and humane.

But bold changes were not for them. The German civil service is renowned for diligence and rectitude, but innovation has never been its pride. Little has been done to supplant the ancient Pennsylvania prisons which still dominate correctional programs. The solitude which their Quaker designers provided in the nineteenth century no longer prevails. But the structures still stand, and programs are accommodated to them. What cannot be done in a Pennsylvania prison is not done. Because the idea behind the old Walnut Street Jail of Philadelphia was salvation through solitude, most German prisons must provide solitary work. Whatever values can be gained from group work will not be imparted in prisons designed to prevent it.

The sight of an elderly prisoner, alone in his cell, painting faces on wooden dolls' heads, produced in quantities which attested to his diligence, summed up the unsolved problems which confront the German prison administrator. Whether the Pennsylvania prison can be adapted to the twentieth century has never been proved, though proof has often enough been attempted. It is doubtful that the judges and civil servants who run the German prisons will accomplish this feat.

Blocked imagination is by no means the only handicap of the German prison service. The fearful impact of the Nazis disorganized it. Criminals and political prisoners were inextricably mixed. Records were profuse but unreliable. Many facilities were destroyed; others were commandeered by the occupying forces. The task of bringing the system back to the standards of 1933 was enormous. It was attempted and largely accomplished. The honestly and decently operated prison of the Weimar republic was resuscitated, with faults and virtues not noticeably different from the prisons of other Western European countries. An overlay of American and English correctional concepts is evident, but these influences have not sunk deep. The idea of change and the use of the correctional institution to bring it about do not seriously influence the correctional leadership or the rank and file.

Everybody works. The full-employment economy of West Germany has work for all hands, even the least capable. In addition to the solitary work going on in cells, every nook and cranny that can be converted into workshops is crammed with inmates making things. Most of the work done is unskilled and repetitive; few men can be released from a German prison more capable than they were for conventional employment. The most that can be said is that during the time of their confinement they were productive and had some experience of the demands of a day's work.

They will not be much richer. The work is contracted for with private entrepreneurs. Unlike similar plans in the Netherlands or in Finland, the German plan is not designed to approach a wage scale comparable to free employment. The pittance allowed was not related to productivity. We inferred that the prisoners resented this situation; exploitation by and for the state is unpalatable enough; when it is by the state and for the benefit of a profit-making enterprise abuses will be thought to occur.

It is noteworthy that this practice continues despite the efforts of the occupying forces and their consultants to uproot it. In 1951, Richard A. McGee, then the Director of Corrections in California, surveyed the progress made in the German prisons out of the chaotic aftermath of World War II. He made many recommendations, and some, we observed, have been carried out. But his observations on the issue of employment of prisoners in private enterprise are still relevant:

There are two types of prisoner employment used in German prisons which have been outlawed in most of the American states for many years. The first

. . . is the contract system wherein a private business man provides raw materials, equipment, and supervision, and the prison furnishes the labor. The prison is paid a stipulated rate for the finished product. The prisoner in turn is paid a nominal amount for his work. This system is open to the possibility of many abuses such as improper collusion between the contractors and prison officials. It also makes possible for not only the state but private persons to profit at the expense of the prisoners who are not free agents in the arrangement.

The second type of employment is similar to the contract system in that private persons may benefit at the expense of prisoners. It involves an arrangement whereby individual prisoners or groups of prisoners are hired out by the prison authorities to private farmers or other private users of labor on a day-rate basis. This system is subject to the same possibilities for abuses as the contract system.

It is recommended that these two methods of employing prisoners be gradually reduced and replaced by more production for the direct use of government.

We could not discover such a revision.

The kind of prison which results from this mixture of ancient institutions, full employment, an obsession with custodial security, and a few American ideas is exemplified at Bruchsal. A Pennsylvania-style structure, this institution is as authoritarian as any in Germany. Every able-bodied inmate is engaged in an active, demanding work program. Bamboo fishing rods, wooden sandals, and baskets are among the products we noted. Recalcitrant inmates are put to work on the basket weaving, a low paid and relatively unpleasant task, carried out in cold and dismal shops under the eaves of the prison.

Armed guards patrol the walls at night. The corners of the prison yards are painted white to prevent escapers from lurking in them. To make security doubly secure, vicious watchdogs are turned loose in the yard and accompany the patrols around the walls. Inside, a pleasant, relaxed program is under way; music, drama, hobbies, and school classes are available, and the atmosphere is almost jolly. We were at a loss to reconcile the austere day-time program with the amenities of the evening, and we fancy that the superintendent wasted little time in considering the contrast. For a culture as preoccupied with metaphysics and theory as Germany, precious little time seems to be allocated to the conceptualization of correctional process.

The situation is not without enlivening aspects. At Hanöfersand, a youth institution near Hamburg, the influence of a pre-Nazi pioneer of modern corrections in Germany, Curt Bondy, is still to be seen. On an island in the Elbe River a complete correctional program for adolescent offenders is carried out. With a conceptual thoroughness not usually evident in German institutions, progress from maximum to minimum custody is managed in terms of gains in responsibility. The boys are moved from steel to wood, and from locked to unlocked quarters. The differences are emphasized as much as possible; as the boys move from phase to phase they are reminded of the significance of the movement.

Life centers on an *Erziehungsgruppenleiter* (group leader). At the point of reception, this group leader is a psychologist, whose task is to understand and plan for the newcomer. Later, in the other units, the group leader is a teacher and counselor. Housefathers in the cottages assist him in the management of the daily routines.

The program for the most part is aimed at apprenticeship training. Cabinet-making, masonry, tailoring, shoemaking, blacksmithing, locksmithing, welding, and gardening are taught; inmates are expected to pass the usual trade examinations when they are released. A farm completed the picture; some boys, presumably those whose aptitude or motivation for apprenticeship is insufficient, are assigned to it.

Upon arrival on the island, the new boy is assigned to the newcomer group. When he is not engaged in supervised activity he is isolated in a cell with steel bars and door. Psychologists test and interview him, and there are some limited group activities. This phase usually lasts four weeks, by which time a thorough evaluation has been completed by the professional staff.

From the *Zugangsgruppe* the newcomer might be sent to one of three *Häuser*. In *Haus* 1 he finds that he is thought to be dangerous and to be kept under close supervision in school, recreation, and work. In *Haus* 2 he is placed in a small dormitory. The outside door is locked, but inside the cottage he has considerable freedom.

Haus 3 is reserved for those who are thought to be long-term risks to the outside community. There are both cells and dormitories in this *Haus*. The notion is that the process of socialization is uneven and that some flexibility must be provided for those who are not in all respects ready for the program available in *Haus* 2.

When, in the opinion of the staff, a boy is ready, he is accorded the status of a *Freigänger*. He is moved from locked supervision to *Haus* 4, which has neither bars on windows nor locks on the outside doors. He comes and goes freely, but he is expected to meet obligations at work and at school.

Finally, after he has successfully completed this experience, he achieves a transfer to the *Dorf*. This village consists of five small houses which provide for four or five boys each. The villagers continue their work and school programs with the rest of Hanöfersand, but otherwise they are expected to shift for themselves. This is carried out through the requirement that they pump their own water, collect their own fuel, cook some of their own food, and govern themselves in the process. They elect a mayor and house elders, and may consult an educational group leader as necessary.

This institution is a legacy of the 1920's. At the time it must have been as much of an innovation as the Junior Republics and the Boys' Towns in the United States, or the open borstals in England. It still seemed to us to be a good and imaginative institution in many respects, though informants told us that it is now far from the vigorous and dynamic institution that it was in the time of its founder, Curt Bondy. Like so many correctional institutions, the mechanics have been faithfully preserved, but the vision that made the mechanics possible has diminished.

The horizon is marked with some portents of a significant correctional advance. Near Frankfurt-am-Main the new Gustav-Radbruch-Haus has just been completed. With a capacity of 340 inmates it serves as a sort of immense half-way house. Situated near major industries, this institution gives its residents access to private employment. About 300 of them are given free rein to work at jobs found for them by the institution's staff. Surveillance continues to be maintained, but it is kept as unobstrusive as possible. During the evening hours inmates are left mostly to their own devices. They can retreat to the privacy of their rooms or join in whatever is going on in the day rooms.

The focus on the transition from the prison from which the residents came to the community to which they are returning is made with a minimum of counseling. In the three or four months that an offender will reside at Gustav-Radbruch-Haus he is expected to demonstrate his ability to manage in the community at large by his responsible behavior under restricted freedom.

Professor Albert Krebs, Director of Correctional Services in Hesse, is responsible for the ideas behind this new institution. In an interview he explained to us that the basic idea grew out of his experience with Rudolfschule, a converted elementary school near Frankfurt. This place was used for the overflow of the overcrowded prisons. Permission was given to employ men in the industries around the establishment rather than to keep them in aimless idleness. The obvious values gained from this program supported the design and building of Gustav-Radbruch-Haus at the considerable cost of DM 5,000,000. As a generous and progressive measure, the institution speaks for itself. What its future potential may be is difficult to predict. Germany is a conservative country in this epoch, and bold new departures are hardly to be expected.

Under the leadership of Dr. Alfons Wahl, now a referee in the Federal Ministry of Justice, the transformation of judicial clemency into a modern probation system has taken place. Wahl's initiative and perseverance have made possible an adaptation of English and American probation concepts to the German social services. Still applied conservatively, still limited for the most part to probation only, German field correctional services have made remarkable progress in a decade devoted to familiarization and experiment.

Wahl had been active in youth work in Bavaria before the Nazi seizure of power. After a long military interlude, he returned to social service after the war. Participation in various correctional enterprises in association with English and American specialists convinced him of the need for the introduction of a modern probation service.

He had to start from scratch. The history of clemency in Germany goes back to 1895, when the first law authorizing the suspension of sentences was enacted. It is an uneventful history. The Weimar republic provided for pardon for certain cases in which reputable citizens undertook supervision. This service presupposed a presentence investigation, usually conducted by a charitable organization. In 1933 the National Socialists, with their infallible perversity, put a stop to this program. During their regime there were no further developments.

In 1951, Dr. Wahl undertook to persuade a few criminal courts to experiment with a probation system compounded from the old law and a private organization, the *Bewährungshilfe Bonn*. The experiment found general favor. While it was under way, Wahl and his colleagues drafted a new probation law for juveniles and adult offenders which was promulgated in August, 1953.

Probation officers handle both adult and juvenile cases. Eligibility for probation is limited to adults found guilty for crimes for which a sentence of no more than nine months is prescribed, and to juveniles who are neither recidivists nor major offenders in the view of the court.

Probation officers are attached to each court; the hope is that a standard caseload of forty-five can be maintained. Generally probation officers have been trained as social workers and are expected to work with wards of the court in all aspects of their social situations.

Dr. Wahl views the future with confidence. In our interview with him, he expressed this belief:

We have to think over the whole penal treatment system more and more. The question is whether a prison is able to change a person. Today the prison's meaning is for the security of the public. It tries to bring him order and discipline, to teach him, to help him improve his educational status. But the prison is never a life-like environment; this is the main reason why we should see probation and parole as a distinct part of the whole system of penal treatment. We must look ahead to the point that probation and parole are not merely ways of bringing freedom to the offender, but are necessary ways to help him. Normally what the offender has done is the result of his inability to make good decisions when he was free to make them. If we are to find out why he makes bad decisions, we must see how he behaves in normal life. We can't see that when he is in prison. . . .

We must reach the point that what the judge, or the prosecutor, or the probation officer does will have the same meaning to the offender. They must aim at the same goal. If the offender sees that that is the way it is, he will not try to excuse himself as soon as he finds someone who shows him a different attitude.

Dr. Wahl's leadership and persistence made the probation law possible. It is clear that more than a law is necessary. To us he expressed the view that "we should make legislation not only by making laws but also by taking practical steps."

There are many to be taken in Germany which, in this respect beyond all others, is uncertain and in need of ideas and leadership.

A GLIMPSE AT THE SOVIET
CORRECTIONAL PATTERN

In the year allotted for our travels, we were charged with the task of making our survey as cross-cultural as possible. The ultimate criterion of culture-crossing in this inflamed age is the ideological barrier which separates the USSR from the West. Our goal was to reconnoiter the broad outline of the Soviet correctional apparatus. We could hardly hope to do more.

Even if language and national sensitivity had been no obstacles, the examination of correctional practice across this particular boundary presented formidable difficulties. The ideas of "offender" and "resocialization" have different meanings from those which the same terms carry in the West. What is the problem which the speculator, the social parasite, or the hooligan present to the correctional practitioner? What needs to be done to restore the individual who is guilty of a crime against the state to a society whose unofficial consensus regarding such crimes is unknown? What does resocialization imply in a social order which has always been subject to coercion at levels which have been unknown in the West for centuries? There are basic philosophical issues which must be explored before we can understand the Soviet correctional practice. We did not make any inroads upon them.

A further problem was that of getting at the truth of correctional realities. In other countries, our colleagues had not hesitated to show us the complete range of their apparatus. We had seen prisons and training schools of which our hosts were ashamed as well as those of which they were proud. Problems as well as achievements had been candidly discussed. There is an awareness throughout the countries of North America and Western Europe that the whole field of corrections is shifting rapidly from its heavily punitive traditions to new patterns whose exact outlines can only be vaguely discerned. But in the Soviet Union there was no question of our looking at a range of practice. With elaborate courtesy which concealed the inconvenience of many explanations and clearances, we were allowed to visit two juvenile institutions and one corrective labor colony. A variety of criminologists, correctional administrators, jurists, psychiatrists, and ordinary citizens made themselves available to us. But we were always aware that best feet were probably being put forward. Statistics were never available except in the form of percentages of unstated integers. Correctional problems contained few unknown quantities; those that remained seemed to be of a basically practical nature, such as, the implementation of Leninist doctrine on corrective labor, or biological, that is, the biochemical causes of alcoholism.

The basic position which was often repeated to us proceeded from the proposition that in a social order in which personal satisfactions are increasing, personal tensions are decreasing so that there will be a decline in the causes of crime. Such a social order is communism. As the Soviet Union approaches this goal, crime must necessarily diminish.

Such crime as still persists in the consequence of the residuals of bourgeois capitalism and the after-effects of World War II, which wrought enormous dislocations on the occupied areas of the country.

The visitor to the great cities of the USSR sees many incidents which are virtually impossible to evaluate in the context of this theory or, for that matter, in the context of hypotheses based on a hostile analysis of Society society. What is the significance of the almost ubiquitous speculator, offering to buy dollars, the shirt off one's back, or the socks off his feet? What is the meaning of the insolent farrago of abuse which Soviet citizens address to the patient militia assigned to direct traffic, control queues, and guard public buildings? How do we account for the fist fights and brawls which are seen so frequently in the best restaurants and hotels? What should we think of aimless groups of young men standing on street corners on a pleasant evening instead of engaging in the cultural, educational, athletic, or political opportunities so easily available to all in this regime? And what of the *druzhina*, that voluntary organization conjured up by the workers of Leningrad to prevent crime and increase public order in a country in which crime is rapidly disappearing and public order is insured by the advance of society toward the utopia promised by the Communist party?

All these questions arise in the mind of the casual visitor. They are not effectively answered by reference to the official theory that crime is disappearing as the social order moves to a triumphant apotheosis of complete communism in our time, as we were insistently told. Nor can we reconcile what we saw with the hostile version that in a highly repressive alienated society fear will dictate compliant behavior. Moscow citizens are not more disorderly than those of Paris, but they are neither the happy lot of which we hear from Soviet apologists, nor the terror-ridden victims of oppression described by Western critics of the Communist regime.

With this background evident around us as we pursued our correctional reconnaissance, we tried to get at the theoretical position of Soviet penology. We began with interviews at the Moscow Institute of Forensic Psychiatry, presided over by Dr. G. Morozov. Our objective was to determine the extent to which psychiatric concepts had influenced the treatment of offenders. This seemed to be a bench mark from which some cross-cultural inferences might be made. Seated with a friendly staff, none of whom spoke English, and a bored Intourist interpreter we found the inquiry rather heavy weather. Nevertheless, certain principles became clear and were supported in English abstracts of publications in forensic psychiatry.

First, with the position of Soviet psychiatry being essentially anti-Freudian and nondynamic, the psychiatrist has no basis for treating anyone who is not psychotic or brain-damaged. Neither Professor Morozov nor any of his colleagues saw that the psychiatrist could play any part in the treatment of an offender based on any of the diagnoses of deviant behavior familiar in the West. While the psychiatric concepts of psychopathy or character disorder or sociopathy might be allowed in the theoretical framework of psychiatric nosology, there was no treatment which the psychiatrist could offer patients so diagnosed. That being the case, it would be harmful to confuse such patients by attempting a treatment for which no rationale exists. To inform a person that he is ill but that no reliable treatment for his condition is available will only excuse such a person from the effort to comply with social norms which all good citizens should make. Much better that such psychopaths as are encountered by the psychiatrist should be subjected to the influences which the ordinary course of criminal justice may exact.

If this is the basic position of Soviet psychiatry, it follows that the forensic psychiatrist has a special responsibility to rule out psychosis or brain damage in any offender whose behavior might suggest such causes. On the referral of procurators or defense attorneys, the Institute of Forensic Psychiatry makes many diagnostic studies of such persons. Where a diagnosis of such major disturbance is made, a recommendation is sent to the procurator that proceedings should be suspended or dismissed and the offender committed to a hospital for the mentally ill. Except in the gravest cases, prosecution is dismissed, and the offender is treated from that point on as a mentally ill person, no different from any other mentally ill person. In the rare exceptions, the procurator may require that proceedings be merely suspended so that the offender, presumably an exceptionally dangerous person, would not be released from the hospital without notice and review by the court.

For the offender who is not mentally ill within the definition of Soviet law, full criminal proceedings must ensue. Upon commitment to a correctional institution, such a person would have no psychiatric attention unless he became mentally ill. Otherwise, the psychiatrist has no part, either direct or consultative, in the affairs of a correctional institution.

Unaccustomed to such a restricted definition of the role of the psychiatrist, we inquired into the management of offenders whose behavior might be attributable to a psychoneurosis. Surely, we asked, the psychiatrist might participate in the treatment of the compulsive offender, the hysterical or depressed person in difficulties with the law, or the many varieties of sexual offender who are mentally responsible? Our questions elicited uncompromising negatives. Such explanations of deviant behavior have no place in Soviet thought; they represent the unacceptable theories of Freud. A person whose crime expressed a psychoneurosis could not be helped by relieving him of responsibility. The consequences of his offense should be the penalties which are applicable to all offenders. To make exceptions merely creates a situation in which the offense is excused and the offender exempted from correction. Again, it does no good to anyone to explain behavior in terms of sickness if the doctor has no remedy to offer the patient. It seemed hardly within the scope of our survey to account for the antipathy of the Soviet psychiatrist for the working hypotheses of Western psychology. Regardless of our success or lack of it in the application of dynamic explanations of human behavior to the special case of the delinquent, the Soviet social scientist will have none of them.

Finally, we ventured the possibility that the special training and experience of the psychiatrist might be of value in the administration and organization of correctional institutions. For example, we suggested, to know something of the sources and treatment of grossly abnormal behavior might furnish the correctional administrator with clues to the better management of prisoners, living as they did, in highly abnormal social situations. Neither Dr. Morozov nor his colleagues could see that they could make any contribution on these lines. The operation of correctional institutions is another specialty for which appropriate training is available. Nothing in a psychiatrist's experience or professional education would qualify him to deal with the problems of the correctional administrator.

This firm but clear delineation of the division of labor in the control of deviant behavior prepared us for the explication of the corrective labor scientist. At our request, we were afforded an intensive discourse on the basic concepts of this new offshoot of Soviet social science. Under the efficient tutelage of Dr. Nikolai Alexeyevich Struchkov, the elements were conveyed to us as a special case of the social theory of Lenin. The foundation of corrective labor science, we learned, is to be found in a little known publication by Lenin entitled, *Summary of the Essence of the Section Concerning Punishments of the Judicial Point of the Party Programme of 1919*.[38] This summary is neatly reduced to these points:

The administration of criminal justice should rely on the principle of the conditional discharge of the offender.

Courts should express the attitude of society toward crime and the criminal through the exercise of social reprimand.

Punishment should be without deprivation of liberty, as for example corrective labor on special public projects.

Prisons should be transformed into educational institutions in which offenders are educated rather than isolated.

Correctional institutions should rely on the support of the neighboring communities to strengthen the educative aspects of their programs.

These are the foundation stones of Soviet corrections. As for the superstructure Dr. Struchkov described in some detail the present administrative model. About 10 per cent of Soviet prisoners are confined in prisons (*tyurmy*), in which a conventional program of containment is carried out. Such persons may be awaiting trial, or unsuited for confinement in a corrective labor colony, or have committed such grave crimes that the risk of their placement in a colony cannot be taken. We were not encouraged to visit a prison. We were informed that several prisons inherited from the tsarist regime have been demolished, and that there are actually very few such institutions left. It seemed unlikely to us that had we inspected a prison we would have found examples of advanced correctional practice. All officials insisted that nearly all prisoners are confined in corrective labor colonies, and even those confined in prison at first are eventually released after a transfer to a colony.

Therefore we turned our attention to the corrective labor colony. This kind of institution has existed from the earliest days of the Soviet Union and in principle at least has followed Lenin's five-point program. Each Soviet republic operates a system of colonies of whatever dimensions are needed. The Soviet Union does not maintain all-Soviet colonies. Criminal law in the Soviet Union is reserved for the republics within certain constitutional limitations prescribed by general laws.

---

[38] V. I. Lenin, *Collected Works* (Moscow: Marx-Engels Institute, 1960), XIII, 85.

Corrective labor colonies are established in accordance with three regimes, described to us as mild, general, and strict. All inmates start with the general regime and are either advanced to the mild regime or relegated to the strict regime as their conduct warrants. Colonies of the mild regime are not guarded, and some colonists are permitted to live off the reservation with families. Most inmates are placed on the mild regime if they have less than three years to serve. Colonies of the general regime are subjected to an armed perimeter, but are allowed liberal visiting and correspondence privileges. In the strict regime housing is in cells, and contacts of any kind with the outside world are severely restricted.

Each colony is organized into detachments led by a detachment commander. His responsibility is to know and influence each inmate in his detachment and to insure that the work commitments of the unit are discharged. Detachments vary from fifty to two hundred; the average is about one hundred and fifty. The size principally depends on the work assigned. Work units are housed and fed together; such collectives are concentrated in an intensive group experience in which each inmate is responsible to the group while the group assumes responsibility for each member. Cohesion is stressed, and it is the task of the detachment commander to insure that the cohesion works in the interests of the colony as a whole.

Terms in the corrective labor colony tend to be long. According to Dr. Struchkov, this is a subject of intensive study among corrective labor scientists. The code specifies a maximum term of fifteen years for most major crimes of violence and for crimes against state property. For crimes against personal property, the maximum term is ten years, as it is also for lesser crimes of violence, including murder without aggravating circumstances.[39] The courts assess the sentence at the time of conviction, within the maximum sentences applicable. With the approval of the district court in which the colony is situated, conditional release may be permitted after half to two-thirds of the sentence is served, depending on the nature of the offense.

The legal structure, in general outline, contains few novelties, and

---

[39] For further details on the sentences in force for major crime categories, see P. S. Romashkin (ed.), *Fundamentals of Soviet Law* (Moscow: Foreign Languages Publishing House, 1962), pp. 413–442.

very little in it would be out of place in a conventional western code.[40]
Corrective labor colonies, as described in the code and the literature
are not strikingly different from conventional medium and minimum
security prisons in Western countries. In practice, however, as we saw
at Kryukovo, the corrective labor colonies are vastly different from anything encountered in any Western correctional apparatus.

Our inspection of the corrective labor colony at Kryukovo had some
of the flavor of a minor state visit. Arriving in a limousine in the company of an official interpreter and a regional inspector of colonies, we
were met at the gate by the colony chief, his deputy chiefs, and a pho-
tographer. From the first we were assured that we would be allowed to
see what we wanted, to talk with whomever we wanted, and to have
access to all available information. Our enquiry proceeded in an atmosphere of friendly candor, clouded to some extent by the unavailability
of statistics and an unwillingness on the part of the regional inspector to
permit responses to questions which might give clues to the numbers
of inmates in custody.

The colony itself is a collection of untidy barracks behind a double-
barbed wire fence. Its capacity is one thousand, but we were told that
on the day of our visit there were only eight hundred inmates. This was
due to the decline in the crime rate in the Moscow region, and it was
added that only during the last year it had been possible to shut down
four other colonies of the same size. How many did that leave in operation? Very few, we were told by the regional inspector in the manner of
a man who is coping with a too inquisitive outsider.

The regime is general, and the average length of stay is from three to

---

[40] Nevertheless, there is some significance, which we cannot begin to assess, in
the fact that corrective labor is but one of a series of sanctions, including death (for
nine different offenses, including murder, terrorism, banditry, embezzlement of
state property, and issue of counterfeit money or securities), deprivation of liberty,
exile, restricted residence, corrective labor without deprivation of liberty, disquali-
fication from office, fine, and public censure. See Romashkin, *ibid.* pp. 414–417. How
courts distribute sentences from this unusual range of penalties we could not study.
The principle, as stated by Romashkin, is: "Individualized punishment is a most
important principle of Soviet Criminal Law: the courts impose penalties in accordance with the . . . social danger of the crime, the degree of guilt of the
accused, his personality, and attendant circumstances." How such a principle of
individualized punishment might influence the process of selection for corrective
labor colonies is obviously a determinant of the quality of the experience of corrective labor.

five years. The chief, Major Artamanov, thought that most of his charges should be classified as "dangerous recidivists," guilty of such offenses as robbery, housebreaking, assaults, and persistent hooliganism. Through the process of inculcating the offender in the "joy of socialist labor," most of these recidivists would be restored to society.

The particular labor which the inmates were to learn was metal fabrication. We were escorted through large shops in dingy sheds but equipped with modern and evidently productive machinery. On bulletin boards in each shop charts were posted showing the production norms for the shop as a whole, the production norm for each inmate, and the relationship of actual production to the norms established. Noting that there was an air of bustle about the place, we enquired whether the inmates always worked so hard. No, said the chief, he would have to admit that this day was unusual because it was the end of the month and everyone was trying to meet or exceed by as much as possible his norm for the month. We noted that the previous month's chart showed that most norms had been exceeded by wide margins, some by as much as 200 per cent.

We were told that the heart of the program is work. Each man is interviewed immediately upon arrival by the deputy chief for corrective labor and assigned to work in accordance with his skill or lack of it. Each man was expected to learn a trade, and indeed, an essential prerequisite for release was qualification in some skill. For some, this might require extensive education, and the standard Soviet "ten-year school" was available for the enrollment of anyone needing it. Many pupils, we were told, not only completed the ten-year school but went on to training in technical institutes or the university. But whatever else a man might do at Kryukovo, he would certainly work, and at the speed expected in outside industry.

Everyone was paid in accordance with a formula based on rates prevailing for regular industry. For highly skilled inmates, the scale might be about 75 per cent of the ordinary rates; for less skilled inmates the rates would be no less than 45 per cent. The deductions made (difference between paid rate and full rate) were for the cost of maintenance of the colony. The inmate was free to use the earned money as he liked. He could send his earnings to his family, save it for his release, or spend it all in the canteen. The major was obviously proud of his work program and thought that he was succeeding in conveying the joys of labor, even the joys to be found at a punch press or an automatic stamping machine.

Discipline was no problem. Perhaps there were two or three rule violations a week, but almost always they were trivial infractions of such regulations as those proscribing spitting on the sidewalks or smoking in prohibited places. Several months before there had been the only fight which the major could remember, but that had ended in hands shaken and mutual apologies. It seemed to us that this level of discipline was remarkable enough under any circumstances, but especially so when the small staff of seventy or eighty was kept in mind. This was where the most unusual Soviet correctional innovation came into play. To advise the chief regarding matters of discipline a Commission on Corrective Labor was organized. Colonists were required to nominate members to the commission from each work group. This section is responsible for calling to the attention of the administration any condition which might interfere with maximum productivity in the shops. Such conditions might be anything from insanitary maintenance of the bath house to an inmate's obstructive behavior. Particularly open to the commission's activity was any kind of sloth or inefficiency. Any such deficiencies were to be discussed by the commission in the presence of the inmate concerned. While overt punishment was not permitted the commission, it could reprimand a fellow inmate, expose him to ridicule in a wall newspaper, or call undesirable behavior to the attention of the administration.

A second device for inmate participation in colony management was the Commission on Professional and Vocational Education. This commission was responsible for helping the deputy chief for education by bringing its influence to bear on untrained colonists to motivate them for special efforts in vocational education. Where the administration might have incorrectly evaluated the capacity of a colonist to fill his job responsibilities, this commission would call the situation to the attention of the chief so that corrective action could be taken.

Both commissions operated in a manner parallel to Russian industrial organization outside the colony. Workers' collectives in Soviet industry proceed on the assumption that it is the duty of each member of the collective to assist fellow members to maximum productivity. If this amounts to a situation in which it is a national duty to mind other people's business, then here is one of the special distinguishing marks of Soviet society. If we are to credit the Kryukovo administration with a factual account of the colony structure, its inmates will certainly learn to support community norms by special attention to the affairs of fellow workers. In this as well as in other respects, life in the Soviet corrective labor colony closely matches the conditions prevailing outside the institutions. Patterns of control which are effective with the Soviet worker can be applied with comparable results to the Soviet criminal.

Because of these controls or because of the additional security built into the institution, there has never been an escape from Kryukovo. Major Artamanov pointed out that there was really no reason why an inmate should want to leave Kryukovo; in his domain a prisoner had good work at reasonable pay, comfortable quarters to live in, good comrades, opportunities to improve his education, regular visits from his wife, family, and friends, and generally as few disadvantages as could be arranged for a man in custody. Besides, he added, there was that double barbed-wire fence with armed perimeter guards under orders to shoot anyone who approached it.

Our tour of the institution took us to the visiting room, a barracks converted for that purpose. A long table on one side lined with chairs provided the usual facilities for the preservation of outside relationships. On the other side of the barracks a line of cubicles had been established for conjugal visiting. These pathetic islands of privacy in an otherwise entirely public condition of life contained only the bare necessities: a sagging double bed, a commode, a straight-backed chair, and a cheap samovar. Throughout the barracks the redolence of bygone cabbage lingered from meals prepared by inmates' wives. Major Artamanov told us that his policy was to permit seven conjugal visits per quarter for each inmate. On the way out of the building he noted that one cubicle was occupied. He knocked and opened, to reveal a sheepish looking young man frantically getting into his clothing while his wife, in bed, clutched the blankets about her and glared balefully at the intruders. We concluded that while conjugal visiting offered undoubted satisfactions to the couple concerned, its hazards were also considerable in the hands of an insensitive staff. We asked Major Artamanov if it presented any problems. He could think of none and considered that it made possible a more natural and humane kind of life for his colonists. It seemed probable that this concession to normal sexuality had eliminated the degrading preoccupation by the staff with homosexuality which prevails in most Western prisons. We asked the major whether this problem was much encountered in his institution. Our interpreter had some difficulty with the question; the major's puzzled expression indicated that he was unfamiliar with the word. When it was defined by the interpreter, the major brushed the question aside as referring to behavior that did not exist in that institution.

Our tour of Kryukovo ended with an inspection of the recreational building, a multipurpose unit which served as a gymnasium, theater, and social hall. On this particular day, however, a special court was in session to consider the conditional release of inmates recommended as ready for return to society. In the rather dingy hall were gathered about fifty cheerless looking inmates who stared at us during the moments of our intrusion. On the platform sat a bench of three judges. Before them stood a youth in the uttermost stages of anxious tension. His knees shook, his teeth chattered, and he grimaced as he tried to deal with the questions of the court. The major explained to us that when a man came up for consideration of release his detachment was encouraged to attend for the support of their comrade and for their edification.

Release is arranged by taking full advantage of the authoritarian organization of Soviet economic society. Two weeks before the scheduled date for release, the chairman of the Soviet of the inmate's home town is notified. The full dossier on the inmate is forwarded together with a recommended employment plan. It is the responsibility of the Soviet to locate for the inmate a place of residence, an appropriate job, and to make such other arrangements for his return to the community as may be needed. This system never raises problems. The possibility that the Soviet might not welcome back a malefactor or that it might not coöperate in his restoration to the community could not arise.

After release, the major told us, the colony must maintain some contact with the former inmate. Detachment commanders would visit him when they could and help with any problems of readjustment he might be encountering. Through reports from the police, from the chairmen of workers' collectives, and from family members his progress would be watched. We were shown some of these reports, most of which were meager and perfunctory, but at least represented contact. Recidivism after Kryukovo was very slight, the major thought. Only 2 per cent of his releases returned to his institution; he doubted that many more got into trouble taking them elsewhere. After all, he pointed out, the problem of resocialization of the Soviet citizen is not difficult; in these times all citizens identified with the aims and philosophy of the Communist party and the Soviet state. This being the case, criminal behavior would be exceptional, and recidivism would be rare. He could look forward with confidence, he thought, to the happy day when Kryukovo, too, would close and he could return to his ordinary trade as a machinist.

How typical is Kryukovo of the Soviet corrective labor colonies? Ever since Potemkin created model villages of muzhiks for the reassurance of Catherine the Great, tourists in Russia have been wondering whether that which they are allowed to see represents reality. Certainly these suspicions will be warranted until the whole society is open for inspection. Throughout the rest of our travels in other countries we were allowed to see what we wanted; no requests, including some which were awkward to arrange, were denied. In the Soviet Union it was clear that Kryukovo was the colony which Westeners were allowed to visit and that they might draw such conclusions as they liked from what they saw. Our interest in visiting other colonies was sympathetically received but no action was forthcoming because of various vague inconveniences.

Yet we think Kryukovo is significant. Even if other colonies fall short of this model, this is the model which the official literature prescribes. It also represents in its position as the colony open — to some extent — to Western visitors, a picture of the way the Soviet establishment would like such institutions to appear to outsiders. It is therefore reasonable to take Kryukovo seriously, for it represents the official correctional theory.

It seemed to us that Kryukovo was a conscientious attempt to normalize the life of the offender. Group influences are even more important in the determination of the conduct of the Soviet citizen than they are in Western cultures. The same kinds of group influences which are exerted in regular Soviet living are practiced in the institution. These include the commitment of groups to the achievement of objectives, the assignment to each group member of a significant role to play on the achievement of the common goal, and the assumption by the group of a responsibility for the group member's performance. Where such an organization of interlocking responsibilities conforms with the official norms, it would be an exceptionally abnormal individual who would be able to resist the influence of his peers. The almost continuous staff-inmate group interaction which was implied by Kryukovo's organizational scheme would reduce both occasion and support for deviation to a bare minimum. We saw no groups gathered in which a staff member was not conspicuously present. Someone is always watching the Soviet inmate. It is Big Brother, as represented by the staff or the inmate's own peers, who exacts conformity. At least in theory, this is the kind of life to which the offender will be released when he goes to his workers' collective. Life in a corrective labor colony realistically prepares the inmate for an adjustment to peer group control not only of work productivity but of personal conduct.

Such a system could hardly be effective if a comparably realistic role in life were not built into the system. There is neither unemployment nor made work at Kryukovo. The real problem of employment is to get all the work done for which the colony has been committed by its administration. Much work undertaken by the colony requires a high degree of skill, and as everywhere else the level of skill of prison inmates is not high. To get out the required work, both staff and inmates must work hard, skillfully, and coöperatively. The various commissions, the frequent meetings of collectives, the insistence on trade training not only prepares the inmate for effective participation in community and economic life upon release but are actually necessary for the day-to-day operation of the colony.

The inmate's productivity meets a real social need. It is not an embarrassment to which society must accommodate in the interest of enlightened treatment as in the United States or England. When an inmate collective is exhorted to meet its production norm and to exceed it by as much as energy and ingenuity can arrange, the source of the exhortation is the fact that the truck engine parts, the kitchen utensils, or the office chairs which the collective may be making are urgently needed. To reinforce this need, an appropriate system of incentives is brought into action. The provision of regular pay at prevailing rates implies the expectation that regular value is expected.

Similarly, the sexual drives of the colonists are realistically respected. Abstinence is neither required nor encouraged. An occasional interlude with a wife in a dismal little guest house scarcely meets the conditions of romance or even of dignity, but as maintenance of marital realities and as relief of infectious sexual tension it makes more sense than the cat-and-mouse homosexuality so common in Western prisons.

This is preparation for a society in which the range of choice is narrow. Whatever the occasions for crime, they must occur within a framework of regimentation which is largely similar to the organization of the institution itself. With the Russian tolerance for coercion and the culture's incessant exposure to officially endorsed norms, the Kryukovo model seems likely enough to succeed. It would indeed be surprising if it were not followed elsewhere in the country, so compatible is it with the Soviet social system.

To round off our observations of the Soviet correctional apparatus we also visited a juvenile correctional labor colony at Pushkin, a suburb of Leningrad. Over its entrance arch is inscribed in bright red and white Lenin's ubiquitous exhortation, "*Uchitsya, Uchitsya, Uchitsya!*" (Learn, Learn, Learn!) Precepts by the currently admired Soviet prophets are colorfully placarded up and down the walks and around the recreation yards. Otherwise the grounds are dreary. The institution is housed in an eighteenth-century monastery heavily battered by artillery during the war. It has been inexpertly restored, as though the project could not be justified for a major investment. The result has been the appearance of untidy desolation.

The demeanor of the staff was something else again. Its chief, Colonel A. A. Anastas, had the manner of a man who rather fancies himself as a martinet but for all that lacks the required rigidity of personality. The remainder of the staff, from what we could see, were friendly, optimistic educators in uniform, much like school teachers of the best kind the world over. The boys themselves looked cheerful and hardly the sullen young delinquents so often seen in training schools for this age group.

But Colonel Anastas assured us that they were typical Leningrad hooligans. There were 391 of them, organized into four detachments of a hundred each. Each detachment was divided into units of about twenty-five; each unit had a staff member assigned to guide, instruct, and advise. The age range of the boys ran from fourteen to eighteen, with an average of about fifteen. The length of stay would not be fixed by the court at the time of sentence; this decision was for the management of the institution, to be approved by the committing court. Probably most inmates stayed about a year, but the range was from six months to two and one-half years. There was a large staff, compared to Kryukovo; in all there were one hundred and sixty-six employees.

Unlike Kryukovo, the program was basically educational. Each inmate was required to learn a trade before he could be released. Vocational training was available in the building trades and the metal trades. Completion of an apprenticeship was not required, but a reasonable competence qualifying the boy for employment is expected. We noted that the trades offered were usually considered quite difficult to master; Colonel Anastas agreed. Nevertheless, he assured us, difficulties must be presented to the delinquent so that he can see what he might become through application and diligence.

While the core of the program is the school rather than the shop, the assumption is that the school will enable the boys to experience the joys of socialist labor, about which one hears frequently in the USSR. These joys are experienced as a consequence of the influence of the community on the individual. The classroom is permeated with zeal because each boy sees social restoration as a satisfying goal. In this sense, at least, juvenile corrective labor colonies have taken leaves from the works of Anton Makarenko, whose work with delinquent boys in the chaotic days following World War I was one of the first improvisations of a correctional community.[41] For years in disfavor, Makarenko's work has been restored to official approval. His picture may now be seen on most correctional walls as a modest figure in the Soviet hagiology.

As revised by the corrective labor scientists and understood by practitioners like Colonel Anastas, the Makarenko system is based on persuasion rather than coercion. The persuasion is reinforced by reliance on community opinion which must support the official aims of the institution. Colonel Anastas thought that the system as applied in his institution depended on three stages. First, the institution preserved the boy's self-respect by giving him as much responsibility as possible. Conventional methods which were designed to humiliate the boys were carefully avoided. A serious effort was made to see to it that the boys should learn to take responsibility for each other. This familiar Soviet theme runs through the entire program.

Second, the system requires the delinquent to learn to work. The culture of work is fostered by recognizing success and achievement in each boy's training assignment in every way available to the institution. Throughout the program, everyone on the staff insists on the maintenance of a normal industrial speed. Trade unions are organized and councils are put to work on serious issues of management in the institution. The trade-union organizations are put into active collaboration with trade unions outside. Vocational training is reinforced with demonstrations by advanced workers from famous plants in the Leningrad area. So far as the institution can pursue this goal, satisfying work achievement is presented to each boy as a realistic personal objective.

---

[41] Anton Makarenko, *The Road to Life: An Epic of Education* (Moscow: Foreign Languages Publishing House, 1955).

The third stage of the Makarenko system is the inculcation of cultural interests and standards. Local Komsomol chapters visit the institution to conduct group discussions of political and economic problems. Theatrical schools send productions to be tried out before this critical audience. Committees of parents visit the school to keep abreast of the programs in which their sons participate and to exchange views with the staff. And throughout it all, there is kept before the inmate community the image of the Ideal Inmate. This ideal is attained by the inmate who: does not violate regulations; studies well in school or shop; fulfills work norms and produces objects of the best quality; shows conscientious respect for instructors and elders; behaves like a cultured gentleman at dances and other social occasions; behaves on week-end releases consistently with the standards of the institution; reads good literature and arrives at an opinion of his own about what he reads.

Colonel Anastas indulgently estimated that about 90 per cent of the boys released achieved this ideal. During the two years immediately following release boys are still under the institution's control. Contact is maintained through the police and through various trade-union and cultural organizations. Like all our Soviet correctional colleagues, Colonel Anastas was vague on the percentages of recidivism. What mattered to him was that the system worked in terms of his part in it. Its ultimate effect in the community for the restoration of his boys was not a matter for which he was expected to take responsibility. As at Kryukovo, it is reasonable to conclude that in a society in which individual choices of conduct could be severely limited, in which surveillance could be intensive, and in which group expectations could be mobilized in support of norms, there should be a high rate of success. If this reasoning is correct, it is especially mystifying that there should be such reluctance to publish statistics which may well be highly creditable to an intelligent and humane system worthy of Makarenko, the imaginative and courageous man who founded it.

In concluding our observations of Soviet correctional practice, we know that we end very near the point at which we started. Our reconnaissance was obstructed not so much by the willful secretiveness of our hosts as by mutual inexperience. We had no personal experience of the Russian bureaucracy or in the observation of Russian social phenomena. Our Soviet colleagues had no experience of the itinerant American social scientist, his frame of reference or his methods of gathering data. The three weeks which we were able to devote to Soviet correctional institutions could not be enough to do more than expose the inquirer and the phenomenon to each other. It was a reconnaissance, but, we think, a successful reconnaissance on which there might be built a more extensive inquiry into the nature and effect of Soviet group control methods. What is needed is a program for the long-range study of Soviet corrective labor practice, developed in collaboration with Russion social scientists. It may be naïvely optimistic to expect that such a program would be welcomed by the Soviet establishment. But certainly nothing can be expected to develop in this important area of social science until we make definite proposals for study to Soviet officials.

Essentially a cross-culture study of Soviet corrective labor would be based on the following elements:

A thorough review of the relevant literature, most of which has not been translated.

The assignment of a team of Russian-speaking social scientists to a series of discussions with the leaders of corrective labor science.

Observations of all levels of institutions in which correctional clients are confined. Such observations should include formal interviews with staff and inmates and attention to group processes of all kinds occurring in the institution. Particular care should be given to the identification of possible typological categories.

A comparable opportunity for Russian corrective labor scientists to observe and study American correctional institutions and to interview leaders of correctional thought in the West.

Through a series of studies of this kind, probably extending over at least five years, much new light could be thrown not only Soviet correctional institutions but also on Soviet society itself. Conducted with attention to objectivity, a study at this level of intensity might not be objectionable to the regime and might greatly enlarge the general theory of group influences. It is so important a venture that it should be pursued with the utmost diligence. It might even provide answers to the questions which we took to the Soviet Union and brought back unanswered.

CONCLUSIONS

We have traversed far and wide and found standard correctional practice in many forms:

It is an American probation officer in a big city with a caseload he does not quite know yet. He is threading his way in a compact car in heavy traffic, getting information for a report, looking for someone who is hard to find, encouraging a faltering ward, admonishing a boy who is up to something, and making his way back after hours to an office desk piled high with referrals, messages, and dictated reports to proofread.

It is an English borstal governor at a battered desk in a converted drawing room trying to arrive at a constructive adjudication of the infractions committed by a series of insolent, slothful, aggressive, feckless, or apathetic boys.

It is the governor of a Scottish women's prison having daily tea with her inmates in the belief that this kind of contact must be helpful in a situation in which few other helpful elements exist.

It is the vice-director of a Danish youth prison, still young enough and fit enough to suit up for a football game with his inmates, and feeling that on the whole this is a good thing to do.

It is a Swedish correctional officer doing a two-hour stint before a battery of television tubes, watching for something out of the way to show up. If something does show up, he will broadcast instructions to fellow officers strategically placed with walkie-talkie radios.

It is a Soviet detachment commander in a corrective labor colony supervising a meeting of his unit at which the candidacy of a member for release is under consideration.

It is all these people and thousands more. They are working in institutions which are mostly obsolete, improvised, overcrowded, and inconveniently situated. The administrative structure is cumbersome and bureaucratic, hard-pressed to keep things going. Maintenance of present services keeps the staff busy; there is little inclination and less time for innovation.

People, buildings, organization charts.

They are for the control of hundreds of thousands of grand and petty offenders. Deterrence, retribution, incapacitation, and even treatment may be the objectives expected by the administration of criminal justice. But the essence of correctional practice as now administered throughout the world is *control*. Within this framework much else may be done. Much else must be done, if only in the name of humane standards of behavior by the state toward its citizens.

It is control, but it is seldom permanent control. For nearly all offenders, no matter how grand or how petty, the day of discharge eventually comes. For quite a disconcerting number, the day of release comes frequently and meaninglessly. The law and the correctional apparatus must presume the offender "normal" when admitted, and "normal" he is when released. He is normal with all the rights, privileges, and disabilities attaching to the term. The assignment of the correctional apparatus is to make the human fact correspond as closely as possible to the legal fiction. To do this quite impossible task, treatment programs have been improvised, borrowed, and sometimes thoughtfully developed. Programs are designed to do two things; to offset the damage done by the artificial experience of confinement, and to change the offender into a person no more likely to commit an offense than any other *normal* citizen. To test these programs statistical tables of recidivism of increasing sophistication are developed. A good program will be reflected somehow in lowered recidivism; an inffective program will not.

This is the standard practice of corrections. It controls offenders directly and it aims for their indirect control as a consequence of the experience of direct control. It is a simple model. By introducing a variety of complexities to facilitate the objective, the model works, usually with somewhat more success than failure. An irrational equilibrium is maintained. At least some credit, but no one can ever establish how much, can be claimed for the successes. Likewise, blame for the failure can be apportioned to circumstances beyond the control of the apparatus, but no one can judge where error left off and inevitability took over.

Perhaps the practice of corrections can continue forever on this unstable footing. Many other human institutions no more rational have survived for much longer than the two centuries of correctional history. But here and there in our wandering inquiries we saw evidence of a trend toward a different model of correctional practice. In some cases it is too soon to be sure that these evidences are more than the aberrant exercise of common sense. But in others we thought we saw the application of a new rationalism to an old problem.

IV

TOWARD A
RATIONAL PRACTICE IN
CORRECTIONS

The standard practice of corrections, wherever we went, centered on the containment of the correctional client. Whatever else was done for him, this client was held, as considerately as possible, within arbitrary limits. Much more was done for many clients: They were educated, put to remunerative work, given remedial surgery, and provided with various kinds of psychotherapy. Even more was attempted: A frequently encountered phenomenon was the good idea put into play with inadequate resources. However, control was the guiding consideration of the correctional apparatus. All other operations were shaped to meet the patterns dictated by custody and surveillance.

Here and there, however, correctional innovations have departed from the stress on control for the exclusive sake of control. These innovations generally follow the reasoning that the traditional instruments of the correctional apparatus too severely limit the possibilities of social restoration.

This perspective implies a radical change in the perception of correctional objectives. It assumes that the apparatus has a mission far more complex than the mere control of the client for the period assigned by retributive justice. Instead, the mission of the correctional agency is the optimal social restoration of the offender to as constructive a part in society as he is capable of playing. To accomplish this end, the whole correctional apparatus must be reoriented in philosophy, methods, and organization. Control alone, no matter how efficient or how sensitive, is not enough.

If control is all we expect, the standard practice of corrections works very well. Not many inmates even try to escape from institutions. Probation officers generally manage to keep in touch with their caseloads for the limited value which contact has. But nobody evaluates the effectiveness of correctional service by the criteria of mere control. What the community wants is obvious enough from the incessant attention to the statistics of recidivism. It wants *change* — the change of the offender from a person whose behavior is intolerable under the normal conditions of community life to a person who can function within the limits of public tolerance. This is an expectation which overrides the traditional assignment of control. It is also an expectation which no one can now reliably fulfill.

Correctional leaders have dealt with their impossible assignment by reasoning that for most offenders the experience of control contains enough unpleasant features and enough conditioning elements to produce the change which the public wants. When English correctional apologists write that "some three-quarters of those who serve a prison sentence for the first time do not return to prison," the inference to be drawn is that a system of control augmented by opportunities at education will produce the desired after-effects.[1] We shall not attack this conclusion. There is evidence enough in the statistics of recidivism of English borstals and approved schools to show that control is not a reliable instrument for producing change in behavior.[2] Similar evidence can be marshaled from the uncompromisingly maintained data of the California Bureau of Criminal Statistics, and the Departments of Corrections, and the Youth Authority. The real conclusion is inescapable that whatever control does to offenders, no one can relate specific positive effects to be defined changes in any clearly described class of correctional clients. Speculations about the benefits of control for the sake of control have been repeated for so many generations that conjecture has been stiffened into conclusion. The correctional apparatus still rests on a crude foundation of expedient hypotheses, precariously assumed to be true. In the simpler and less numerous society of the nineteenth century and the first four decades of the twentieth, the social and economic cost of the errors concealed in an irrationally organized correctional system could be tolerated. The soaring costs of

---

[1] *The Treatment of Offenders in Britain* (London: Central Office of Information, 1960), p. 27.

[2] *Report of the Commissioners of Prisons for the Year 1960* (London, HMSO, 1961), pp. 187–192.

crime control in the postwar decades insistently tell us that the time has come to rebuild correctional process on a more rational basis than emotionally satisfying hypotheses about the rigid control of the criminal.

To assemble and test conjectures about alternatives in correctional practice, we are bound to the present. The innovations in this standardized field are inextricably linked to the traditional assumptions. No one can pound his fist on behalf of a good idea and say he *knows* how good it is. The application of any rationally conceived innovation is confounded by tradition, incompatible practice, and imperfect execution. We still do not know how to test correctional innovations surely enough to relate effects to causes. The survey of innovations to be found in this chapter represents an inventory of promising notions. They have been formulated from experience and the findings of the social sciences. They are, in fact, as hypothetical as the standard practice which they may some day replace. How shall we identify promise in the modest variety of innovations to be surveyed? The question plagued us from the first. A frame of reference by which the advanced practice of corrections could be recognized when we saw it does not exist. Though the canons of efficient and humane control are contained in such publications as the *Manual of Correctional Standards,* no one has proposed an integrated statement of advanced practice. The many scholars who have contributed to correctional thought have mostly concentrated on the obvious defects in the framework. The improvements which they have proposed have been based on the traditional assumptions. Their adoption has improved the control systems which constitute standard practice. By such improvements the correctional apparatus *holds* the offender more surely and with less danger from the noxious influence of punitive barbarisms. But most correctional reformers assume that the practice of corrections will not receive a change in assignment.

We decided that the assignment must be altered to provide for the objective of optimal social restoration. It is a view shared by a scattering of practitioners all over the world. It does not imply the abandonment or even the relaxation of control. No utopia of education, therapy, loving-kindness, or magic is in sight for the offender or his keeper. For the foreseeable future, correctional clients will need external control. This control will be certainly coercive, and no attempt can be made to disguise that fact from the client, the staff, or the public. For our goal is not to release our motley collection of thieves and cut-throats from coercion. Rather, we must accommodate what coercion is necessary to a rationally conceived plan for making as good purses as we can out of the sow's ears we have to work with. This is quite different from contriving as good a plan as we can in accommodation to a system of control which has been conceived without reference to what a client may need before he can be safely returned to society.

If we could make the objective of social restoration the touchstone of advanced practice, were there any specific signs by which we could be sure that we were in the presence of advanced practice? We thought that there were some indices beyond the good-will resounding in the aspirations of correctional officials to improve their clients. These indices seemed to us to include the following:

1) A deliberate, conscious emphasis on social restoration as the primary goal of correctional practice. The evidence of such emphasis would be the existence of a rationale for the item of practice which could be connected with the social restoration of a differentiated class of clients. Such a rationale would identify a problem, propose its solution, and account for the solution in terms of cause and effect.

2) The maintenance of aseptic social conditions in the correctional experience. We kept in mind the admonition of Florence Nightingale that, "Whatever else hospitals do, they must not spread disease." Similarly, delinquents must not be made worse by the institutions to which they are sent, nor must probationers be further alienated from legitimate authority by the kind of supervision which they receive.

3) Built into the structure of an advanced correctional innovation there should be a system for its evaluation as an instrument for the social restoration of the classes of offenders to which it is to be applied.

No one could say that these were easy conditions to meet, nor that a quick glance at this agency or that would uncover advanced correctional practice by reference to these principles. Experience was to show us that nowhere were we to encounter a correctional apparatus which met all these conditions. Most seriously lacking nearly everywhere were systems of self-study. Good criminal statistics are rare but good correctional statistics hardly exist. Therefore we still cannot say in this chapter, "This is the correctional future, and we have the data which show that it works!" Worse still, we saw little evidence that pioneers with good ideas were being afforded the resources with which to evaluate the application of their concepts. It happens, but innovations in treatment method are preceding by far the development of methods of correctional measurement. The trusting willingness of parliaments and legislatures to give correctional innovators the means to do something new without requiring adequate evaluation of the results is impressive testimony to either the credulity of fiscal parliamentarians or the persuasiveness of correctional administrators. Still, a good idea, rationally conceived and executed, is worth relating in this chapter, even though we have no way to prove how good an idea it may be.

In what follows, then, we shall describe some of the actual elements of rational practice as we saw them in our travels. Put together, the isolated practices and concepts which we found would still fail to constitute the full scope of an advanced practice aimed at social restoration. But a correctional apparatus so oriented would include systems of classification related to correctional problems to be solved, methods of case management designed to produce optimal solutions within the limits of present knowledge, and access to research operations for the improvement of both classification and services. Here and there correctional enterprises can be found which promise such a future. Its achievement depends on the ability of correctional leadership to innovate comprehensive models providing for the three basic indices of advanced practice for all correctional clients. Such models will have to contend with the sources of public satisfaction with a control-oriented system, however irrational such a system may be shown to be. The fragments of the rational model are all we can show here. They may be considered to be mere adjustments to the irrational equilibrium of contemporary corrections. We prefer to think of them more optimistically as the portents of a more rational civilization to come.

CLASSIFICATION

The great correctional reforms of the past hundred years would have been impossible without systems of classification. To eliminate the cruelty of treating all offenders alike some differentiations had to be made. Once the community was persuaded that the object of criminal justice was to hold rather than to hurt the offender, it followed that no one should be held by control greater than his case required.

Further, the conviction that industrial employment, education, and, later, psychotherapy should be afforded the offender while he was under correctional control required a system to allocate these services according to need. A classification system based on matching test results and diagnoses with the services available became generally accepted as a necessity in a well-run institution. By 1947 classification concepts were well enough crystallized for official publication in an American Prison Association handbook.[3] Comparable ideas were generally accepted in European institutional planning, as for example the intricate distribution of population in English correctional institutions. Juvenile institutions borrowed heavily from the practice of educational guidance. Classified residential treatment in juvenile institutions throughout the world is grounded on the formal case study followed by periodic review.

While field practice has lagged far behind the institutions in the development of systems of differentiation, the influence of classification as an essential tool of the correctional institution was beginning to be seen in the postwar probation agency. Administration learned to differentiate caseloads by the nature of the risk, the need for service, and the problem presented. Through the increased use of presentence investigations, a focus was brought on the dimensions of field service in corrections. If the court was to be advised as to its disposition of a defendant, there had to be some definition of the capacity of the probation service to control him.

This is neither a history nor a handbook of classification. Our object here is to examine the trend of classification practice. The baseline from which such trends must be projected is easily established. The elements of the new departure in classification are more difficult to describe. Nevertheless, just as the great reforms of the past began with classification, we must begin our excursion into the correctional future with an appraisal of the advanced thought in the differentiation of the offender population.

Classification, generally, begins in the court. Some courts carry the process farther than others, but all courts classify offenders by the nature of the offense committed. Once this is precisely defined, the degree of retribution, as aggravated or mitigated by circumstance, can be measured out. No court, not even juvenile courts, can disregard the demands of retributive justice. The very act of making a finding and a disposition implies retribution. For some courts, the exaction

---

[3] American Prison Association, Committee on Classification and Casework, *Handbook on Classification in Correctional Institutions* (New York: American Prison Association, 1947).

of payment for wrong-doing overrides all other possible considerations.

Courts must also consider the need and requirements for social control. The impossibility of appraising this need from the bench has brought into the practice of probation an emphasis on the presentence investigation which sometimes overshadows the supervision and treatment of the offender. The increasing use of probation investigations will probably bring to judicial attention the claims of social restoration as an essential consideration in the disposition of cases.

The first dimension of classification is retribution. The second dimension is control. While the courts make the first differentiation, by which offenders are distributed to the various arms of the correctional apparatus, the second determination is carried out by the correctional agency itself. It is concerned to classify offenders by the degree of control the offender needs. The correctional decision maker now has the responsibility to keep the offender safely or to maintain certain required contacts. He must make this decision in accordance with the minimum amount of control needed to achieve these objectives. Data are gathered to enable the decision maker to choose from the available options as safely and as economically as possible. "Programs" — to use the all-purpose word of corrections — are needed to implement control. They also serve to mobilize services in preparation for discharge. Programs are the product of classification systems. Most such systems are based on periodic syntheses of subjective estimates, almost always made in interdisciplinary groups. Indeed, it would be hard to think of any human activity quite so interdisciplinary as correctional classification.

Programs are built from determinations of myriad questions. How much surveillance will we have to provide for this man to be sure that he remains under our control? What kind of housing behind what kind of perimeter is the minimum needed to prevent him escape? What kinds of industrial, educational, medical, and psychological services will be most suitable to facilitate his present control and to improve his future conduct after release? These and many other questions are incessantly asked in correctional institutions. They are indispensable for sensible control.

But control for what? The emphasis shifts with the institution. In the immense prisons so unhappily characteristic of the United States, the staffs rightly expect trouble and wish to prevent as much of it as possible. The peaceable accommodation of the inmate to the apparatus becomes the objective. Watching the classification committee of such an institution in action, one has the sense of large units of little-known psychopaths being marshaled and deployed through a system in which only the past and present exist. The future, a time when the inmate will once again try to be his own man, is a distracting irrelevance. What has to be done is to work this man, house him, educate him, and, maybe, treat him as a psychiatric patient. All this has to be done now with the scarce resources of the institution, the scant knowledge of the man, and in some way consistent with the hundreds or thousands of other programs to be set up for other offenders. This is control, and, when thoughtfully carried out by a sensitive staff, it can minimize the havoc which incarceration in a large institution can wreak. Classification at this level is essential to the difficult, almost incredible task of containing several thousand felons on one reservation.

In the smaller juvenile institutions and in many European prisons classification can take the future into account. When the classification committee convenes in such an institution, the present realities are weighed with an eye to the future. Release will take place some day, and it should be part of a program leading to that critical event. Successive relaxations of control form the basic structure of that program. Readiness for release can be appraised by the response to each relaxation as reflected in the inmates' progress in other aspects of the program. This process needs intimacy between staff and inmate as an essential ingredient. It goes on all the time in a matter-of-fact way in small institutions blessed with staff with an appreciation of the opportunities. The most cogent exponent of the process encountered in our travels was John Gittins, the headmaster of Aycliffe approved school in England. Aycliffe is a classifying school which receives approved-school commitments from the north of England. It also maintains a program for "very dull" boys, as Mr. Gittins frankly describes them. In a day spent at Aycliffe, we heard much about what Gittins regards as the comparatively simple process of initial classification:

If you have a given boy coming to the classifying school, you spend four or five weeks in a comprehensive diagnostic procedure. You work out a treatment plan for the boy, and by and large it's true to say that the style of report coming from a classifying school is in advance of anything that is possible in the way of treatment. It is much easier to tell people what to do than it is for them to carry on and do it. The next phase in our development is to go into the administrative difficulties of carrying out a consistent treatment for each boy. I call it "working at the coal face," and I mean working with people who are doing the job — organizing their work for them so there is a planned treatment process for each boy.

The "planned treatment process" has two distinct aspects: institutional and individual:

During the training period a boy can be first, second, or third class; this decision is made entirely according to his overt behavior. If the boy keeps himself clean and tidy, does what he's told, and coöperates, he can be the biggest rogue in school but he'll be rated as first class and rewarded accordingly. His promotion is determined by the points he has earned for character development, according to a program which has been thoroughly discussed with the boy. We make a very sharp distinction between rewards for overt superficial bearing and taking him along the promotion line according to character and other defined progress. Remember that with these boys we've got to dramatize all the time, and this is one of the devices we use for dramatization. On the deeper side, there's a good deal of manipulation of these points and classes. What we try to do is to get the boy to a recognizable peak. I think it's quite important that the peak should come shortly after the boy's license.

"License" means eligibility for release. After this determination is made, the boy is moved into a different house in preparation for his return to his family or to the community. He may be found a job with some employer in the vicinity while on license at the school. We asked for an example of the operation of this process.

Let's take the case of a boy who came here. He had a terrible behavior record although he came from an exceedingly respectable family. After we got him here, we uncovered a most grotesque, sordid situation in the family which nobody knew anything about, and we brought the whole thing to the surface. That produced great disillusionment in the boy and in everybody else, but we gradually put the pieces together. Now we've got to the stage when the parents are collecting what was really a shattered marriage and doing something about it. They're putting the home straight, and it's beginning to become a place to which the boy could go. We have made it clear that this home is not a place to which the boy should go permanently. There is a long story behind this — a very complicated story. This was an adopted boy with more than his share of the problems of adopted boys. But now he's on top of the world; he's one of the best boys we've got in the school. It's important to license him while he's doing awfully well, because there's always the chance that he'll get into some minor scrape. If at this particular point in time anything happened to that boy which would make him feel that he was lowered in our estimation, I think it would be quite traumatic. He's only been in the school for about thirteen months but I think he's got to go on license. For a relationship has developed, you see, in which if a problem should develop outside, he can bring it to us and ask for advice. I think there's a great danger in getting "over the hump" — once you get over the hump it's awfully difficult to get on to another hump.

The minute scrutiny necessary to the procedures described by Gittins requires not only intimacy but awareness. Only with the confidence which comes from real knowledge of the individual can a dual set of standards for both control and social restoration be manipulated without confusion. In the system described, control is achieved by relating full information about the past to the events of the present and the reasonable options for the future.

In most large systems, this kind of knowledge is out of the question. Seen as a unit in a mass, the offender will be classified on the basis of easily assembled information. The category in which he falls will be settled by the amount of control indicated by the information at hand. When he is docile enough to need no control, the correctional administrator is likely to think him ready for release or discharge. Similarly, as a term progresses toward its judicially pre-determined conclusion, controls are relaxed unless some exceptional situation requires their maintenance. Simple considerations of this kind are at the heart of most correctional classification in the large systems in the United States, and, to some extent in England.

The new departure in classification adds to the dimension of control requirements the prospect of social restoration. Though this prospect has always been in sight in institutions such as Mr. Gittins' establishment at Aycliffe, it has not been a feasible scale to apply in large institutions until recently. But recent technical developments have added much to the potentialities of classification. From the findings of social science the techniques of *individualization* and *prediction* have been added to the correctional repertory. Through these instruments it has at last become possible to think of classification in terms of the job to be done rather than as the adjustment of the offender to correctional control. The application of these techniques is still experimental. Not all connections between findings and theory and between theory and practice have as yet been made. But new materials are at hand, and here and there correctional administrators are learning to use them. The new approach to classification is the foundation for the rational practice of corrections.

Let us begin with the part which prediction plays in making possible a system of classification that points beyond control to social restoration. We do not intend to review forty years of complex and highly technical work in the statistical analysis of criminal experience.[4] The fundamental aspiration of social science to discover methods of predicting human behavior has been pushed toward realization by many scholars in many countries. Their hypotheses have varied widely and their data have ranged from molehills to mountains. Though many resulting methods have been validated with statistical experience, few have been put to administrative use. It is useful to examine the reluctance of the courts and the correctional apparatus to accept these fruits of statistical science.

First, many still question the propriety of using statistical interpretation of experience to set prison terms and guide the award of probation. This is an ethical issue on which controversy is continuing. Mannheim and Wilkins attempt to settle the fundamental problem of the connection between justice and statistics with the following analysis:

Justice is not a function of statistics. Statistics only ensure that rational decisions may be taken with known risks. Nothing is perfect in this world and we must take our choice of taking risks and more often than not coming to the right decision, or of not making any decisions. . . . It has been demonstrated in this study that the statistical classification into likely failure and likely success groups results in more than twice the accuracy of intuitive methods based on the judgments of highly experienced assessors. This means that if the assessor has access to the statistical tools and uses his judgement to supplement these (where and in such ways as such supplementation is valid) the two methods together are likely to result in better classification than any one alone.[5]

---

[4] For a comprehensive but concise review of the literature cf. Hermann Mannheim and Leslie T. Wilkins, *Prediction Methods in Relation to Borstal Training* (London, HMSO, 1955), pp. 1–27.

[5] *Ibid.*, p. 47.

A similar point is made by Barbara Wootton in a review of the status of prediction studies:

Once it is established that statistical methods applied to a particular type of problem give consistently more valid results than the intuitive judgments of even wise and experienced men . . . then the claim of those men to wisdom can hardly be sustained, if they still insist on the superior merits of their own intuition in relation to that particular problem.[6]

A second and related issue is the status of a statistical prediction of delinquency as a self-fulfilling prophecy. This concept, given currency by Merton,[7] is of particular relevance to correctional prediction. Where a prediction is made whose consequences place the correctional client in a class for which definite expectations are entertained, these expectations will have a tendency to be fulfilled. The child who is predicted to become delinquent on some such scale as the Gluecks[8] have provided will be more likely to become delinquent simply because this eventuality is expected by those in authority around him. However valid this concept may be for the "predelinquent" child, it bears special significance for the offender handled in accordance with his probable recidivism. To be placed in a class of correctional clients for whom failure is predicted must enhance the probability of failure, unless carefully considered steps are taken to offset the prediction. In this connection, the admonition of Merton himself is specially relevant: "The self-fulfilling prophecy, whereby fears are translated into reality, operates only in the absence of deliberate institutional controls."[9] The moral obligation of correctional administrators to install such controls when prediction devices are adopted is inescapable.

A third obstacle to the general use of predictive methods is technical. Even the simplest prediction devices require a considerable technical facility to construct and a considerable organization to administer. Only with the advent of electronic data processing has the

---

[6] Barbara Wootton, *Social Science and Social Pathology* (London: George Allen & Unwin, 1959), p. 199.

[7] Robert K. Merton, *Social Theory and Social Structure* (Glencoe, Illinois: The Free Press, 1952), pp. 421–436.

[8] Sheldon and Eleanor T. Glueck, *Unraveling Juvenile Delinquency* (Cambridge: Harvard University Press, 1961).

[9] Merton, *op. cit.*, p. 436.

application of prediction method become practical for most correctional agencies. Now, of course, it becomes not only practical but inevitable with the revolution of automation. Our problem now is to
assure that our concepts are as wise as our technique is sophisticated.

Finally, the principles underlying prediction method, particularly the
refined mathematics, are difficult for the lay administrator to grasp well
enough to acquire confidence in their application. It has been hard to
swallow the notion that a mathematical model can be constructed
which could provide a more accurate view of the future than the clinician, on whose judgment the decision makers have relied for so long.
The manipulation of masses of data, none of it clearly related to personality dynamics, is not so emotionally satisfying as the psychosocial
evaluation in which the clinician relates an intimate knowledge of the
individual to his professional perspective. But even if such authorita-
tively based evaluations were more commonly available than they are,
reliance on them would not be likely to turn out as well as the cold,
impersonal tables of the statistician. For as Mannheim and Wilkins
point out,

> perhaps those who are likely to have the best results in treating delinquent
> behavior are those who are able to believe the best of their cases. If this is so,
> the good therapist is an optimist and may not, therefore, be the best person
> for prognosis. . . . In the intuitive systems we cannot separate within the
> mind of the assessor the various aspects of his personality, and his optimism,
> desirable in one field, may be undesirable in another.[10]

For these reasons and perhaps still others correctional practice has
for more than a generation had many tools proffered for its use in ra-
tionalizing practice, only to ignore them for the less effective instruments of clinical intuition. Nevertheless, prediction methods cannot
be longer resisted in an electronic age. It is up to the correctional
administrator to make certain that the place of the computer is consistent with its capabilities. With the level of data now in use, the
administrator is restricted to those decisions which can be made valid-
ly with reference to the client as he was when he arrived. The
Mannheim-Wilkins system is based on an assessment by scoring of
five kinds of factors: use of alcohol, disposition of prior offenses, nature of past living arrangements, place of residence, and length of

---

[10] Mannheim and Wilkins, *op. cit.*, p. 38.

employment.[11] Similarly, the Base Expectancy system developed by the California Departments of Correction and Youth Authority in consultation with Wilkins, is based on the development of equations to differentiate risks according to similar kinds of demographic attributes. Predictions so based will sort out offenders according to the prospects for behaving themselves after exposure to some standard correctional experience. Nothing is said, of course, about the way they can be expected to fare after specialized training or therapy. Much more information will be needed before mathematics will be able to give us answers of that kind. As matters now stand, prediction tables and systems can be valuably used for the following purposes:

First, they can sort out the correctional population according to an estimate of the prospects of each member for resocialization. The value of this instrument for the rationalization of practice is considerable, even though some problems are created which are far from solution. But as long as time and confinement are dimensions of the disposition of offenders, we need reliable means to decide between probation or institution and to determine the time required for each. What prediction systems can tell us about good risks and bad can influence the courts when they award probation and the classifying centers when they decide on institutional placement.

Second, prediction systems can be used to assist courts and paroling authorities regarding the nature of the risk ahead for any particular offender. The cliché of the "calculated risk" is a rationalization for the correctional administrator who is doing what his intuition tells him is best. The prediction system introduces an actual calculation, but does not entirely complete it. It is still up to the administrator to weigh the risk as calculated against the kind of hazard to be expected. This calculation is much more apt to be made if the mathematical prediction is available as a point of departure. The assessment of an individual as a member of a category with a 70-30 prospect of success insistently raises the question of what the implications of the 30 per cent prospect of failure might be. A 30 per cent prospect of homicide must be viewed in a different light than an equal prospect of shoplifting. Nothing in sight offers the administrator complete relief from the burden of the risk-laden decision.

Third, a prediction system increases the precision of evaluation. To

---

[11] *Ibid.*, p. 158.

know the success of a correctional apparatus in terms of the recidivism
of a population at risk is to know more than most administrators.
But it is not a level of knowledge which tells anyone where the
strengths and weaknesses of a system lie. If the population can be
stratified by the classes of risks confronting the apparatus, the results can some day be compared with expectations. Investments in
program can be shifted, reduced, or increased according to what is
found from the comparisons made. No prediction system goes far
enough to include elements more sensitive than demographic items.
In another generation of refinements expectancies can be based on the
nature of the problem to be solved and, perhaps, some assessment of
the adequacy of the available solution.

In this section on innovations in classification, we are concerned
with the use of predictive machinery for the allocation of offenders
to programs. We encountered no system in which this system was
used by the courts to determine sentencing practice. Some use has
been made, notably in Illinois, of the predictive method in granting
parole.[12] But the most impressive use of prediction methods for the
allocation of offenders is in the institutional systems of large correctional apparatuses. It was the English borstal system on which the
Mannheim-Wilkins scales were standardized, and it was on this system that it was first put to regular administrative use. Publication
of the Mannheim-Wilkins study stimulated the notion that it could
be put to a first test in the opening of a new borstal in 1957. This
was Pollington, established at a decommissioned RAF base in Yorkshire. The governor had completed a course of training in group dynamics at Tavistock Institute in London. It was thought that under
his specially prepared leadership an experiment could be conducted
whereby the allocation of inmates to Pollington would be limited to
the two best risk categories in the Mannheim-Wilkins scale. With an
expected success rate of about 75 per cent, would it be feasible to reduce the length of stay at Pollington from the then prevailing average
of more than two years? The answer is related in the governor's account to us:

We very much wanted to see that by taking good prediction risks and
giving them a very short period of training if we appeared in any way to re-

---

[12] Lloyd E. Ohlin, *Selection for Parole* (New York: Russell Sage Foundation,
1951).

duce the chances of success. We have worked pretty steadily since the time that we opened on the basis of keeping lads for a period of about ten months training, counting right from the very minute that they were sentenced to borstal by the court. This means that in practice it is about seven or eight months in Pollington itself.

We asked if there was an significance in the period selected in terms of the program offered by the institution. He went on:

No, I can't honestly pretend that. Originally we did start for the very first months by working on one year. We soon felt that the kind of boys we were getting could just as effectively be trained in ten months. . . . We decided not to tell the boy as he came in that he could get out in the absolute legal minimum provided for at that time, that is, nine months. We made that a little vague to provide some incentive.

What kind of homogeneity was achieved by limiting the intake to a special group in the upper ten or twelve percentiles of the Mannheim-Wilkins scale? No one had pulled together all the details at the time of our visit to Pollington, but there were some impressions:

The impression one has is that they are rather simple, poised young men. They don't seem uneasy when visitors meet them or when we talk with them. It's a pretty easy relaxed kind of a relation which they seem to have with us and others outside. Between themselves, the first thing that strikes one is the strength of feeling of each dormitory toward itself. Dormitories are family groups formed of twenty boys. I think it's true to say that there is quite a spirit of common helpfulness among the boys toward each other. There is some real concern, I think, about whether other boys are likely to get into trouble — whether they can play some part in helping other boys to behave more sensibly or to see things more sensibly. There isn't a great deal of fighting. . . . It is a common thing for a boy who has been segregated in the punishment cells to be asked for by his counseling group and to meet with the group in the evening.

At any time, a number of boys stand out in the community by reason of their excessively hostile and aggressive attitudes toward staff. I think that especially in this last year there has been an astonishing ability on the part of the staff to tolerate this kind of thing without taking counteraggressive attitudes. My own belief is that where these hostile, aggressive attitudes spring from a personality difficulty, such a boy acquires quite a reasonable adjustment. Where I think we make absolutely no headway at all is with those boys who have acquired a pretty hardened view of themselves as the result of the culture in which they've grown up. This is a culture in which you've just got

to play a recalcitrant part — the term here is the "shrewd man." We aren't
awfully successful in getting this kind of recalcitrant to change his views.
He's much too heavily invested in the maintenance of these defenses.

Remembering the ideal inmate of the Leningrad Corrective Labor
Colony, we asked whether with this homogeneous intake subjected to
a specialized and uniform program a model Pollington inmate emerged
at the end of the line.

I haven't the faintest idea what a model Pollington inmate would look
like. I always feel that there is an enormous danger in group pressures — this
awful business of suggesting that everybody has got to conform to some kind
of standard. We have a camp meeting mechanism which seems to apply to
this problem. You must understand that we have no boys in leadership positions to which they have been appointed by the staff. Every boy who has a
position in the camp has to be freely elected by the other boys. Now, one of
the things about this is that a recalcitrant often gets elected. At once, his
occupancy of such a position subjects him to pressure to do as all leaders have
to do — to conform to group norms much more closely than he wants to. This
is a powerful influence which the lads themselves bring to bear on him. The
camp meeting tends to swing from electing the very normal well-adjusted
boy to choosing as its next chairman one of the more difficult boys in the
place. I think the more difficult chairmen are brought to heel by necessities of
managing this camp meeting and doing a good job of it.

In this borstal of one hundred and twenty boys selected as the best
prospects for success in the system's intake, it has been possible to
take some short but clear-cut steps toward innovation in an otherwise conservative apparatus. Since the staff had the assurance that
this was a picked group conditions were established under which a
group counseling program could be started with little technical leadership. Community meetings could be started, in spite of the hazards
which correctional clinicians have traditionally foreseen in the use of
this device. And the low risk of failure supported the staff in a release policy which more than halved the average length of stay in
borstals.

The results so far have extended far beyond Pollington. The group
counseling program has been extended throughout the British apparatus. Prisons as dissimilar to Pollington as Dartmoor, the ancient bastille for long-term offenders, or Wandsworth, London's "tough nick,"
have incorporated the practice in their programs. The average length
of borstal terms has been reduced to about sixteen months for the

whole system, a trend which is at least partly based on the Pollington experience. The use of a predictive system to establish a population on which experiments can be made has justified the system. How much farther the British Prison Department can carry the application of the Mannheim-Wilkins scale to the development of program remains to be seen. It is easy to think of improvements to institutional practice with good correctional risks. What to do about the poor risks is a problem which has baffled not only the British.

PREDICTION AND INCREASED CORRECTIONAL EFFECTIVENESS

One of the first tasks of the Research Division of the California Department of Corrections when it was established in 1957 was the development of a system of base expectancies. With the consultation of Leslie Wilkins, the statistical innovator in the Mannheim-Wilkins partnership, the thorough and advanced system of correctional housekeeping accounts set up by Ronald Beattie was put to use as the base for an elaborate predictive system. As in the Mannheim-Wilkins scale, essentially demographic data were selected and subjected to correlative manipulations. The result has been a series of base expectancy scales applicable to various correctional populations. Inmates could be ranked according to the risk of recidivism which they presented. By 1960, each of California's adult offenders was being assigned a base expectancy which represented a multiple correlation of such information as arrest histories, use of alcohol and narcotics, patterns of residence, and previous confinement. With the aid of computers it would not be long before every living soul committed to the Department would be rated as to his expectancy of future major criminal activity. What would be done with this information?

A strategy was adopted similar to the one which brought Pollington into being and made it quickly into a unique component of the English borstal system. The population was divided into three sectors: high, middle, and low base expectancies. Based on the assurance that inmates with a high expectation of parole success are likely to succeed regardless of the length of incarceration, a program of "Increased Correctional Effectiveness" (inevitably contracted to *ICE*), was brought into being. High-expectancy inmates were identified and programed for release as soon as possible after minimum sentences had been served. To reduce the stress of vicissitude and the accidents of fate when social restoration is unplanned, a special program

of release preparation has been devised. Despite the practical difficulties, parole agents are incorporated in the life of the ICE groups
at the institutions. Their day-to-day familiarity with the problems of
parolees on the streets becomes a ready resource from a familiar face
rather than impersonal news from a remote, almost unimaginable
world.

Middle-expectancy inmates are also included in the program, on the
principle that this kind of purposeful treatment structure, as contrasted with the mere serving of time, justifies earlier release of even
the less-promising release prospects. In a mixture of benevolence and
good economics which is probably peculiar to corrections, intensified
social treatment produces monetary savings to the state by facilitating
shorter institutional sentences.

So far, this is a small program, mostly consisting of forestry camps
of sixty to eighty inmates. Again, intensive group-counseling, community group methods, and the concept of completely integrated
treatment dominate the process, just as these ideas prevail at Pollington. Progress in treatment, rather than the passage of time, determines
eligibility for release. To settle on such a principle would have been
impossible without predictive methods to reduce the risks of failure and
to limit the contamination of the hopeful by the hopeless. But though
the number of inmates actually assigned to ICE programs is only a
few hundred out of many thousands in California, the test of the
treatment concepts would only have been possible with the assurance
that a strong underpinning of prediction furnishes the correctional decision maker. From these tests, more can be learned about the efficacy of various social treatment procedures as they apply to offenders
grouped according to the degree of their criminal identification. Much
more can be inferred for future tests regarding the impact of such
case management on personality types.

The further use of predictive techniques in California corrections
depends on the development of appropriate program concepts. Because it is reasonable to suppose that expectations of a narcotics ad-
dict or of a violent offender may be grounded on a different quality
of criminal identification than is common to the property offender,
efforts are under way to establish a system of base expectancies related to the peculiarities of these delinquent careers. With some experience in their use, base expectancies may play an important part
in developing new distributions of these classes of offenders.

CONCLUSIONS ON THE USE OF PREDICTION METHODS

Despite their long incubation in the universities of several countries, prediction methods have only begun their useful career in corrections. We shall later examine their usefulness for research, but here we must summarize the actual and potential uses for correctional operations:

In court: Sentencing practice now depends on a composite of the legal requirements of the statute, the judicial policy on retribution, and the professional opinion of the probation officer regarding the prospects of the offender for reclamation. The use of base expectancies could eventually add a fourth determinant, a comparative statement of the prospects of any given offender for social restoration by any of the available alternatives. In this way, courts could consider the statistical experience of the community in sentencing a particular class of offenders to prison, jail, or probation. The possibilities might also extend to analysis of experience on length of term. To our knowledge, nothing like this use of base expectancies has yet been attempted. While such a system would never relieve a judge of his responsibility for making a decision, his chance of making the right decision would be considerably enhanced.

In probation agencies: So long as financial and training resources of probation are as meager as they now are, any improvement in probation administration will depend on differentiation of caseloads. Some agencies emphasize differentiation, based mostly on the elusive factor of professional judgment. The distribution of caseloads by the risk of failure will afford the probation supervisor with information by which he can allocate his resources of personnel and time in accordance with the calculated hazard to the community. Under no circumstances can this principle be allowed to degenerate into over-simplified risk categories. A sex offender with a high base expectancy will still need more attention on probation than the shoplifter with a low expectancy. Further, base expectancies will provide probation supervisors with an experiential basis on which to recommend discharge. There is no point in encumbering probation caseloads with clients who have favorable prospects of success without probation.

In institutions: In institutions, base expectancy systems assist in the allocation of inmates to the available programs and provide support for the design of new forms of treatment. Where the latitude of an indeterminate sentence makes it possible, release decisions can be guided by the expectation of success. These potentialities are partly realized in England, California, and Illinois. They can powerfully contribute to the advance of any system of correctional institutions which can justify the cost of the statistical paraphernalia.

In parole: Parole decisions generally resemble those which face the probation officer. Large caseloads must be divided among a usually insufficient number of personnel. Case requirements vary between a desperate attempt to provide as frequent contact as possible and the perfunctory maintenance of legal requirements for a parolee who has found a reliable place in the community. Base expectancies can assist in making the same order of judgments for the parole supervisor regarding the allocation of work as for his colleague in the probation department. No matter how rich the agency's resources, the use of base expectancies in making informed decisions about the choice of supervision methods is essential. To practice without the intelligent use of this instrument limits decision-making to inspired guesswork at best. Inspiration is not an abundant commodity in any correctional agency.

A further use of the base expectancy system in parole operations lies in the decision-making in a parole violation. While this decision has sometimes to be made by the probation officer, too, any parole agency finds itself incessantly faced with judgments about the advisability of a return to the institution. This decision cannot be made by statistics alone, but a statistical estimate of the probable success of a plan to maintain a paroled person in the community as opposed to his return to prison could add support to the painful judgment which must ultimately be made on the basis of other factors.

Base expectancies will solve no problems by themselves. They will not even provide hints as to how problems should be solved. From such a calculation no one can derive a plan for the appropriate management of any particular class of offender. The allocation of an institution to some particular level of offender graded on the expectation of success will not tell the superintendent what he should do next. Some administrators, indeed, will derive from their analysis of the accumulated expectancies of their clients the conclusion that what they do is irrelevant; their inmates are bound to fail or succeed as the case may be. Others, awarded a clientele with apparently even chances of success or failure will accord small thanks to a system that tells them so. What base expectancy systems offer correctional administrators is an estimate of the risk which will enable the decision maker to plan control for so long as the risk is his. To plan programs, information of a different order is needed. Prediction schemes assume that there will be no change in the phenomena about which predictions are made once the predictions have been formulated. When change is to be provided for, we must shift to a different system of sorting out the clientele. For want of a better term, we refer to such systems as treatment typologies.

THE USE OF TYPOLOGIES

In the correctional apparatus measures must be taken to classify offenders according to the degree of control needed and the risk to society and the system if the restraints imposed should fail. Similarly, there must be a system which determines what measures of change are likely to succeed and assures that those measures are carried out.

No news in these propositions. Classification committees have pooled their knowledge about offenders in conscientious, interdisciplinary fashion for a long time. Determinations have been made regarding the educational, vocational, and psychological capabilities and needs of clients with due regard to test results of considerable variety. In a well-regulated correctional system, probationers and inmates are probably the most tested segment of the community. The value of testing is not challenged here; indeed, it may well be that future correctional advances will add to the battery of tests now administered.

What is new is a different perception of the task of change. Conventional correctional practice relies on classification to decide how large a dose of education, vocational training, industrial employment, or psychotherapy the client can absorb. In the coercive operations of the total institution, motivation is of slight relevance. The treatment of the unwilling client has been subjected to some modest exploration, most significantly in psychotherapy.[13] The profusion of tests of achievement, aptitude, maturity, and personality winnow the population of correctional institutions for prospects for kitchen, mill, classroom, or psychotherapy. A correctional institution in which programs are planned along these lines becomes a combination of school and hospital, a hybrid from which inmates learn that they have deficien-

---

[13] See particularly, Melitta Schmideberg, "Training the Unwilling Patient," *British Journal of Delinquency*, IX:2 (October, 1958), 117–122.

cies which they can correct if they apply themselves. Often enough, a correctional client does apply himself to the offerings of the institution. Through educational effort or psychotherapeutically induced insight he may improve and be released, to be seen no more by his keepers. The joy in correctional high places over such successes is great. The failures are dismissed as inevitable. When everything possible within the conventional framework of corrections has been done there can be no reason for chagrin.

Correctional theorists have been aware that the widely differing results which the conventional institution produces may be expected from the process of exposing widely differing offenders to basically similar treatment methods. Though classification may have physically separated offenders from one another and found good and sufficient reasons for varying the degrees of their control, the treatment they get once separated is more remarkable for its similarities than for its differences. To many theorists, improvement of correctional results depends on the development of reasoned diversification of treatment.

The need for differentiation of offenders has intensified the search for relevant typologies. In a concise but thorough review of the subject, Marguerite Grant has identified twenty-three separate typological approaches distributed among five general categories.[14] These categories are:

Prior probability approaches: Already discussed (pp. 189–193), the Base Expectancy method provides the administrator with the power of establishing the risk and gauging the results. It does not identify the problem or prescribe its solution.

Psychiatrically oriented approaches: Most significantly applied in child guidance or psychiatrically programed institutions, such typologies are of limited value for general correctional use. They provide the psychiatric treatment team with a distribution of the patient caseload in accordance with clinical experience and the configuration of symptoms encountered. They do not furnish the correctional specialist with a basis for planning programs to solve the problems of individual offenders to be restored to the community.

Reference-group and social-class typologies: Indispensable for the study of criminal identification and the organization of client groups

---

[14] Marguerite Q. Grant, "Interaction Between Kinds of Treatments and Kinds of Delinquents." *Proceedings of the 90th Congress of Corrections* (Denver, Colorado: 1960), pp. 455–465.

both in and out of the correctional apparatus, such studies as those of Schrag [15] or Sykes [16] are not intended to indicate how the social types described should be managed.

Behavior classifications: Such classifications identify significant symptoms (and group them together). Eventually they may be of considerable predictive value. There is much need for the development of typologies of this kind for research into the effectiveness of treatment. If we can describe the abatement as well as the aggravation of symptoms we may also gain further knowledge of the processes by which treatment achieves its effects. Such classifications tell us little, however, about the problem the client presents in achieving restoration to the community.

Social perception and interaction typologies: These typologies are based on various theories of accounting for ego strength. Such classifications differentiate degrees of ego development or personality integration, as accounted for by arrests in psychological maturation.[17] Through an identification of the modes of interaction with the social environment characteristic of particular levels of personality development, various strategies leading to the social restoration of the offender can be devised. Such strategies do not necessarily aim at cure. A much more modest goal — optimal function within the limits of a social handicap — is both realistic and enough. Cure, in the sense of substantial personality change, is evidently beyond the capability of the correctional apparatus except for a few kinds of clients. But within the community locations can be found for the isolated to be sheltered, for the manipulator to obtain satisfactions without recourse to operations damaging to others. It is the task of the correctional apparatus to locate such situations for its clients and to prepare them for different ways of achieving the same satisfactions. It is enough that the client should be safely returned to society through a compensation for the defective interaction which caused his delinquency.

Fundamental to interaction typologies is the assumption that defective personalities abound in general society. Sometimes they thrive,

---

[15] Clarence Schrag, "A Preliminary Criminal Typology," *Pacific Sociological Review*, IV (Spring 1961), 11–16.

[16] Gresham Sykes, *The Society of Captives* (Princeton, N.J.: The Princeton University Press, 1958).

[17] Sir Julian Huxley, ed., *The Humanist Frame* (London: Allen & Unwin, 1961), pp. 147–165.

sometimes they manage precariously. To enable the delinquent to function as well as his equally defective but nondelinquent fellows is a realistic correctional goal. It is all that can be done with the means at hand; for all but a few, the defects themselves can hardly be touched.

Here, then, we concern ourselves with typologies of interaction. Efforts in this direction have been few and modest. Results so far are meager; theoretical development still rests much more heavily on speculation than on facts. But the advance of corrections depends on the improvement of treatment. Merely to improve control, whether in the institution or in the field, is relevant to social restoration only so far as humane treatment or the lack of it may motivate the offender to conform. The most hopeful avenue for increasing the effectiveness of corrections is in the direction of diversifying service in accordance with the client's problem in social restoration. The use of social interaction typologies defines the client's problem. It also provides a base for solutions. To define the offender's problem in terms of experience with similar offenders previously dealt with is to arrive at some notions as to possible solutions. The shotgun sprayed at the whole offender group is replaced by a rifle aimed at a specific problem with a specific intended effect.

The use of social interaction typologies is not only consistent with the requirements of control. Through increasing the credibility of the treatment administered, control is enhanced. Further, the ultimate objective of the correctional apparatus, the effective self-control of the offender, can be achieved most reliably by plans for treatment to make self-control possible.

Social interaction typologies depend on studies of ego strength. In clinical psychology such studies have been proceeding for many years, but their application to correctional problems is recent. The first venture of this kind was undertaken by Clyde Sullivan, Marguerite Grant, and Douglas Grant in a project carried out under U.S. Navy auspices at the Retraining Command in Camp Elliott. This project, initiated in 1952, has been described, in part, by the investigators in a recent publication.[18] The investigators developed a theory of interpersonal maturity by which seven successive stages of maturity were identified

---

[18] J. Douglas and Marguerite Q. Grant, "A Group Dynamics Approach to the Treatment of Non-Conformists in the Navy," *Annals of the American Academy of Political and Social Science*, 322 (1959), 126–135.

as the ordinary course of personality development. Fullest ego strength is realized when the complete sequence has been traversed.

The range of the stages of maturity extends from the first level, at which perceptions of self and environment are like those of earliest infancy; this describes a condition which virtually precludes the commission of a crime. The seventh level, at the other extreme, provides for the ultimate in personality integration. This enviable condition is described by the authors as the "integration of relativity, movement, and change." So fully realized is such a person by hypothesis that the authors thought that "no one completes this stage in the society of today." Obviously, any such persons, if they exist, would be most unlikely to be confined for nonconformity.

In the intermediate levels of maturity various defective interactions are identified. At the second and third integration levels children are preoccupied with problems of gratification and denial which must be solved before an advance to higher integrations. In sequence, children find through experience that denial of demands must be attributed to rules and to interpersonal conflict. Later, in the fourth and fifth integration levels, standards are internalized, and some of the complexities of social relations which affect the realization of standards are successively understood.

The integration level theory accounts for delinquency and other deviant behavior by assuming arrests in normal emotional development. Those who suffer such an arrest in the early stages of maturation are particularly prone to delinquent behavior. Denial of gratification arouses violence at the second level and manipulation at the third level. At the fourth level, fixation renders the individual vulnerable to the stress of guilt and feelings of inadequacy; the authors believe that gang delinquency and professional criminality are characteristic of this stage of maturation. At the fifth level maturation is nearly complete and such delinquency as occurs is "situational," the bad luck involved in faulty estimates of complex social situations.

No attempt will be made here to provide a theoretical buttressing for what is still an incomplete scaffolding. For an account of the system, such as it is, the reader is referred to the authors' original paper,[19] which concludes on this modest note:

---

[19] C. E. Sullivan and J. Douglas and Marguerite Q. Grant, "The Development of Interpersonal Maturity: Applications to Delinquency," *Psychiatry*, 20 (1957), 44.

This effort to understand personality through modes of experiencing inter-personal relationships is not presented as a complete theory of personality; rather it is offered as a first step in a program of personality investigation. Its value lies not in the absolute truth it contains, but in its ability to raise specific questions to which there are specific answers, which will aid in the scientific approach to truth through approximations.

Questions on the nature of the arrests which fixate individuals at early stages of maturation are answered in terms of fear, guilt, and anxiety. The influences exercised by culture, the social structure, and chance learning experiences are scarcely touched. The typology divides up the universe itself, but particularly classifies the interpersonal sources of delinquency. As the earliest such attempt it is a landmark in the still inadequately charted domain of rational correctional practice. We may not find in it many clues as to what should be done with immature young thugs floundering their way through life at the second integration level, but the identification of such a group is a valuable contribution in itself.

Nevertheless, light though the scaffolding is, it has served already as a base for a significant demonstration of the need for differentiation of treatment in accordance with modes of social interaction. At Camp Elliott, the investigators classified naval prisoners by integration levels and made comparisons of differential responses to treatment not only in accordance with the integration levels found but cross-classified by kinds of supervision administered. Differences in the effectiveness of treatment were predicted on the basis of the investigators' estimate of the group supervisors' competence. The validity of the estimate might be questioned, but the existence of some difference in the way the groups were handled is beyond doubt. It was discovered that prisoners with high maturity levels were far more successful when restored to naval duty than those with low maturity levels when assigned to companies whose supervision was rated best. On the other hand, the success of prisoners assigned to companies rated worst was much lower for high-maturity individuals and much higher for low-maturity individuals. The significance of this experiment in supporting the proposition that what's good for some may be bad for others is not lessened by the lack of replication. Investigations of this kind are difficult to conduct, require years to complete, and must be pursued under controlled conditions which do not exist in every correc-

tional setting.[20] Because the classification of offenders into this scheme
by the methods now available is prohibitively costly, further experiments of this kind will probably have to await the validation of test
methods which can be rapidly applied. Interest shown in this typology
in areas as far apart as Denmark[21] and California should eventually
carry its potentialities further toward practical usefulness.

A "second generation" lineally descended from the integration-level typology is the Interpersonal Maturity Level Classification for Juvenile Offenders proposed as the theoretical base for the California
Youth Authority's Community Treatment Project. This typology was
derived from the original formulation by Marguerite Q. Grant, one
of the three investigators responsible for the basic integration-level
theory. Its present practical application to an active research project
demonstrates the utility of the approach and some of its difficulties.

Mrs. Grant distributes the delinquent population into nine categories, each tied to levels of perception corresponding to stages in
maturation identified in the basic conceptualization. Before we proceed to a description of the project itself, a brief outline of the nine
categories on which it is based will be needed. Mrs. Grant begins
at the "I-2" level with the following pattern:[22]

Aa (I-2)   unsocialized personality, aggressive type: "demanding"
Ap (I-2)   unsocialized personality, passive type: "complaining"
Cfm (I-3)   conformist, immature personality type: "conforming"
Cfc (I-3)   conformist, cultural type: "conforming"
Mp (I-3)   manipulator, psychopathic type: "manipulating"
Nx (I-4)   neurotic anxiety type: } "defending"
Na (I-4)   neurotic, acting out with no felt anxiety: } "defending"
Se nonneurotic, situational emotional reaction: } "identifying"
Ci neurotic, cultural identifier: } "identifying"

With such a finely screening classification system available for use,
the next step was to work out a treatment model. The matured concept in the hands of Mrs. Grant was grasped with alacrity by Heman

---

[20] Grant and Grant, as cited in n. 18.

[21] E. Hoeck-Gradenwitz, "The Use of Anamnestic Analysis: Its Techniques and
Results," unpublished manuscript, 1960, in the author's possession.

[22] Marguerite Q. Grant, *Interpersonal Maturity Level Classification, Juvenile* (Sacramento: Department of the Youth Authority, 1961).

Stark, the director of the Youth Authority. Dissatisfied with institutional care for juvenile offenders and convinced that ways of retraining them in the community should be found, Stark had been casting about for a design to strengthen parole services and reduce the need for what must be realistically called confinement, no matter what euphemism is chosen to disguise it.

Obviously neither law-enforcement agencies nor the general public itself could or should accept the immediate placement of youthful offenders on parole. If correctional supervision were all that control required, the courts would have been able to make a probation order. Something more than conventional field contacts was needed. With Mrs. Grant's typology available it became possible to think of differentiating cases in accordance with treatment needs. With such differentiations made, hazards to the public could be kept at a minimum not only by selecting youths without histories of violence but also by making plans to control and treat them in accordance with their needs. To be sure that these plans had the fullest possible chance of being put into effect, the size of the project caseloads was set at eight as the normal level, with ten as a maximum. The project provided for six caseloads, all situated in the general area of Sacramento and Stockton in the interior of California.

Selection of caseworkers had to be based on those interested and available from the ranks of the Youth Authority's Division of Paroles. Each caseworker selected was given a promotion to the second level of the civil-service structure, partly to compensate for their removal from the normal paths of advancement, partly in recognition of the unique demands which would be made on them, and partly to forestall so far as possible the turnover incident to promotion. Because an understanding of the project's operations depends on some information about the staff, we must dwell further on its composition and problems.

Mrs. Grant reported that the attractions of the project and the unusual, if not unprecedented, nature of the job to be done required a mixed bag of caseworkers. She and the project supervisor, Thomas McGee, "looked for mavericks," she said to us, "and we got them." It was not enough that the staff should be formally trained. There had to be some reason to believe that they had some gifts in influencing young people. Second, there was the need for creativity. Something new had to be developed, and it had to come just as much from the staff as from the project's designers. Mrs. Grant might have found a way to describe and designate the unsocialized personality, and to lay down general principles for his treatment. But only the caseworker himself could build detail onto the principles and determine for the project how applicable they were to the predicament of this boy in this home in this community. To discover creative candidates the question was asked, "How satisfied are you with what you are doing?" What the candidate was doing was the management of a fairly large caseload, usually more than fifty. A certain satisfaction with such a caseload might be all very well for those who worked for a conventional large parole agency. But it would not do for a young man expected to innovate in correctional treatment. Finally a tolerance for uncertainty was sought, by asking the question, "Can you tell us why you're doing what you're doing?" Those who referred with satisfaction to the canons of parole practice were obviously essential to the agency, but hardly equipped for the strains of a task in which early assurances of success could not be expected.

From the casting of this net a team of six caseworkers was drawn in. Two had professional training in social work; two were clinical psychologists; one was trained in criminology, one was a converted teacher. All agreed, after about a year on the job, that the training of none of them had been relevant to the kind of work they were doing. As they absorbed the contributions of various consultants invited to participate in the project they came more firmly to the conclusion that in community treatment of the delinquent, as they practiced it, there are no experts — including themselves. "They all see themselves as learners, learning more from each other than from anyone outside," Mrs. Grant reported.

We discussed the selection and morale of the staff at such length because these factors must be appreciated if the special quality of the program is to be understood. This is not an adaptation of conventional practice, nor do its practitioners see themselves as engaged in a heavily reinforced parole. This is a purposeful search for methods of changing delinquent behavior which can be applied through a close understanding by the caseworker of the client's complete life-space. The boy or girl can be seen daily, if necessary, and so can everyone else in the child's social structure.

Some significant experience of the program is emerging which demonstrates not only the value of the typology but some difficulties for future correctional programs.

The client begins his progress through the Community Treatment Project after he has been subjected to the customary diagnostic studies at the Youth Authority's Reception Center-Clinic. Because experimental conditions must be maintained, he can reach the Project only by way of a pool of eligible candidates. A research team selects him at random from the pool; the remainder of the pool goes on to conventional institutions. Once the client has reached the project there is no turning back. In the life of the project so far, there have been hardly any transfers.

Once in the project, the client must be placed in his niche in the Interpersonal Maturity Scale typology. His caseworker devises a tentative treatment strategy. It is at this point that the project tests the applicability of this typology to community treatment.

For the first eight months (the normal length of stay in a Youth Authority institution) the caseworker maintains almost daily contact. At the end of this period, the rate of contacts is reduced to once a week, or about the pace of early parole. During the second year of assignment to the unit contacts might be once in every three weeks. At the end of the second year, the client is discharged.

So far as can now be determined, the most immature level of maturation, the *Aa's* and the *Ap's* are appropriately managed on programs of foster-home care and daily individual contacts with caseworkers. "These are real weirdies," Mrs. Grant told us, "they're not mentally defective, but they have that appearance. Most of them have IQ's in the neighborhood of eighty, but they don't look it. They're given to inappropriate laughter, uninhibited sexual curiosity, public masturbation, and other kinds of trying behavior. How foster mothers ever manage to put up with them in their homes I don't know, but they do, and they do a remarkable job with them." Such children are not identified with delinquency, "they wander into trouble." They have to be placed in situations in which trouble is less than ordinarily accessible if they are to be controlled. Some group meetings are organized for this type; these are socializing experiences in which some interactions are provided for. "They try to plan something — usually a picnic or a party. . . . They're very oral characters. The agents maintain contact over an endless stream of hamburgers and malted milks."

With the next higher level of integration, the *Cfm's*, the *Cfc's*, and the *Mp's*, the emphasis is on guided group interaction, usually at a rate of three meetings a week. "Guided group interaction," as the term is used in this project, refers to group meetings in which the acceptable limits of behavior are codified, examined, and democratically applied. A fierce insistence on compliance with the limits is exercised. The theme of the groups' interaction is, "you've got to believe in nondelinquency." Passive acceptance is punished, and so is any form of noncompliance with the group's regulations. Members in trouble are voted into custody either at a juvenile hall or at the Youth Authority Reception Center-Clinic. While any group member is in custody the whole group meets with him at his place of custody. When the group feels that his attitude has sufficiently changed to justify release, they vote to release him. Mrs. Grant is certain that for these groups the satisfaction of mutual aid is a powerful cohesive force. The extent of the benefits of this form of treatment is yet to be assessed, but there are preliminary signs that it helps. Generally the children are doing better in school than before, perhaps because of the exercise of group sanctions on slovenly school performance, perhaps because of peer support for adhering to conventional standards.

Group therapy is offered to children in the higher classifications. For the *Nx's*, *Se's*, and *Ci's*, the course of treatment has been uneventful but evidently helpful. The difficulty is with the *Na's*, the acting-out neurotics. It is difficult to keep in contact with them, and they get into much more trouble than the rest of the project's clientele. Generally, they seem inaccessible to the kind of relationship intended and in group situations tend to reinforce each other's delinquent attitudes. The tentative inference is that group treatment is not indicated for them. Mrs. Grant wonders whether for this group institutional care with intensive psychiatric treatment should not be the chosen treatment. Nevertheless, the commitment of the project to exploration is maintained; the staff continues its search for effective community treatment for this personality type which has resisted treatment in many other settings, too.

As for the children's feeling about the program, Mrs. Grant and her staff do not conceal from them that the project is unusual. Some of them have developed a touching loyalty to it: "I thought about running away, but then I thought about the Project and I decided I didn't want to foul it up." Others are less moved by emotional ties to a situation which presents some unprecedented inconveniences: "The pressure in this project is too much for me. I wouldn't mind seeing my agent every month or so, but every day! My God!" However, all agree that somehow each ward got a break. Certainly no one feels that assignment to the project is exemption from punishment, but no one would want to trade his situation for placement in an institution or even for regular parole.

Community treatment is a new effort; its application of intensive relationships and a service-oriented typology offers a potential which cannot yet be gauged. It will certainly not supplant the use of institutions for all cases. Already at least one class in the integration-level typology seems to be resistant to this form of management. But the attraction of control through relationship rather than confinement is hard to resist. Where results are no worse than those obtained from institutional care it will be difficult to justify continued use of costly institutional facilities when the same gains can be made through means which can be built with people rather than with concrete.

The administrative use of community treatment is still to be decided. At present, it is dispensed by a statewide agency which is in a position to assure that standards are established and maintained. But there is nothing in either the law or in the nature of community treatment which cannot be installed on a local basis and under local control. Already some California probation departments are watching the Grant program with a view to its installation. Premature application by inexperienced or unprepared personnel would be deplorable, but it is to be hoped that further experience can be gained with the method in other communities.

Here, then, is the transplantation of a theoretical formulation of some complexity to correctional practice. Many adjustments had to be made in the ideas and policies which govern the agency's operations. Everyone had to get used to the notion of caseloads which by all experience were so small as to be freakish. And everyone had to get used to the idea that clients would be thought of as representatives of typological categories. This was the order of change in the agency's approach which had to be accommodated; the small caseload was essential to the application of the typology, and only the availability of a new theoretical system could justify the size of the caseload.

Systematic classification of the correctional clientele in accordance with interaction typology seems to be peculiar to California correctional research. The Grant integration-level typology is related only indirectly to the service-problem typology proposed by Dr. Elliot Studt.[23] Working through the problem of defining the social worker's part in the correctional process, Dr. Studt based her researches at a medium-size reformatory for young male inmates. She was impressed by the absence of any scheme of classification of correctional clients with which the social worker could define problems and arrive at any standardized solutions. The models of social-work practice common for other arenas in which the profession is active seemed to be inapplicable in the correctional institution. Though the tools of social diagnosis and casework interviewing were generally applicable, the vast difference between the functions of a child welfare agency and an adult prison made itself felt as soon as the social worker tried to make use of familiar implements in the new setting. Patterns of reasoning which constitute professional approaches to foster-home placement for a disturbed child do not have counterparts in the approach granting parole. The social worker needed to think about the correctional client as a person with a problem to be solved before he could be restored to the community. Some generalizations about the kinds of problems to be solved in the correctional caseload were needed as guides for the social worker.

With this search in mind, Dr. Studt established herself at a hospitable, effectively managed institution for young adult offenders in which the objectives and methods of the social worker were familiar. For sixteen months she thoroughly studied the interactions of eleven markedly dissimilar inmates with the various persons on the staff and in the inmate community. Based on this study, five general types of service problem were identified. These are:

----

[23] In the following pages, frequent reference will be made to Dr. Studt's manuscript, as yet unpublished: "Social Work in Corrections," in the author's possession. It is hoped that this important contribution to correctional theory will be published by the Russell Sage Foundation early in 1965. Under the circumstances, our reference will be to chapter location only.

Preliminary Typology of Delinquent Interaction Patterns

Type	Characterization of interaction pattern	Perception of "I-They" relationships
The Isolate	Disengagement	"*They* act by magic. *I* (and others like me) act like an animal (take direct action to satisfy primitive cravings.)"
The Receiver	Exploitation	"*They* are there to supply my needs. When they give pleasure *I* respond amiably; when they make unpleasant demands, *I* run away or panic into destructive behavior."
The Manipulator	Mutual manipulation for differently defined goals	"All individuals act under a system of externally determined rules and obligations. *They* and *I* manipulate by conforming or by conning."
The Love Seeker	Conflict	"*They* give love for being good and rejection for being bad. *I* seek love and approval. If I am rejected I ally myself with other rejected ones to become the enemy."
The Learner	Responses based on a commonly accepted reality	"They act and *I* act as human beings with feelings and in accordance with role obligations. *I* move through stages of understanding, make mistakes, and learn."

Dr. Studt cautions that the designations for each type should not be taken as adequate labels to be applied to personalities. The typology is based on interaction patterns characteristic of an individual's interpersonal relations and especially intensified by stress. The terms which she has tentatively used are indicative of interpersonal impact, not items in a nomenclature of morbidity.[24]

With these classes, a foundation was now available for designing treatment strategies aimed at social restoration. But realities had to be faced. People are not sent to reformatories because they are "isolates," "receivers," or any other class of human being twisted by a distorted perception of the "I-They" relationship. They are locked up because they have been duly sentenced by the courts in accordance with the law. The optimum treatment strategy for a given offender

---

[24] Studt, *op. cit.*, chap. iv, pp. 35–36.

might well be best administered in the community rather than in an institution, but correctional programs must be built from brute facts, regardless of whether the facts seem capable of an optimum of any kind. The question was whether the essentially regressive experience provided by the institution could be made to lead to social restoration rather than to increased incapacitation.

This question has been posed for several decades. Given the necessary ingredients of the correctional institution, the administrator is confronted with unsatisfactory alternatives in controlling the inmates to be confined. They can be kept in isolation from each other, and the result will be disorganization of personalities which were fragile in the first place. They can be allowed to associate with some freedom, and the consequence is the development of an inmate social system whose effect on ego identities is never positive and often disastrous.

To make the best of this bad bargain, most correctional administrators in the United States see their task as one of maintaining as orderly and "aseptic" a community as they can and to encourage inmates to make use of whatever treatment services are on hand. In the community of control there are established various treatment concessions; a psychiatrist, a school, a shop, or a library whose acceptance and use may vary widely but which are not organic to the life of the institution. Like the free community, the treatment resources of the institution are specialized services made available to clients at their option. Natural though this disposition may seem on the surface, the objectives of treatment in the correctional institution tend to come off a poor third against the forces of the inmate social system and the necessities of control. So general is this experience that some analysts of the correctional predicament have concluded that treatment services of the kind now provided create such tensions in the institution as to make them dangerous to security as well as futile.[25] This position is unnecessarily extreme in our opinion, but it brings into sharp focus the pressures which reduce the utility of services in the conventional American prison.

Dr. Studt agrees with the general validity of this analysis so far

---

[25] See Donald R. Cressey, "Limitations on Organization of Treatment in the Modern Prison," *Theoretical Studies in the Social Organization of the Prison* (New York: The Social Science Research Council, Pamphlet 15, 1960), pp. 78–110.

as it goes. To overcome the antitherapeutic value system which results from the opposition of the inmate social structure and the requirements of control, she proposes two lines of attack on the conventional institution. First, a conscious effort should be made to build a true community embracing both staff and inmates. Many correctional administrators think they are doing this, and in a sense they are. But Dr. Studt would have them go much further. Beyond maintaining structured contacts between staff and inmates, she believes that a common culture for both can be brought into being. Second, the fragmentation of the staff into specialties should be stopped, and in its place there should grow an integration of treatment and control operations. There is enough evidence, she believes, to support the notion that these structural modifications in the institutional community would alter the inmate social system sufficiently to enable inmates to use services constructively. She emphasizes that services so employed must be directed toward social restoration rather than provided as pacifiers for the duration of confinement. It is all too easy for everyone concerned to be satisfied with the training of offenders for the improved performance of the inmate role.

Here, then, Dr. Studt has put together a theory of correctional treatment which hinges on the realistic use of social restoration as the goal of both the institution and the inmate. The classification of inmates in terms of problems to be solved preliminary to social restoration is powerfully implemented by her social-interaction typology. If it is recognized that a safe return to the community depends on enabling the offender to live and mature within the limitations of his social perceptions, the aim must be the individualization of treatment. No longer can the stereotypes so ready to the hand of the traditional administrator be considered enough, however humanely they may be applied. The school, the shops, the chapels, and the other customary features of the institution will still be needed. It will not be enough merely to understand; the inmate will have to live, not only in the present, but for the future as well. The standards by which he lives are fitted to his own potentialities, not to the fantasy that he must somehow achieve middle-class expectations as a condition for release.

The influence of this approach on the culture of the institution cannot yet be precisely defined. Dr. Studt's assumption is that so long as correctional institutions are designed for control, no services, however rationally prescribed, are going to be effectively used for social restoration. The individualization of service through the application of typology to treatment strategy redirects the goals of the institution toward social restoration. Through the use of this approach it becomes possible for inmates to assume roles in an institutional community working on a task of mutual improvement. The programs to which inmates are assigned are prepared with an understanding of their characteristic patterns of interaction, which in turn reflect the limitations on their perceptions. From the inmate's program, as he carries it out from day to day, his role in the institutional community takes form. No longer will he be a subject of control and therefore an object to be managed by the staff. As a member of a community shared by the staff, he works in a purposeful group, part of whose task is to help him and to enable him to help others.

A final element of Dr. Studt's model is the integration of correctional process. Difficult though it is in most correctional systems, especially in a system serving a state as large as California, the parole staff must be brought into the institutional community. The liaison with the world at large must be as close as a concern for the future of the inmate can contrive, rather than as distant as an obsession with custody can provide. Without such a liaison, the transition from the total institution to the seemingly unrestricted freedom of the world will be a chasm into which the offender may fall, rather than a bridge to safety. Dr. Studt's model therefore provides for the regular presence in the community of parole representatives, so far as possible agents who will have continuing contacts with the inmates after their release.

The model required a test. Interest generated in the staff of the California Department of Corrections was channeled into an institution comparable to the reformatory in which the original studies were made. The Deuel Vocational Institution at Tracy houses about 1,800 young offenders — some who are wards of the California Youth Authority, some who are committed to the custody of the Department of Corrections as adult offenders. By the operation of a special irony of classification, the Youth Authority wards tend to be offenders who have proved to be or are thought to be too aggressive, too unstable, or too unpromising for confinement within the unarmed perimeters of the standard Youth Authority institutions. Because the vocational and educational facilities of the institution are more varied and better equipped than in any other institution of the Department of Corrections, the inmates allocated as adults are ordinarily a most hopeful and tractable lot. To complicate an already difficult paradox, an element of inverted expectations is introduced by the sentencing requirements applied to the two classes of inmates. For Youth Authority wards, a term of eight to ten months in confinement is normal. For adult commitments, terms average about two years. Thus, the least hopeful inmates serve shorter terms than the well-motivated prospects for success sent as adult cases. That a correctional institution can be managed under such circumstances testifies to the resourcefulness of the staff. That it could accommodate to the exasperations unavoidable in any research project, or that research could be attempted in such a setting, suggests that the conditions necessary for successful research are not nearly as exacting as might be supposed.

A wing housing one hundred and thirty inmates was selected for the project. In addition to a research staff consisting of Dr. Studt and three assistants, a casework service was installed. This unit, designed for maximum staff impact, was much richer in personnel than the staffing pattern for the rest of the institution. A casework supervisor, a specially assigned lieutenant, and three caseworkers were added to the normal complement of correctional officers. Cells were transformed into offices. The project got under way in July, 1960, amid considerable speculation throughout the institution about the unprecedented intrusion of researchers, especially a woman researcher into a housing unit hitherto reserved for inmates and their custodians. Despite a dogged insistence by the staff on the official designation, the Inmate-Staff Community Project, to the rest of the institution it was "Disneyland," a location where unfamiliar and possibly risky enterprises were afoot.

The program was to develop for each inmate a treatment strategy for the period of confinement which would make the experience as constructively supportive of social restoration as possible. So far as this could be done, the strategy would be designed in collaboration with the inmate. All staff, including work supervisors and teachers outside the project, would be kept informed of the strategy's objectives and progress. This individualization was expected to influence the culture of the unit toward social restoration as its objective, simply because people who feel themselves understood are more likely to be amicably disposed to the staff which makes understanding possible. To reinforce the shaping of a community culture of treatment, the unit was encouraged to plan activities together. A unit football team was fielded. Holiday parties, monthly dinners, and various entertainments were planned and enjoyed. A unit welfare fund was organized to which contributions were made for the benefit of unit members needing loans or assistance. Hobby discussion and special-interest groups kept the leisure hours filled with opportunities for self-improvement and fun rather than for the usual descent to the common denominator of crime. A unit newspaper was developed in support of communication.

Only the passage of more time than has elapsed at the time of this writing can determine whether the installation of a therapeutic community based on systematically individualized treatment is effective in the social restoration of offenders. The effects in the institution itself have been striking. Routine disciplinary infractions decreased in comparison with the rest of the institution and racial disturbances which flared up in the rest of the institution occasionally during the life of the project seemed to sweep past the unit without its members playing active parts. Dozens of agitated inmates from other units had to be locked up after a near-riotous incident; none from the inmate-staff community. "We all know each other too well to want to fight about race," one inmate told Dr. Studt. Hostility is a heavy burden for a young man to carry; to the extent that some sort of camaraderie can be substituted, a valid contribution toward a safe return to society has been made.

All three projects described in this section are based on psychosocial classification of inmates. Pollington borstal depends on grouping together inmates with a high expectation of success after release. It is assumed that the culture will reinforce the individual expectations and that inmates with less hopeful prospects and more pronounced criminal identifications will not contaminate those whose promise is brighter. Obviously this scheme leaves unanswered the problem of what to do with the bottom of the barrel, or with several layers above.

Classification by typology does not eliminate the need to devise some relevant program for the less adequate inmates. It does lead to a recognition of the problem in precise terms and provides some clues as to what should be done. Practitioners will be working for a long time with the difficulty of making use of these clues. No one knows to what extent offenders with different problems can be treated in a common setting. In the Community Treatment Project, group approaches designed for a common limitation on social perceptions are at the heart of the program. In the Inmate-Staff Community Project, the separation in an institution of the more from the less disturbed is hardly feasible. A

virtue is made of the necessities of propinquity; so far as possible inmates gain some satisfaction from helping each other. This richly re-
warding satisfaction would be scarcely conceivable without a con-
sciousness by the inmates that help toward resocialization within the
circumstances of confinement was indeed a reality. Only the adequate
individualization brought about be relevant treatment strategies could
confer on these inmates the sense of being helped. With the climate of
confidence in the staff which is thus created, two significant objectives
should be approached by such programs. Resistances to the aims of the
correctional apparatus should attenuate. A true sense of community
should result which will support inmates in pursing the goals of resocialization. Though achievement of these objectives seems probable,
the evaluation of the pilot projects is not nearly complete. Assuming the
validation of the principles, the task of full-scale implementation has
not even been given a preliminary survey. Much more needs to be
done before these tentative advances can be turned into ordinary realities.

TREATMENT

From the exciting work being done by these few pioneers in finding
new solutions of the problem of correctional diagnosis we can derive
clues to improved correctional treatment which have yet to be translated into mature principles. Because most of these investigations have
taken place under conscientious research controls, the correctional
world may expect to have the benefit of examined experience with these
basic hypotheses.

In the meantime, improvements in correctional practice have been
sought through the application of psychiatric principles to institutional
realities. These improvements vary in many significant respects. They
have in common the notion of the therapeutic community. It will be
necessary here to consider briefly the origins, common principles, and
significant practice of this much abused term.

So many clinicians have noted the importance of the milieu in which
treatment is conducted that it is hardly fair to ascribe credit to anyone
for this observation. It seems obvious that the experience in the total
institution must be consistent with the patient's formal treatment if the
treatment is to be effective. The difficulty has been to reorganize the
traditional practice of institutional psychiatry so that the influence of

the institution will reinforce the few hours of each week which can be given to individual or group therapy. The roles of everyone concerned, from superintendent to patient, must be reconsidered in terms of the resulting interactions; the allocation of the working day of everyone in the artificial institutional community must be made in accordance with the impact on patients; communications patterns must be expanded with new channels and customs; relationships with the world outside the institution must be strengthened. All these basic changes must be conceptualized and tested. It has been difficult enough to begin this task in the mental hospital, where the official objectives of resocialization are not in question. The task has scarcely begun in the correctional institution, where much conflict still exists about what to expect. Fortunately, a handful of hybrid institutions exist in which psychiatric staffs are attempting to adapt the institution to the treatment needs of offenders. From the experience which has thus been gained in reconstructing institutions we can gauge the nature of the problem ahead for the correctional apparatus if the truly therapeutic community is to become as widespread as its advocates urge.

Let us begin with the Social Rehabilitation Unit of Belmont Hospital, the English establishment in which the term "therapeutic community" seems to have been coined. Situated on the grounds of a large mental hospital about thirty minutes by commuters' train from central London, the unit itself consists of four wards with capacities for seventy men and thirty women. It primarily accepts patients who are diagnosed as personality disorders, or as psychopaths, to use a term which is more familiar if currently out of favor. According to Rapoport,[26] a study of one hundred and sixty-eight patients in 1955 disclosed that 81 per cent fell into this class. The remainder included psychotics and a variety of neurotics. Most referrals are from medical sources, but the courts, probation departments, and prisons are also contributors. The program is aimed at the difficulties of persons with a weak ego strength. Because the intake policy establishes a patient group which is clinically similar to a correctional population, the program of the Social Rehabilitation Unit has been of extraordinary interest to correctional innovators. Some of its features could not be easily adapted for general correctional practice without an upheaval in community expectations of prisons and

[26] Robert N. Rapoport, *The Community as Doctor* (London: Tavistock Publications, 1960), pp. 39–41.

reformatories. The basic principles, however, are relevant to the creation of a milieu in which the characteristic problems of offenders can be dealt with. A detailed account of the concepts and activities which make up the program can be found in the reports of its original designer, Dr. Maxwell Jones.[27] A more current report is contained in the Rapoport study.[28] Here we shall report our own observations.

The community day begins at 8:30 A.M. with a meeting of all patients and all staff except the night attendants. This event, the "Eight-Thirty," occurs in a bare and battered room filled with wooden benches and canvas chairs arranged in two opposing banks, as in the House of Commons. Attendance is prompt, perhaps because late-comers are likely to be asked to explain themselves. Proceedings begin with a droning of the minutes of work groups and special committees, followed by the log of the nursing sister. With all the coughing and the scraping of chairs, the halting delivery of the committee reporters is hard to follow, but attention is keen and correction of mistakes and omissions is vigorous. The reports contain information ranging from statements of production to the emotional problems of the producers. Absences and tardiness are detailed, often with references to the additional burdens placed on members of the group by the nonparticipation of its less conscientious members. The nurses' log contains the observations of the staff regarding unusual incidents, misbehavior by patients, and unauthorized absences. It ends with a listing of those who were not on their beds and in their pyjamas at 10:30 on the preceding night. This is a violation of one of the few standing rules and calls for an explanation by the culprit to the community.

Sometimes the reports provide the fuel for community discussion. On many occasions during our observation, however, excitement ran high about some issue only marginally related to the formal reports. Is Mavis pregnant, and if so, shouldn't Bert be asked to leave so that he can earn some money and establish a home for his ardent girl friend? What should be done about Jack and Eddie, who were caught yesterday in a clumsy attempt to rob the pay telephone? Everybody knows they need help, but the damage done to the telephone will put it out of action for several days, to the great inconvenience of the whole community. What can be done about Elizabeth, a young, pretty, but very

---

[27] M. Jones, *Social Psychiatry* (London: Tavistock Publications, 1952).
[28] Rapoport, *op. cit.*, pp. 79–99.

disruptive girl who has exasperated the members of her work group beyond the limits of their tolerance for even one more day? Is there a work group left which can put up with her noisy idleness? What can be done about the perpetual mess in the women's ward which the male patients who act as janitors and dustmen report periodically with such sanctimonious disgust? Is it true that Harold, this menacing old lag from Dartmoor with the incongruously upper-class accent, has a gun in his possession? Harold won't say, the staff is worried, the patients ask their questions with gingerly circumspection; even if he is unarmed, Harold is not to be lightly antagonized.

Questions of this kind surge across the Eight-Thirty, engaging attention at many different levels. Defenses are raised and demolished. A young psychiatrist advances an interpretation in the hope of ending the talk about the mess in the women's ward; he is raucously told to come off it — can't he think about anything but sex? A sneer projected across the room from one patient brings its target clambering over the knees and laps of other group members to pummel the tormentor. The prevailing mood is ill-tempered, passionate, absorbed, and oddly tolerant. It is as though everyone expects to be emotionally as well as physically uncomfortable in this crowded, smoky, and ill-ventilated room. Uncomfortable, but no one is to be hurt. One sad little homosexual was the silent, writhing butt of probably well-founded attacks for his tale-bearing interference in the business of others. Scathing comments on his mendacity, his eavesdropping, his sexual aberrations were flung from all corners of the room. His downcast eyes and twisting fingers told more about his misery than he could ever have put into words. But presently matters had gone far enough. An authoritative Yorkshire voice came to the rescue: "We've 'ad enough of this. David's not a bad lad; all he needs is a bit of 'elp. 'E sucks up to some of us because that's the only way he knows to get it."

That was enough. Discussion turned to a neutral topic; should a ramble on the Surrey downs be planned for the coming week end? What could be done to speed up breakfast service? Other matters of community concern could always be relied on to ease the never quite unbearable pressure on any individual. The talk at the Eight-Thirty was always directed at the present concerns of the community. So long as a member stayed in this exposing interaction he must be confronted with the consequences of his patterns of conduct, patterns which must previously have provided for flight from anxiety. Few members of the community escaped a moment of attention in the Eight-Thirty; most of the hundred or so participants would sooner or later come in for extended comment. Doctors, psychologists, nurses, and even the untrained and obviously vulnerable "social therapists" were targets for irreverent discussion. Professional position was no armor against the concern of the community.

That was the Eight-Thirty, a crowded, irritable, anxious hour almost always full of incident. Intended to start the day with a focus on treatment as the goal of the whole community, it seemed to serve three primary purposes. First, the treatment method of confronting the patient with the consequences of his behavior as reflected in the responses of others was brought into play. In this sense, each patient came to act as an agent as well as a recipient of treatment. To what extent this understanding of the new patient role was general would be hard to say. For some the opportunity to try one's hand at psychotherapy seemed to be so attractive as to obscure the aim of receiving help. Rapoport quotes one patient as defending sadistic conduct toward another with the assertion, "I was just trying to therapeut this bloke." [29] Others, the frequent targets of help from patient-peers, must have felt that their responsibilities for treatment were quite involuntary.

The second purpose of the Eight-Thirty was to open communications. No one can say to what exact extent this end was accomplished. An article of faith in the Social Rehabilitation Unit was the conviction that communications should be as free as possible in all directions. The incessant exchange of expressions of feeling, information about events, and interpretations of behavior certainly gave wide currency to materials which are left in the realm of privacy in conventional institutions.

Third, the Eight-Thirty symbolically sustained the idea of community so fundamental to the Unit's ideology. Everyone was there, all staff and all patients. The theme of the community as an entity in whose benefits all must share and to whose welfare all must contribute could scarcely have become so pervasive in the Unit without the daily experience of the Eight-Thirty. No observer could come away from this abrasive hour with the impression that a happy community had been observed. But it was a community, and it was concerned. In the concern there may have been the essential ingredient of therapy; for most

---

[29] *Ibid.*, p. 182.

of these haggard, unhappy, and often defeated men and women concern, whether given or received, must have been new.

The rest of the community day was given to the meetings of smaller groups. There were "doctor's groups" in which the more conventional procedures of group therapy were carried out in explorations of dynamics. There were ward groups in which the members of a ward considered the issues arising from living together. Workshops filled the afternoons and usually ended with group discussions. The day ended with an evening social hour of dancing, card-playing, or chatter. From time to time there were special groups for newcomers, for patients' families, for discussions with visitors, for recreation. On Saturday mornings a volunteer group met for the benefit of community members who wanted still more group experience than they had had during the week.

Length of stay varies widely. Some patients are so horrified by the open, un-English communications that an overnight sojourn is all that can be tolerated. About 15 per cent, according to Rapoport, leave during the first month, though this figure must vary considerably with the composition of the community. Other patients stay for a year, but this is a maximum stay which must not be exceeded. Dr. Jones encouraged a "six-months culture" — patients should think that six months in the unit is about enough for most community members.

To as great an extent as possible, continued participation is voluntary. Occasionally members create problems in the Unit which require the members' removal; occasionally there are patients whose psychological condition is so grave as to require transfer to a conventional mental hospital.

Many stay because they have to under the conditions of probation. Others have nowhere else to go. For some pathetically inadequate people, the harsh and austere life of the Unit is the only adequate adjustment they have ever experienced; they cling to it for as long as they can.

To manage this intricate and demanding exploration of human inadequacies, a microcosm of nothing, but a community for people who never experienced a community, a comparatively rich staff was organized. Its core consisted of four psychiatrists, a psychologist, a psychiatric social worker, and a nursing sister. Revolving around this nucleus is an "adjunctive" staff, which includes workshop instructors, employment counselors, and staff nurses, none of whom have psychiatric training. Finally, in another orbit, are the "social therapists." These are young, untrained, unmarried women, usually foreign, usually expecting a career in social work. In return for their service, usually of about six months, they receive room, board, some remuneration, and tutorial training in psychiatric concepts and practice. The unique role they play is that of the good, accepting, attractive young woman whose influence will be in the direction of acceptance of the world as it is. Because of their status as foreigners they have something in common with patients, who are also outsiders. Their egalitarian approach is reinforced by their situation; unfamiliar with the country and often without facility with the language, they, too, must be helped by the patients in order to help in return.

The Social Rehabilitation Unit is a model which has been in the making since 1947, when it was established for the care and rehabilitation of unemployable "industrial neurotics." It has been concerned with its present patient categories since 1954, with an increasing emphasis on character disorder referrals made by the courts. It has survived organized concern by the neighboring communities concerning its permissive treatment policies; some serious question concerning the validity of its concepts; and, perhaps most hazardous of all, a great deal of staff turnover. England is a more tolerant country than most foreigners imagine, but in any society an institution must be sturdy indeed to fend off such formidable threats.

What accounts for its continued existence? In what lies the strength to go on in spite of concerted attack, considerable professional skepticism, some dismal failures, and few apparent successes? We think the answer is of profound and hopeful significance for the future of correctional practice. The industrial revolution began in England and is older there than in any other country. Its consequences for the human condition are farther advanced and in some respects more grievous in England than anywhere else. Hope does not burn brightly for the urban poor in England; for most it does not burn at all. Its absence is an ironic testament to the emptiness of victories at war and the futility of sacrifice by the working classes which made the victories possible. The consequences of apathy are not predictable, but both altruism and self-interest make it worth while to explore avenues for offsetting it. The rising crime rate in England is tied to the *anomie* of the great conurbations. If in the Social Rehabilitation Unit a part of the solution can be found to the riddle of the good life for the urban worker, the money investment and the community exasperation can be afforded. Perhaps a means can also be derived for helping vulnerable people before they have achieved full criminal identifications.

If this is true of Dr. Jones, it is important to apply research methods. Long-term follow-ups, thorough diagnostic discrimination, replication, and continuous analysis of results are necessary. In Dr. Rapoport's comprehensive study an important beginning has been made. His study leads to the conclusion that patients who have been in treatment more than six months are the most likely to show sustained benefits after discharge. The data also indicate that the benefits are more marked with patients with stronger egos and more organized personality resources. Married patients gain more from treatment and maintain their gains after discharge more significantly than the unmarried.[30]

Much remains to be done before the Social Rehabilitation Unit (now officially designated the Henderson Hospital, to emphasize its autonomy), can be considered a completed model. The assumption that the treatment offered is equally applicable to the wide variety of rehabilitation goals presented by the patients needs examination. Questions regarding the degrees of heterogeneity which can be tolerated in the community will have to be resolved. More than any other problem, that of the transition between the institution and the community, needs to be systematically attacked. Until it is seen what can be accomplished with a sensitive after-care system, it will not be possible to say who can benefit to what extent from the Unit.

Despite its incompleted work, its lack of sustained research capabilities, and its inadequate conceptualizations, the Social Rehabilitation Unit remains for the correctional future probably the greatest single contribution toward advanced practice since the general adoption of humane standards of institutional practice.

The most significant example of its influence is to be found in the Netherlands. At Utrecht, under the leadership of Dr. P. A. H. Baan, the van der Hoeven Kliniek has adapted the therapeutic community approach of the Social Rehabilitation Unit to the problems of long-term prisoners. Dr. Baan, a thoughtful observer of the methods employed at Belmont by Dr. Jones, considered that the most immediate need for this approach in the Netherlands lay in the restoration of violent and sexually deviant prisoners coming to the end of their terms.

Dutch prisons are essentially custodial. For most inmates, terms are not long, and the emphasis in program is on security. Schools and work-

---

[30] *Ibid.*, pp. 220–224.

shops are well equipped, and so are the custody staffs. Generally, the distribution of responsibility between the probation services and the prisons is such that only the most aggravated recidivists and the most serious first offenders are confined in prison. In all, there are about 1,800 prisoners in Dutch correctional institutions. Property offenders are generally kept for short periods, but violent criminals draw long sentences, by the end of which they are often incapacitated by the processes of institutionalization.

In 1955 the van der Hoeven Kliniek was organized as a separate section of an ancient mental hospital in Utrecht. The Kliniek itself is situated in relatively modern quarters, providing for some security, but is not well suited to the operation of the institution as it has developed. It houses about one hundred patients; between twenty and thirty additional patients live in town but receive treatment from the institution. The Kliniek is organized under private auspices, but accepts only patients who have some legal status as offenders. Most are men or women who have completed a sentence and have been "placed at the disposal of the Queen." This is a curious provision of Dutch law whereby some offenders may be detained after their sentences are completed, ordinarily for psychiatric treatment, but sometimes for preventive detention.

The status of the van der Hoeven Kliniek as a private institution for the treatment of public wards enables the staff to maintain a control over intake which is not usually possible for a conventional correctional institution. Program, too, can be developed with a minimum of reference to precedents established and the regulations maintained by official administrative structures. Because of the independence of the Kliniek, it has been able to rationalize policy to a degree we encountered nowhere else. In the few years it has been in operation, policies have been created to govern many issues with attention to consistency with a few basic principles. Though many of these policies would be difficult to apply in a prison, jail, or borstal, they are of interest to the student of correctional advance as examples of the subordination of all organizational considerations to the objective of treatment. No concession has been made to any interest which might conflict with the treatment ideology of the institution. This ideology is uncompromising and exacting. Its difficulties seem to have been resolved with little regard to expense, public opinion, professional differences, or administrative pressures. Dr. Baan emphasized to us his belief that correctional leadership has a responsibility to provide aggressive direction to the advance of practice and theory. In his view, the public will never be ready to accept what they have not seen. In the van der Hoeven Kliniek, the public has something to see. A model has been created\for the treatment of dangerous offenders which is clear, explicable, and rational. The only absent element is a system of evaluation; even here, critics must allow that insufficient time has elapsed to create the model and appraise its effects.

Not much has been written about the Kliniek. Language barriers have inhibited transatlantic interest, and Dutch scholars have not yet felt called on to mobilize for the massive kind of study which Rapoport and his colleagues have given to the Social Rehabilitation Unit. We are relying on our interviews with members of the staff and on one published paper by Dr. Baan.[31] We are particularly lacking in studies of the impact of the Kliniek program on patients. What the Kliniek staff sets out to do deserves careful attention and a full-scale analysis of process. Its operation is so different from that of the Social Rehabilitation Unit that it is hardly recognizable as a conceptual offspring.

Eligibility for the program is determined by the Kliniek staff. Usually referral is made by the Ministry of Justice through the Psychiatric Observation Clinic in Utrecht. This clinic is designed to provide psychiatric recommendations to the courts in cases where the government's retaining control after confinement is in question. Inmates under study may be recommended for supervision on probation, for hospitalization, or conceivably for pardon. Complete studies are made, including interviews of members of the patient's family, his neighbors, and the officials of his community. We were shown records which included files of pictures of the people and places concerned, just to be sure that the staff had access to the details of his life before his coming to the Kliniek. If an individual is considered suitable for the Kliniek, the staff will invite the director to arrange for an interview. At this point the first and most important governing principle determining Kliniek policy comes into play. All patients are voluntary in the sense that they have chosen Kliniek placement from one of several available options. Great stress is laid on the importance of complete understanding of expectations. The nature of the treatment and the requirement

---

[31] P. A. H. Baan, "The Treatment of Criminal Psychopathy," *Canadian Journal of Corrections*, II (January 1960).

that patients make an effort to benefit from treatment are explained. It is emphasized that no promise can be made when the commitment to the "disposal of the Queen" can be ended. While in this status, the patient is subject to confinement or probation, depending on the judgment of the Kliniek staff. However, the staff accepts the obligation to administer treatment with this objective in view. In this sense a "gentleman's agreement" is made, the parties entering into a reciprocal relationship which can be terminated by the failure of either side to satisfy the other that the agreement is being kept. Termination of treatment under such circumstances would mean return to the Psychiatric Observation Clinic for the development of a new plan.

Patients in the Kliniek find themselves in a world different from the highly authoritarian Dutch prisons. The emphasis is on approaching as closely as possible the conditions of life in the community. This stress begins with the insistence on work. Patients are expected to work eight hours a day and are encouraged to make coöperative efforts to manage the conditions of their labors. Most Kliniek employment is undertaken under contract with private manufacturers; at the time of our visit the principal contract under way was the manufacture of picnic tables and chairs. The terms of the contract are agreed to by the patient work group, and the pay is usually at rates specified by the Dutch government for sheltered workshops. It seemed to us in our observation of the pace of work that it was comparable to the pace expected in a conventional shop running under a favorable piece work rate. However, wages are administered in such a way as to make a good rate dependent on appropriate effort. The maximum rate is 50 guilders a week (about $15), of which the patient can receive only 10 guilders, the remainder being retained for savings. Rates are adjusted monthly; about 60 per cent of the inmates qualify for the maximum rate, the rest receiving rates down to 10 guilders a week, the minimum. From their earnings patients must pay for their clothing, their recreation, their furloughs home, their educational materials. Only food, lodging, and treatment is provided by the Kliniek. All patients have some funds; some are comparatively affluent, as public charges go in any country.

The financial solvency of Kliniek patients strengthens the principle of responsibility which is applied in every way the staff can imagine. Punishment for disciplinary offenses is ordinarily a fine. Absence from work can be punished by deduction from wages, but if the absence is extended to the point that the efficiency of the group effort suffers, a fine is exacted to reflect the loss in the shop's productivity. Broken windows are paid for by the patient responsible; as a result, hardly any are broken as compared with two hundred in the first year before the rule was introduced. Even escapes are fined. Unauthorized absences usually result in a 10 guilder fine, a sum which is based on a cost analysis of the average amount of work done by the Kliniek to re-establish contact with the absentee.

Responsibility is not merely fiscal. From the first, patient committees assume a major share in the formulation and administration of rules. The first group of patients, mostly transfers from long terms in prison, were invited to draft the entire code. The result was a set of regulations so stringent as to be unworkable; it had to be modified with staff assistance. However, patients are still encouraged to participate in the administration. No one is allowed on furlough without clearance with a patient committee, though it may happen that confidential information to the staff may rule out this degree of trust even though the patient committee has agreed on it. Much is made of permission to take walks in town. Patient committees determine who is to be granted this privilege and must take responsibility for the conduct of groups which are allowed off the premises for a stroll.

Communications are stressed, as in the Social Rehabilitation Unit. Community meetings occur regularly, but only for the transaction of business, not with emphasis on their therapeutic value. The goal of these meetings, as of all group activity, is the maintenance of an orderly community in which there will be no unnecessary obstacles to treatment. Patients are not expected to treat each other, and for this reason there is little introspection in groups which meet formally or informally. The Kliniek sociologist, Mr. Jan Jessen, provided an example of the distinction between the Kliniek approach and that of the Social Rehabilitation Unit with which he was familiar. During a visit to Belmont, someone had drawn a death's head on the wall of the room in which the Eight-Thirty was conducted. "There was talk for about a quarter of an hour about why the patient had drawn it on the wall. What was his feeling about it? What was its meaning? And so on. But there was no question about how the wall would be cleaned up. Here at the van der Hoeven Kliniek all this would be impossible. Someone would ask the patient, 'How are you doing? If you have having some difficulty, please talk to the doctor, but clean the wall. We don't want to sit in a room with death's heads on the wall. Clean it!' The patients have a responsi-

bility for treatment. They don't treat each other, but they have a responsibility for each other's treatment. There's a difference." Jessen
gave another example. "We had one patient on one of the wards who
used ugly language to everybody. We did not talk about it in group
meeting. No one asked him why he needed to talk like that. We only
said that we did not accept that kind of language. If he wanted to live
in that particular social group he would have to behave well. If it were
difficult for him to behave as the group expected then he should discuss
with his doctor why he used that kind of language."

Treatment is considered to be a private matter between the patient
and his therapist. For this reason, the therapists are entirely outside the
administrative structure of the Kliniek. Most of them are in practice outside the institution and carry a patient load within it as a part of their
ordinary practice. Dr. Baan, who has separated himself from administrative responsibilities at the Kliniek, acts as a supervisor and consultant to these psychiatrists. So far as possible, the functions of treatment
are confidential and carried on in private psychiatric practice. The flow
of information from the therapist to the institution is minimal. No recommendations are made, and the opinion of the psychiatrist regarding
the decisions to be made about patients is not requested.

Responsibility for administrative management is in the hands of the
superintendent, Dr. Henriette Roosenberg. It is her responsibility to organize the Kliniek in such a manner that the principles of voluntary
treatment, normal living conditions, and patient responsibility are reflected in the daily life of the unit. Her responsibilities extend further
to the making of recommendations to the Ministry of Justice regarding
permission to live outside the Kliniek and ultimate discharge. It is thus
her task to evaluate the success of therapy as it is reflected in the daily
life of the Kliniek and in accordance with her estimate of the patient's
capacity for restoration to the community.

Between them, Dr. Baan and Dr. Roosenberg have based the Kliniek's ideology on the proposition that offenders can benefit from psychotherapy. The Kliniek's function is to provide an environment in which
psychotherapy can be optimally effective, and in this sense it is a therapeutic community. Activities in the community are focused on cure
rather than control, and into the administrative structure are built
many unusual features designed to improve evaluation and to increase
the support which the community life gives to therapy. Social workers
are used to maintain contact with the families of patients and to facili-

tate understanding between the patient and the community. Camping expeditions are arranged for small groups of patients for week ends or longer. Occasions are contrived for relaxed conversations among staff and patients as well as formal "business" meetings.

Dr. Roosenberg also supervises some therapeutic activities. From time to time a group of patients is detached from their other responsibilities for two or three days of intensive group treatment. This unusual approach is based on Dr. Roosenberg's view that for long-term patients group therapy has some serious disadvantages. She told us, "Our patients are sensitive, vulnerable, unrealistic, and idealistic. In group psychotherapy they start quickly and with high hopes. Then you have to be careful that they aren't disappointed." She recognizes the advantages of group psychotherapy, especially the comparison of one's own personal problems with those of others who have experienced the same difficulties. But the loss of momentum in group treatment can offset all possible gains; for this reason she believes that it is a method which should be cautiously employed.

The brief but intensive group-therapy experience is still experimental. Eight to ten patients are grouped with two staff leaders for eight hours a day during the period of the treatment. Role-playing, psychodrama, and free discussion are used with liberal resort to tape recorders for play back of the content of the meeting. The value of this approach has yet to be determined; it is intended as an attempt to capture some of the advantages of conventional group therapy without undergoing the disillusion of routines replacing meaningful experience. Dr. Roosenberg is sure these sessions have some effect. They are emotionally exhausting, but seem to result in new insights for at least some patients.

In another effort to maintain a purposeful pace in treatment, considerably more use is made of sodium pentathol interviews than is now customary in mental hospitals. Dr. Roosenberg thinks the rationale can be found in the culture which grows out of such a patient group. The Kliniek patients have in common a life-long experience of repeated and massive failures. Individually and collectively it is easy for the patient group to sink into a resignation to the failure of treatment. Why should anything succeed in their lives when failure has so frequently prevailed? Pentathol interviews do relieve inhibitions; the movement of treatment is perceived, and "a little bit of magic" is introduced into a situation which can easily subside into group depression. Most patients need the authority of the physician. They often voice their perplexity at finding that physicians are ordinary people who neither carry stethoscopes nor wear white jackets.

Change is the great objective at the Kliniek. Its perception is notoriously difficult. From day to day no one can tell for sure what is happening to a patient undergoing the massive therapeutic experience in the Kliniek. With this limitation in mind, the responsibilty for keeping track of events seems to the staff to be important to the attainment of the Kliniek's aims. For this reason, the process of record-keeping is carried much farther than in other correctional institutions. For each patient a meticulously thorough clinical file is maintained with all the customary diagnostic and administrative entries. In addition, a system of accumulating objective data on behavior has been developed from the Kliniek's daily staff meetings. These sessions include as many of the staff as can be spared from their duties, with representation provided from every institutional function. The events of the preceding twenty-four hours are freely discussed. Minutes are systematically kept and transcribed in triplicate. The original copy is preserved in a permanent chronological file. The duplicates are clipped for the mention of each patient. Whatever has been said in the meeting about anyone is placed in the individual file. The third copy is distributed to functional files so that a chronological record of events in the principal areas of the Kliniek is available, as for example, the kitchen, the wards, the workshops, or the group social meetings. Primarily, these records are regarded as the sociologist's working tools. When the evaluation of any patient's progress is needed, the first step is the reference to the record in an effort to discern changes in response to the institution and to others over an extended period of time. The patterns which can be extracted from such a record are used to determine the effectiveness of treatment as objectively as possible. When decisions are to be made, the professional impressions of the administrative psychiatrists and a record of trends are available. This method of data accumulation has a secondary value in training the staff to observe and communicate data relevant to the evaluation of change.

The optimistic emphasis on treatment is in contrast to the usual correctional emphasis on rehabilitation. As Rapoport stressed in his analysis of the Social Rehabilitation Unit, the objectives of that institution combined in a blurred fashion the goals of treatment or psychological change, and rehabilitation or social change. It was apparent that for some Belmont patients treatment was essential to rehabilitation. For others rehabilitation seemed to be accomplished without significant psychological change. The separation of therapy from resocialization at the Kliniek seems to eliminate the blurring of the two objectives. What goes on in therapy contributes to resocialization by increasing the adequacy of the patient's insight. What goes on in the institution makes possible an experience consistent with the goals of therapy while at the same time providing a life experience consistent with the aim of resocialization.

Dr. Baan and Dr. Roosenberg believe that the patients received in the Kliniek must be treated in order to be restored to society, and that such restoration must be on terms which are independent of control. They recognize that patients are permanently handicapped, but their ideology assumes that patients will be enabled to seek and find needed compensating support from the conventional institutions of society rather than from permanent recourse to the Kliniek.

As for results, records are being kept, but no statistical reports are published, nor will any conclusions be attempted for years to come. Until enough patients have gone through the process of Kliniek treatment and a significant period of after-care under the supervision of the Meijers Society,[32] nothing valid can be said about the success of the program. Dr. Roosenberg supports her optimism, however, by pointing to patients who before treatment were unable to manage without episodes of criminality, but who after treatment have been able to maintain themselves for significant periods of time without offense. Despite the high potential of the patient group for aggressive crime, no one has yet committed an offense of violence after release or during an absence from the institution.

While the Kliniek staff firmly believe that significant results are being achieved by their program, they also believe that these results show that much more could be done if the Dutch public were serious about the prevention and control of crime. The long lapse which now occurs between the commission of the offense and the treatment at the Kliniek is a serious and unnecessary obstacle to the success of treatment. The lapse of time is compounded by its long passage in the security conditions of Dutch prisons, as a result of which both the original condition which brought about the commission of the crime and also the dehu-

---

[32] Cf. Chapter III., pp. 117–119.

manizing effects of institutionalization have to be treated. In the view of the Kliniek staff, the foundations are being built in Utrecht for the rational treatment and control of offenders, one element of which is the reduction in the passage of time between offense and treatment.

A THERAPEUTIC COMMUNITY IN DENMARK

No account of the development of the therapeutic community approach to the treatment of offenders would be complete without reference to the Institution for Psychopaths at Herstedvester. Under the long-established leadership of Dr. Georg K. Stürup, an imaginative attack on the control-oriented institution has been under way since 1935. Much of the ideology of the "therapeutic community" was approximated years before that fashionable term was coined. There are some superficial resemblances to the van der Hoeven Kliniek, but the differences in official structure and treatment policy are basic. Herstedvester must be regarded today as an institution which represents the boundaries of the therapeutic community within conventional correctional structure. Though it serves much the same class of patients, both policy and practice have been limited by the requirements of control to a degree which has not been necessary at the van der Hoeven Kliniek.

Herstedvester is one of two institutions in Denmark for the medical treatment of psychopaths. Another, at Horsens, Jutland, deals with substantially the same kind of caseload as Herstedvester with the same general approach. Both institutions are administratively subordinate to the Ministry of Justice and are separate from the national prison system. Between them, the two institutions house more than 350 inmates. Herstedvester usually contains about 200. In addition, the Herstedvester keeps in touch with about 300 ambulants through its social workers.

Herstedvester's functions are clearly defined. In Dr. Stürup's language, they are formally set forth as follows:

> The institution at Herstedvester has two functions. Its first and primary function is to protect the community against the dangers to public security which these criminals would present if they remained at large. Its second function is, within the limits set by the first function, to attempt to influence these persons in such a way that the risk of further criminality becomes less, preferably very much less.[33]

---

[33] G. K. Stürup, *Herstedvester Papers* (Herstedvester, Denmark: 1957), p. 13.

The difference from the van der Hoeven Kliniek's functions is important. Herstedvester must take who comes, keep him at all costs, and treat him if it can. The Kliniek will only take those it believes it can help, will keep them as best it can within the physical structure of the institution, and will send those patients away whom it finds inaccessible to help. Actually intake is not entirely beyond the control of the institution. When a convicted offender is thought by the court to be in possible need of care at an institution for psychopaths, a referral is made to a Forensic Medical Council. A thorough psychiatric investigation is made, upon the conclusions of which the Council determines its recommendation to the court. If it is decided to commit the offender to an institution for psychopaths, an indeterminate sentence is pronounced. No change or release can be made without action by the committing court. As the institution is now represented on the Council, and as Dr. Stürup is psychiatric adviser to the court, considerable weight is attached to the institution's views on the appropriateness of a release. Nevertheless, Herstedvester and its sister institution must in principle take who comes. It is a principle which Dr. Stürup emphatically supports. From the beginning, the patient is in the position of having to do what he can in his own behalf. He must show a willingness to be treated. There is no "gentlemen's agreement," as at the Kliniek, to give or receive treatment. Dr. Stürup said: "I tell the new patient, 'You're sentenced here for the protection of society. I have no responsibility for your cure. I am allowed to do what I can to influence you to change.' But my great advantage over out-patient clinics is that at Herstedvester I have the power to influence a man to coöperate in treatment."

From the point of acceptance by the institution, the program proceeds, whether the inmate coöperates in his treatment or not. Dr. Stürup thinks of the essential elements of the program as consisting of the following points:

Situational approach. — Each inmate's situation is examined individually to determine what elements brought him to Herstedvester and what elements will have to be introduced to get him out. From this analysis a plan is made with the inmate's active participation, so far as it can be obtained.

Staff group collaboration. — As in any therapeutic community, attention is given to the flow of information. Dr. Stürup sees the maintenance of this flow as his first responsibility. He told us:

In order to be informed by staff, the first and last requirement is that *you* must inform *them*. If you don't, they will never know that you need help. I stress how little we know; I stress that without knowing what goes on in the inmate's daily life, we cannot help him. When they ask me anything, I speak as to a fellow doctor, whether they can understand me or not. So much the worse for them if they can't. They get so irritated when they can't understand that they try harder. They get to asking questions. We try to get these questions out in group meetings; we hold such meetings once a week for anyone to attend who is interested in trying to understand what goes on in the institution.

Then we have a staff conference every day. The custodial captain, his deputy, and two work foremen participate with the entire clinical staff. We have no staff meeting with doctors alone, nor for psychologists alone. We are all together, the whole staff. Everything is discussed openly. Some people don't understand everything that goes on, but after they have heard our discussions for a while, they start to take an interest and try to understand.

We attended two of these daily staff meetings, and heard the specific kind of issues dealt with. It seemed that most action decisions regarding patients were made in this conference. A social worker reported that a patient had just returned from leave in Jutland where he got drunk. He had not been prescribed antabuse; in the future he must have this treatment before going on leave. Another inmate was paying for his wife's furniture from earnings (although she was able to pay for it herself), hoping thereby to demonstrate his responsibility to Dr. Stürup. The staff were unconvinced, and it was decided not to release him, despite the inmate's charge of broken faith. Another inmate refused to work, to which Dr. Stürup philosophically rejoined that he must have freedom to go down as well as up. And so forth. The whole staff being present, or represented, decisions taken were fully understood, although they might be preceded by considerable difference of opinion. When discussed with the patients affected there would be as little opportunity as possible of playing one staff member against another.

Motivation and trust. — Anyone who has been defeated as often as a Herstedvester inmate must develop a feeling of hopelessness. It is essential to help the patient to the idea that he can be useful to society despite all indications to the contrary. He must also acquire the feeling that the staff can be trusted to try to help him — sometimes a difficult achievement for individuals who have neither trusted nor been trusted for most of their lives. Dr. Stürup thought this situation could be epitomized in the patient's willingness to run the risk of frustration once more. He who cannot trust can hardly be capable of tolerating frustration.

Recognition of limits. — Dr. Stürup is fond of a nautical metaphor, used frequently with patients. Some personalities, he says, are like ships which can cross the ocean; they can reach a distant port on their own power. Others are like coast-wise vessels, too fragile for the high seas, but adequate for navigation within sight of lighthouses and the shore line. Patients must learn to place themselves in the continuum of this metaphor. For most, a life-long dependence on Herstedvester is a necessity. "I try," said Dr. Stürup, "to be sure that no one leaves us as an ambulant without understanding that he will continue to need Herstedvester, probably for the rest of his life." This much more limited view of the patient's future contrasts with the expectation at the van der Hoeven Kliniek that therapy will result in cure to the extent that the patient will be able to function independently. Dr. Stürup does not exclude this possibility for some of his patients, but most of them will need to keep close to the shore line; periodically they will need the assistance of navigators from Herstedvester.

This view of the correctional institution's role as a supportive agency tends to permeate the thought of Danish correctional staff. In child-welfare schools, in borstals, and in some prisons the point was repeatedly made that most inmates had no one else in their lives on whom they could depend. It was essential, at least for some, that they should be discharged with the feeling that at a future crisis there was a staff member at the institution to whom they could turn for counsel. While this experience is familiar, we suppose, to anyone who has ever worked in a correctional institution in a constructive capacity, in Denmark this dependency was most overtly encouraged. To what extent and with what kinds of inmates it is most usefully achieved we could not determine. The frank recognition of dependency as a fact of the delinquent's life which must be provided for is at great variance with the dour insistence on independence as a treatment objective in Anglo-Saxon correctional institutions.

Responsibility. — In the application of Herstedvester's treatment approach, the acceptance of personal responsibility by everyone is stressed. In every way possible, staff members are held accountable for their share of the group effort. In turn, responsibility is forced on inmates as a consequence of the staff's facing the demands made on it. In the areas of assigned work, as in the workshops or in the physical maintenance of the institution, the question of accountability is relatively easy to settle. For treatment, individual responsibilities are harder to determine. But everybody keeps in mind that there must be a plan for every inmate to meet his particular responsibilities to his utmost capacity. Some will be unwilling to engage in formal treatment, but all must work or face the consequences of idleness, which at Herstedvester are loss of pay and status. To Dr. Stürup, responsibility is a cardinal element in every decision leading to any action affecting a member of the institutional community. No one must ever feel that it does not matter what he does. But unless constant attention is given to assuring that the consequences of an action are appropriate, the feeling can easily arise that within the institution a not wholly unpleasant irresponsibility is possible.

Integration. — The sense of community which is so carefully built up at Herstedvester rests on a foundation of acceptance. "Everyone who comes here belongs here," Dr. Stürup explained; "nobody on the staff or among the inmates can be allowed to say that this or that individual doesn't belong here. Nobody can be eliminated because he is untreatable or because he's violent and destructive. No one will ever be sent away from Herstedvester for any reason other than that we believe he is ready to go back into the community." It is clear that this principle removes a considerable latitude for manipulation. At Herstedvester, the consequences of what one does will have to be faced on the premises, not at some other institution or in some other community. The difficulties of correctional administration within such a context are obvious, but so are the advantages for effective treatment.

Small Groups. — Herstedvester is built around the small living group of fifteen inmates supervised by two custodial officers. Dr. Stürup believes that the essence of correctional treatment is positive interaction between all members of the community. Such interaction cannot exist unless contact with staff members is close and continuous. No one can have a feeling of closeness in a group much larger than fifteen. The kind of individualization essential to treatment goals is impossible in situations where preoccupation with control prevents the staff from achieving intimacy with the inmates.

The Pro-Therapeutic Community. — Much attention is paid to elements in the community which might have an antitherapeutic influence. Groups which seem to be oriented to objectives inconsistent with the aims of the institution are broken up, whether they are giving "trouble" or not. Considerable thought is given to placing strong inmates with antitherapeutic perspectives in groups which contain members able to compete effectively. Institutional norms are carefully nurtured in all groups; it would seem probably that in a protherapeutic group the strong dissenter usually promotes cohesion. No one even knows of a way to demonstrate the optimal composition of living groups in a correctional community. Few places in the world give such careful attention to the individual influences which inmates exercise upon each other in living groups or the effect which each member has on the group as a whole. Facilities for the study of the methods of using the small correctional group as a therapeutic instrument are not lacking in Denmark, but projects of this nature are not under way. We believe that there is hardly any contribution to correctional research to be made in Denmark comparable to the systematic study of Herstedvester living groups. The institution, the staff, and the groups themselves have a continuity of approach which cannot be matched anywhere else. Procedures which would be innovations elsewhere are established practice at Herstedvester, and therefore much more reliable objects for study. Unfortunately, the energies of the staff have been diverted into research of phenomena of relatively minor importance, as we shall see. Whatever can be done to examine the unsensational but formidable problems of social structure within a system deliberately planned for many years to achieve the ends of a therapeutic community should be undertaken without further delay.

The Indeterminate Sentence. — In Dr. Stürup the indeterminate sentence has one of its stoutest defenders. Convinced that the prisoner will work harder at therapy when the goal of release is determined in part by his own efforts, Dr. Stürup thinks that the indeterminate sentence is the crucial feature of his program. He believes that without it, inmates could not be induced to assume the responsibility for their lives which is fundamental to successful resocialization.

At Herstedvester, the indeterminate sentence is fixed by the Minister of Justice. This decision is grounded on the superintendent's evaluation and recommendation. The responsibility devolving on the medical director is great and multilateral: To the public he owes a reasonable assurance that released inmates will not be continuing risks to life and property; to the inmate he owes a professional determination of eligibility for release as soon as sufficient improvement is discerned; to the institution he owes a treatment program so effective and so clearly understood that confidence in his recommendations to the Ministry of Justice will reinforce the effectiveness of treatment. These three obligations seem to be inescapable in the management of an indeterminate sentence, and it is seldom that the observer has confidence that they are met. It would be pleasant to report that a clearly defined system can be discerned at Herstedvester, with a well-established procedure for inducing, measuring, and reporting change. Unfortunately, just as in a less sophisticated correctional atmosphere, change is determined by clinical intuition. Based on long and reflective experience, this intuition is undoubtedly more valid than hunches or a politically appointed parole board. It is no easier to define and illustrate. For example, Dr. Stürup told us:

The first objective is to bring the patient to a situation in which he is willing to work hard and accept advice and some help. It is important to reach a point at which he will be able to expect something worth while of the future. Too little emphasis is put on these personal expectations. "What is possible for me as a miserable among the most miserable, deemed by the court, the newspapers, my family, and my friends to be a terrible person?" In most cases, such a person will think to himself that this judgment is correct, but at the same time he will try to hide this opinion of himself from himself and from other people. Because of this he will often act aggressively. But when one day this man feels that it is fine to talk about the "old life," then it is a good sign; we are getting down to business.

We face many problems in this period. Very often a criminal will be told that he should not be so self-centered, that he should not concentrate so much of his energy in dwelling on the past, that he should not be so egocentric. We go in just the opposite direction. We try to make him consider in detail his intentions and the patterns of his behavior. He will begin to understand how his mind works, and what sort of difficulties he must try to avoid because these difficulties are too dangerous for himself.

The prisoner will have to find out and accept his own possibilities. He must realize that for this project he will need to undertake a time-consuming and difficult study of his personality. If we *force* decisions on a man, he will usually react aggressively or immaturely; he will prove that he does not understand himself. Soon he will resume his former pattern of behavior. Much will be needed before he can plan his future life. He will have to go through the same problems again and again with himself and his advisers. Often he needs to feel that he is left alone. He may realize that it is really up to himself to decide when and if he will accept more help. In such cases we try to show our willingness to assist, that we are healers and not judges.

In Dr. Stürup's account we can hear a rationale for change, a series of intuitive insights concerning its external signs, and some confidence that experience has adequately supported judgment. It does not tell us how change is induced, nor do we have an analysis which relates symptoms to a broad range of diagnoses. It is not clear at what point the patient can be entrusted to the institutional after-care system, largely carried out by social workers employed by Herstedvester.

To most correctional observers the program of castration for sex offenders is probably the most familiar feature of the institution's practice. Because of the controversies which this practice has aroused, and the considerable skepticism in many other countries regarding its usefulness or propriety, meticulous attention has been given to accounting for its consequences. A comprehensive review of the Herstedvester experience with castration has appeared in a recent American publication.[34] We shall not here attempt a review of the statistics. Comparisons of recidivism for castrated and noncastrated offenders show a wide difference in favor of the castrated. This difference not only shows up in a much lower rate of relapse into sexual crime, but also in much earlier release; the castrates are ordinarily released within two years, but the noncastrates ordinarily serve more than four years.

Such figures are superficially impressive, and anecdotal accounts of the experience of castrates after release are, usually, reassuringly benign. The operation is voluntary in Denmark, though one castrate told us that he had felt that his volition was compromised by the explanation that with the operation he could expect release within eighteen months, but without it the term might be as much as ten years or even more.

One can hardly argue with success, even with this radical program, particularly when it is voluntary. Comparisons of castrates with noncastrates are not instructive, however, when the only controlled variable is the commission of one of many possible sex offenses. Further, the relatively favorable experience with noncastrated sex offenders in other countries raises a question as to whether many Danish castrates could have been successfully treated without surgery. A foreign observer cannot erase the impression that the availability of a simple and mechanical control for the sexual offender is irresistibly preferable to the ardor of

---

[34] G. K. Stürup, "Sex Offenses: The Scandinavian Experience," *Law and Contemporary Problems*, XXV:2 (Spring 1960), 361–375.

psychotherapy, both to staff and patients. If it is to be continued, and in the present climate of opinion in Denmark it seems certain that it will, the castration of sexual offenders should be studied on a more sophisticated level than accounting for comparative recidivism. Attitudinal studies are needed, and some analysis of the consequences for different personality types should be undertaken. A large volume of data is available but unevaluated, dealing with obscure psychological and physiological problems. The ethical issues cannot be resolved without reference to a better understanding than we now have of the consequences of castration.

Like the Social Rehabilitation Unit and the van der Hoeven Kliniek, Herstedvester lends itself to superficial description. All three establishments are consciously planned for the maintenance of therapeutic communities. In all three much thought has been given to the essential conditions. None of them is research-oriented, and there is no way of empirically supporting an appraisal of either the idea of a therapeutic community or its special application in any of these institutions. Studies which will facilitate such an appraisal are urgently needed for the refinement of the programs at these institutions and for the validation of the idea of the therapeutic community, so attractive to the correctional theorist and reformer, so difficult and expensive to install in a conventional correctional apparatus. These models are rare; they embody numerous impressive hypotheses; though the populations which they serve are highly specialized, much can be learned from a study of the clinical and organizational consequences of the assumptions on which they are based. It is to be hoped that resources will eventually be made available for such studies, preferably applying the same research designs to all three institutions.

GROUP COUNSELING AND THE CORRECTIONAL FUTURE

One avenue of advance in corrections is through the construction of test models. Enterprises like the three we have described are valuable laboratories in which ideal conditions can be maintained indefinitely and improvement can be sought for application to the general conditions in the entire correctional apparatus of a state. Not all correctional systems have the leadership or the resources to provide such a laboratory. The future may be approached from a different direction.

One such possibility is the piecemeal improvement of an institution or a system. New programs are somehow installed, studied, and integrated within some long-established and familiar operation. The difficulties are formidable; the resistances of any bureaucracy to change are well known, but the resistance of the correctional bureaucracy is heavily fortified with imagined hazards, folklore, and, sometimes, justifiable apprehension about the consequences of the introduction of a new element in a precariously unstable situation. For this reason, novelties are rare in long-established correctional systems. Correctional necessity has never been a fecund mother, but it has produced a few innovations.

Such an innovation is the group-counseling movement. Wherever we went, our California origins had only to be known to raise questions concerning the mushrooming practice of group-counseling in the prisons, training schools, jails, and field agencies of our state. The use of this simple treatment model is widespread in the more advanced correctional systems in the United States. It has been impressively adapted to the markedly different correctional scene in England. Under vigorous leadership its practice is to become general in Sweden after a thorough training program has been completed. Despite some natural skepticism, many other northern European countries are planning to experiment with this powerful reinforcement of correctional practice.

More than most programs in the correctional field, group-counseling is moving through a transition. Founded on faith and propagated by enthusiasm, it has managed with a meager theoretical endowment. Problems of apparently formidable theoretical significance have been deferred for solution, evidently with no serious harm done. Administrative obstacles have been handled on a basis of expediency or brushed aside. Under the circumstances, the movement can scarcely be found in ideal conditions, and often languishes in a perfunctory state, maintained for appearances rather than the benefits it is capable of conferring.

Descended from the psychiatric practice of group therapy, group-counseling uses the group meeting of correctional clients, not to exert professionally grounded influences, but rather to bring to bear on individual offenders the reservoir of good will and constructive interpersonal relations in staff members and the offenders. The distinction is important. Group-counseling looks exactly like group therapy. A small gathering of inmates or probationers is gathered with a staff member. If the staff member is a psychotherapist, the content of the discussion when we get close enough to listen, includes introspection, interpretations, and a deliberate application of professional experience to the discussion with the object of achieving insight. In the group-counseling session, the leader may be a work foreman, a correctional officer, a probation officer, or, in at least one institution, an inmate.[35] The content of the discussion is on the surface, dealing mostly with current problems, and bringing to bear on each participant the life experience of the group members. The counselor usually acts as a facilitator rather than an agent of treatment. From this experience insight and other therapeutic objectives may be reached. These achievements are often the random results of every-day living in the ordinary course of events. But the group-counseling movement is satisfied with much more modest goals. The application of good will and orderly discussion to personal problems is a valid objective regardless of psychological aims of a more ambitious order. In the otherwise undirected discussions in prison cell blocks, recreation yards, and subculturally delinquent communities, the premises for problem-solving often includes assumptions of hostility, aggression, and destructive motivations leading to impulsive behavior. Understanding is limited to the projection of the ill-will felt by the actor onto everyone in the environment. Defenses against the hazards presented by life in such a community must consist of a wary eye out for unprovoked attack and a ready hand for defense against it. In the total institution the safety of each inmate depends on cohesive adherence to an inmate code which protects inmates not only from the staff but also from each other. It is a code which makes life possible in circumstances in which inmates are left to their own devices. It is also a code which notoriously places huge obstacles in the way of resocialization.

In group-counseling a method has been developed to divert the influence of the inmate or delinquent code and at the same time to bring to bear influences of good will and orderly, conventional standards of human relations. It is not the only way in which these objectives can be attained, nor is it an infallible way. But properly used, it appears to be helpful to some classes of offenders, and impressions are general that the elusive factor of institutional climate is improved.

It would be idle to trace group-counseling back to its first origins. Doubtless a practice identifiable as such could be located far back in

---

[35] Under the leadership of Dr. G. Lee Sandritter, Atascadero State Hospital, a California institution for the treatment of sexual psychopaths and mentally ill offenders is experimenting with patient-led groups. No reports of results are as yet available, but staff impressions are favorable.

the annals of penology. But the contemporary group-counseling movement is readily traced to a time and place of origin and to an originator. The year was 1954, the place was Folsom Prison, California's grim old bastille for maximum-security recidivists, and the innovator was Dr. Norman Fenton, at that time Deputy-Director for Classification and Treatment of the Department of Corrections. A high intake of prisoners and the chronically undernourished condition of correctional industries had combined to produce an ominously large number of idle inmates in the Big Yard. In a prison with a tradition of violence and a population with a predilection for aggression it seemed clear that the safety of all was at stake and that major disorders were a distinct possibility. The concern of Warden Robert A. Heinze spread to the officials of the department. As an expedient to help with an anxious situation, Dr. Fenton volunteered to undertake some experiments in group-counseling. It was not expected that this enterprise would transform Folsom into an island of tranquillity. But it succeeded far beyond expectations. Inmates participated with interest and, what was more important, a significant number of employees responded to the invitation to observe and learn.

Dr. Fenton brought to the group-counseling enterprise a broad background as a clinical psychologist, notable gifts as a teacher, and a skill at administration which surprised associates accustomed to believe that the practice of a helping profession incapacitated the practitioner for the responsibilities of "getting things done." The initial success of the Folsom group-counseling venture inculcated in him an evangelical enthusiasm for the process. With the support of the Adult Authority, California's parole board, inmates were encouraged to apply for inclusion in a counseling group in far larger numbers than could be accommodated. A crash program of training was designed and more counselors were thus made available than could be accommodated in the rooms suitable for group meetings.

From Folsom the group-counseling movement rapidly spread to the other institutions of the department on the general principle that if it could be effective at an institution for the worst and least-motivated prospects for resocialization then it should be even more successful with more hopeful prisoners. With Dr. Fenton's personal efforts, staff in each institution were trained. Professional social workers at each institution were trained to train beginning counselors. The group-counseling movement became domesticated. Its success in California could not be readily demonstrated in statistical tables, but it seemed obvious that the transformation of hard-bitten old guards into paternal and friendly counselors was a gain worth making even if it would be years before results could be shown in terms of rates of recidivism. So attractive was the idea as propounded by Dr. Fenton that it has been borrowed for implementation in most countries committed to contemporary ideas of corrections.

As now practiced in California, group-counseling is usually voluntary. We shall have more to say presently about compulsory group counseling. Most groups vary in size between ten and twenty. Most counselors are correctional officers, but employees of every class can be and have been used, including wardens and female clerks. Some counselors make heavy use of various aids, the most important of which is the text prepared by Dr. Fenton, *What Will Be Your Life?* [36] This book presents in simple language enough basic psychology to start an offender to thinking about the causes of his predicament. Its use as a text provided a simple and familiar class-room situation for the Folsom inmates who were first exposed to it, and offered support to the correctional officers who were insecure in their new roles. Moving pictures, articles in the newspapers, visiting experts, and the ingenuity of the counselors themselves were used to enrich the experience. Generally, though, the groups have learned to rely for material on the incidents of the day, the frustrations and occasional satisfactions of institutional life. At first a group may use the unfamiliar freedom with the staff for the expression of grievances against the institution or the system. With the passage of time and the development of a certain cohesion, the groups turn into small forums for the discussion of emotional problems confronting their members. One man may have received notice of his wife's intention to file for divorce; another may be about to go out to an uncertain and unfriendly world with profound doubts of the sincerity of parole agents; still another may voice his lingering fascination with the idea of escape. Most groups tend to have a rather skeptical response to the contributions of their members; it is as though insincerity was to be expected from fellow inmates. Little is taken at face value; the usual response to an assertion is a challenge. It would go too far to claim that the typical challenge is based on concern for each other. More likely the

---

[36] Norman Fenton, *What Will Be Your Life?* (Sacramento: The Department of Corrections, 1955).

atmosphere of healthy doubt arises from a common familiarity with the processes of self-deception, rationalization, and projection. It is not often left to the counselor to voice skepticism; frequently he is more easily deceived than the inmate members of the group.

Not all groups are effective, nor are all groups equally effective with each member. Staff turnover and, in California, the inmate turnover resulting from transfers made to effect population adjustments, destroy the impact of many groups. For most group counselors, the activity is secondary to the primary occupational commitment; in the nature of an avocation, it is an additional string to the bow. Skill in group-counseling is only marginally significant for promotions; the rewards for a job well done are not money and status, but the gratitude of a group of inmates and the occasional approval of peers. In Western society the attractiveness of intangible incentives varies greatly; the pursuit of money and security tends to reduce the energies which can be devoted to altruistic undertakings.

It is not surprising then to find that for many counselors the spirit is willing enough, but the flesh weakens after weeks or months have been devoted to an activity whose value has to be taken so largely on faith. Meetings are missed, thoughts wander, and initiative atrophies. What may have been originally a weekly exchange of brisk discussion decays into desultory bull sessions wearily continued for the record.

Because of its nature as a voluntary, peripheral activity, group counseling needs unusual administrative implementation. Supervision must be skilled, training imaginative, and problems shared. These postulates are not usually met; indeed, the tendency is to settle for as little supervision as will insure that minimum training is available, that there are chairs to be sat on, and records of attendance kept. Even in California, the leadership of a renowned ranking expert in the agency has been supplanted by social workers with little status and modest training in the perplexities of group management. In other places, as for example in England, reliance is placed on the occasional visit of a consultant supported by whatever enthusiasm and expertise the governor of the prison or borstal can muster. The trappings of group counseling are easy to simulate; the substance is hard to produce.

Whether group counseling should be a compulsory feature of correctional programing is still an unresolved issue. The doctrine that psychotherapy is necessarily voluntary is persuasive to many; it is reasoned that a man will hardly benefit from a service he neither wants nor understands. To emerge from the group-counseling experience with a change for the better presupposes at least be a desire to change.

Nevertheless, the advocates of compulsory group-counseling have comprehensive experience to offer in rebuttal. Perhaps the most significant demonstration of compulsory group-counseling is to be found at the California Institution for Men at Tehachapi. Here, in 1956, it was proposed to convert a minimum-security facility into a prison suitable for housing medium-security men. To do this, the installation of an armed perimeter was planned. After a review of the plans, Dr. Fenton proposed that, as an experiment, the medium-security men be sent but that the security be provided through compulsory group-counseling. The only restriction was that men be sent who were deemed psychologically and culturally capable of responding to such a program. Mental defectives and inmates not speaking English were ineligible. Six years have passed, and though Tehachapi has had two or three escapes a year, the rate has never been so high that the Department of Corrections has had to reconsider this plan. In this way, the expense of manning four gun towers, a considerable item at about $30,000 each in personnel costs, was saved through making group-counseling the basic feature of the institutional program. The superintendent, G. P. Lloyd, comments that the reason for the exceptionally low escape rate at Tehachapi lies in the fact that "before a man hits the fence, he has to run a gauntlet of four hundred head shrinkers."

But whether the inmates are stirred by the experience to a new perception of self and others or sit in vacant silence, it is hard to see that group-counseling has done any harm. The apprehensions of psychotherapists that reversals of the rehabilitative process might occur with counseling in such untutored hands do not seem to have been justified. Boredom and the failure of participants to make the most of the occasion appear to have been the most adverse consequences. Group-counseling may produce an occasional cynic, but it is unlikely that in the corrosion of personality it can ever match ordinary imprisonment.

Though hopes for individual resocialization may fall short, some general benefits seem to ensue from the process. First, the roles of all participants are changed. The counselor is no longer simply a guard or a work supervisor; he is a helper, sharing from his experience and his strength in the process of resocialization. This change undoubtedly produces role conflicts which are difficult to resolve. Many counselors find some value in resolving anew the problems of personal identity.

The fact that such resolutions can be made is seen in the many men and women who have managed to sustain the role of group counselor in addition to their regular occupations for many years. In their example may lie some indication of the correctional future. The role of the future disciplinary officer in a correctional institution is uncertain but the experience of group-counseling will undoubtedly produce a metamor phosis.

Not only the role of the employee who acts as a counselor is changed; the role of the inmate is changed too. It has been many years since the role of the inmate of the correctional institution has been simply to receive punishment. He has been the student, the industrial worker, the medical patient, and, under some auspices, the mentally ill person. Group-counseling makes of him a person who is being helped, and who is expected, as a part of the process of being helped, to make such contributions as he can to the helping of others. Gone is the concept of "doing one's own time." The modern correctional client is his brother's keeper, whether he likes it or not. Neither he nor anyone else may know very well how he can best help his fellow offenders. But from the experience of his efforts can be extracted the principles by which his goodwill, too, can be put to use.

The second benefit of group-counseling is the change in the character of the correctional institution. This arises from different order of communications among the elements of the community. The existence of a group-counseling program puts the relationships of the persons involved onto a footing different from that which exists in a conventional institution. The relations between staff members and inmates in the group-meeting becomes informal, permissive, and concerned, at least in principle, with resocialization as an objective. As for inmates in the conventional institution the content of communication will be those issues in which inmates have a common interest: generally, such issues will be in the areas of resistance to the staff and of crime itself. An old-timer in a close security Federal prison described the difference which groups made to him:

We have a group here which is one of the best things I've ever seen in an institution, and I've been in seven of them. It's what we call a Self-Improvement Group. We meet each Saturday, sometimes with outside guests, and each week we have a different subject. For instance, it may be, "How to get along with your fellow workers," or "What is expected of a person in a community." I think we need this kind of program. Without it, we wouldn't have too much to talk about. We used to talk about the past, what we're going to do when we get out. Let me give you an example. I went to jail first when I had just turned seventeen. There were a lot of old-time cons, and I had a little trouble because of my age. I had a number of fights, but I was pretty husky for a kid. I didn't do too bad. When some of the older fellows saw that I didn't want to indulge in sex in prison, they invited me to join their group. And one of the leaders — I'll never forget the man; he's still living today — he told me: "Jimmy, this life is no good. Why don't you get straightened out and learn something and go on home and behave yourself. Look at me, I'm over fifty years old and I've spent half my life in prison. This just ain't good." And I said, "I'm gonna steal — *I'm* gonna steal." So then he said, "Well, if that's the way you feel, then I'll try to teach you the right way to steal." Of course, there is no right way, but he told me what he knew. Now there was a man, even in those days, an old professional criminal, who didn't want me to be a thief because I was just a young kid. But when he saw that I was determined to be a thief, then he tried to teach me what he called the "right way to go." If I had been a little older, if I had listened to what he really wanted to tell me, my life might have been different.

But you have a different type prisoners now than you had in those days. I can only speak from my own observations. But, for example, when I first came here, seventeen years ago, the first thing I noticed was the fights, you know. I'm telling you, I was scared, I kept wondering, "What have I got into here?" Every week there'd be a fight of some kind. And the older guys would say to you, "Buddy, take it easy, slow down a little." But I'd say, "It's none of your business. I'm doing my own time." Nowadays you talk to some young guy, and he'll listen to you.

No one should conclude that even in this evidently well-organized prison an entirely harmonious community has been created. There are still fights, there are still officers who shout and curse, and there are still inmates who tear up cells and have to be transferred to a maximum-security setting. But the prospects of successful social restoration are much improved because, as we were told, "we have different things to talk about."

Among staff, too, relations change as an investment of time and concern goes into group-counseling. A chief officer at Pollington Borstal was specific:

I'm responsible for the staff, and obviously if you haven't got a happy, contented staff you certainly can't hand much on to the lads. I treat the officers as I would like to have them treat the lads under them — they aren't just following firm, grim orders. By treating them with a friendly attitude I hope they will pass that on to the lads. We're unique in that we have weekly staff study groups. All the lads are in group counseling, and the staff needs training for that. You must realize that a lot of this has to be done in the officer's spare time. For both the group counseling and for the study groups the officer is not due in until one in the afternoon, but he comes in anyway at 9:30.

I'd say that probably 5 per cent of our staff think we've gone a little bit too far; they'll say that we're too helpful to these lads and that now and again they'll want a bit of the stick — but I don't think that they really *think* it. The great majority of the officers in here, if they're asked to do something to help the camp, which inevitably is to help the lads, will do it without any grumbling or fuss at all.

The governor of Pollington, then, added:

One of the most important issues to solve is this question of how much confidence the various ranks of staff can acquire in each other. Disciplinary officers were always dominated by the fear of the big mistake — a fear that a boy will run away and you couldn't say when you last saw him. Even with counseling groups, the fear that the inmate would be able to take away their authority was always present. Our training had in part to be directed to removing this kind of fear and anxiety. The basic design of training has been the weekly study groups. They are voluntary and there is usually a reasonable attendance. Many of the formal status edges have worn off; I *think* my officers feel quite happy about talking freely in front of me. They're not worried, as they once were, that this was going to be stored up in reports about them.

We've been fortunate in securing the help of a chap who has had some experience in taking groups as a consultant. He runs two groups entirely outside the establishment for us to go to. I go along with everybody else, just as a learner. The intellectual stimulation has been considerable. Two members of my staff went off last summer to study, completely at their own expense. Other officers take courses in group psychology and group factors in crime and punishment. This has been a remarkable liberation of staff.

The inference from this kind of observation seems to be that if a correctional staff is given a professional task, it will begin to act professionally. This means that a responsibility will be discharged, not by rote or by reference to personal experience, but rather from what has been learned from an organized body of knowledge. The increase in self-respect which arises from professionalization is reflected in the altered respect which can be extended to fellow professionals. A shared concern about a professional role to be performed leads to entirely different staff relations than will be encountered in situations in which communications among officers can have hardly any other purpose than the correction of a deficiency in control. Staff members who are learning from experience will communicate among themselves a vastly different feeling and content than what was communicated when they were merely obeying orders. What they transmit to each other will inevitably be transmitted to the inmates, sometimes in groups, but really throughout the days, months, and years they are all together in a community.

Much needs to be done to capitalize on the opportunities of group counseling. Its form in California, in England, and wherever lay staff members are used, has been the heterogeneous group of ten to fifteen inmates meeting once a week. Some groups have been assigned for a definite period, usually three months; others have been set up for indefinite duration. In some situations the Belmont model, consisting of a community meeting preceding small group meetings, has been adopted. Some groups, as in the Community Treatment Project or in Pinehills at Provo, Utah, have been action-oriented, with a definite part to play in the formulation of decisions about confinement and release of inmates. Other groups have been specifically prohibited from the assumption of any action role. The variants on the general idea of group-counseling are numerous. The standards of practice are so fluid as to be unidentifiable.

This conceptual disarray is disturbing because it occurs in an era of evaluation. From the first, there has been an eagerness to prove that this one or two hours of the week of the offender has enough impact to make a difference in the outcome of his confinement, regardless of what happens during that hour or two, and regardless of what happens during the rest of the week. The fact that the content of group counseling ranges from the near-didactic to the near-permissive has seldom been faced squarely; neither has the question of the relative competence and motivation of the counselors, a variable of even greater significance. California study has shown that inmates with middle base expectancy in long-term group-counseling under one leader seem to show a more favorable outcome than is experienced by inmates with a low base expectancy.[37] Studies of this kind are steps in the direction of sophistication. But the impact of group-counseling on the correctional apparatus can not be appraised until some models

---

[37] Paul F. C. Mueller and Robert M. Harrison, "Clue Hunting in Group-Counseling," Department of Corrections (Sacramento: 1964, mimeographed).

can be set up for test. The task now is not to prove that group-counseling works. Eager advocates of research must be patient with an era of experimentation in group-counseling. Nothing will be settled in any massive study which could conceivably be executed now. Dozens of small issues must be resolved before group counselors can be adequately trained. In the meantime the gains which the correctional apparatus makes from the mere existence of this practice within its gates should sufficiently reward its tolerance.

In this section we have examined the major innovations in correctional treatment. Our frame of reference has been the hypothesis that the addition of a special program of psychotherapy, education, or industry is irrelevant unless the community itself is oriented to social restoration as an organizational goal. Two methods of producing this re-orientation have been examined. First, new institutions can be designed so that the complete impact of the institution can be therapeutic. In such a therapeutic community a rational application of all resources of staff and inmates is made to the individualized problem of each inmate. Clearly, none of the three samples described yet meets this objective. But both the physical and organizational models are contrived to take advantage of what is known about the change and control of behavior, and to incorporate what is yet to be discovered.

Second, the hundreds of old, ill-designed, and often dilapidated institutions which survive from a more punitive age must still be used, and for a long time to come. Usually the structure of such an institution is a negative influence to be offset, rather than an asset to be capitalized upon. From the introduction of group-counseling, major organizational changes become possible through the role changes of the staff and inmates.

Community and group methods in the treatment of the offender derive from what has been aptly called the "third revolution in psychiatry." [38] This development is characterized by the recognition of group influences on the individual through the maintenance of an atmosphere in which these influences can be strategically deployed for the benefit of all. It would be tempting to refer to milieu treatment as

---

[38] Rudolf Dreikurs, "Group Psychotherapy and the Third Revolution in Psychiatry," *International Journal of Social Psychiatry*, 1 (1955), 23–32.

the first revolution in corrections. Such a revolution has not occurred; the most that can be said is that experimentation with these borrowed methods promises to add components to a new, and as yet incompletely conceptualized practice of corrections. In this sense milieu methods may be more appropriately seen as the first steps in the evolution of correctional practice to a rational performance of the correctional assignment.

ORGANIZATION

With imagination and professional skill available in the right places, the effectiveness of the correctional apparatus can be greatly increased with relatively little cost. The further investigation of treatment typologies and strategies will probably demonstrate that better results can be gained with many classes of offenders without costly confinement in institutions but rather through intensive and discriminating field supervision. Correctional advance can move far within its present structure. All it needs is leadership.

Leadership can also execute major revisions of the structure in which the entire apparatus is charged with achieving resocialization. In the following paragraphs we want to discuss some organizational innovations which have radically changed the nature of correctional process. We are addressing ourselves to the difficult question as to how the correctional apparatus can be organized to take the fullest advantage of what is now known about treatment and what we seem likely to find out if present research trends continue. There are a few principles which seem to be accepted for correctional advance in most industrial countries. The principles we have distinguished are:

Institutions should be small. Units in institutions should capitalize on the socializing values of the small group.

Life in institutions should be as normal as possible so as to counteract the regressive influences of institutionalization.

Every effort should be made to integrate the institution with the community.

Wherever possible, the resources of field supervision should be employed to effect resocialization without confinement. To this end the correctional apparatus should make available massive resources to reinforce field supervision so that it can be exercised effectively wherever the public safety permits.

When institutional confinement is necessary it should not last for longer than the purpose for which it is intended requires.

Recognition of the handicaps of stigma and inadequacy, which particularly affect recidivists but also impose burdens on occasional offenders, should be given in the form of hostels, half-way houses, and labor colonies.

These principles derive from a basic doctrine, difficult to validate, which might be stated thus: Restoration of the correctional client to maximum community life requires that the ordinary course of his existence should be interfered with as little as possible, consistent with the public safety and his own. This doctrine is the foundation of most current thought. Its origins in common sense and humanitarianism are obvious. Its application to individual and institutional situations is difficult and in many respects open to conflicting inferences. Its influence as a base for advance is powerful, partly because of the humanitarian implications of an increasingly egalitarian society, partly because in corrections a direct and persisting relationship between benevolence and economy exists.

Most examples in this section will be fragmented advances, attacks on one or two sectors only of the organizational arrangements of corrections. The only broad approach to correctional change we found in Sweden; even there, as will shortly be seen, the advance is partial, leaving probation and after-care mostly untouched. But as an example of faithful application of principle with as little compromise as possible, the Swedish correctional institutions for adults and children present models which are in most respects far ahead of other Western countries.

Swedish progress in corrections seems to be attributable to three influences. First, for reasons that confound the theorist, Sweden has a rising crime rate. Other Scandinavian countries are little affected by whatever influences caused the increase in Swedish delinquency since World War II. Second, Sweden, a nonbelligerent in two wars which impoverished other countries, has money to spend on public services and a well-established tradition of spending it. Third, Sweden has the gifted and energetic leadership of Torsten Eriksson, one of the most resourceful correctional administrators of our time.

Eriksson is new to the director-generalship of Swedish prisons, but his ideas have been influential in their planning and organization for many years. His touch is everywhere to be seen in adult and juvenile institutions.

He identifies four basic ideas in his program for the reorganization of Swedish corrections. They are neither new, nor surprising, nor tested. They have been adopted on a basis of the common sense that they provide more hope for the future and more relevance to present conditions than an attempt to make anything out of the legacy of the past. Shabby relics of the nineteenth century, such as Stockholm's grim bastille, Langholmen Prison, are scheduled for demolition. In their place are rising a series of modern institutions embodying Eriksson's four-point program as fully as it can be actualized within present knowledge. This program consists of the following principles:

First, prisoners must work. To dramatize this point for the general public, Eriksson points out that all Swedes have to work in order to live and that prisoners should be no exceptions. They should work to build a better Sweden, and they should work to preserve and increase their own skills. Therefore, the slogan on which prison-planning in Sweden is based is, "first we build a factory, then we add a prison to the factory." The first step in planning a new institution is a consideration of an appropriate industry. A new women's prison, elegantly situated in an eighteenth-century mansion remodeled for its new occupants, will do all laundry and dry-cleaning for nearby governmental installations; another new institution is built around two factories, one for the manufacture of furniture, the other for production of uniforms for the Swedish Army. Other institutions are planned which will produce prefabricated houses for government posts.

Inmates in most Swedish prisons are paid liberally, though not at full rates paid by outside employers. Plans are under way, however, for the establishment of new institutions in which wages will be paid at prevailing rates, with deductions for maintenance. Eriksson's emphasis on realistic employment in prisons is clearly carried to the extent of providing the conditions in which realism can be expected, which includes a normal system of incentives. The result, at least in the more modern institutions, is the maintenance of an industrial pace which approximates the requirements of regular industry in the community.

This approach to prison industry contrasts with the situation in Anglo-Saxon countries, where make-work, slow-motion employment, idleness, and, worst of all, punitive hard labor, virtually assure the deterioration of skill, morale, and contact with economic reality. Eriksson is frank to admit that in the economic situation of Sweden since World War II it has been easy to persuade the public of the logic of his position on correctional industry. With employment at such a high level that the labor shortage requires Sweden to import thousands of workers from the rest of Europe every year, there can be no reasonable opposition from any quarter to putting all prisoners to constructive work. What will happen in the event of economic adversity remains to be seen. Eriksson hopes that by that time, if it ever comes, the Swedish unions and the general public will be sufficiently accustomed to a high level of prison employment that no change will be demanded.

Eriksson's second principle provides for the psychological health of the institution. To him, a good prison plan must minimize the unhealthy aspects of confinement. People feel better in the open air, work better in good light, get along better when they are not crowded into spaces in which confinement is emphasized by unnatural and involuntary closeness to others. Privacy must be a part of the plan rather than the object of inmate-scheming. Swedish prisons have walls, but they are not obtrusive, oppressive reminders of mistrust. The space which the walls enclose encompasses not only the cottages in which prisoners reside but also acres of playing fields. This is not to say that monotony, alienation, and institutionalization do not produce the negative effects found in other countries. Inmates described hostility, boredom, and fear of the outside community in terms quite reminiscent of those heard in hard-pressed American institutions. Nevertheless, avoidable negative effects are avoided in the design of the institution, rather than left to the staff to minimize.

The third principle of institutional design is the use of modern technology. Wherever anyone's work can be made more efficient by electronic devices, mechanical conveniences, and strategically organized communications, great pains are taken to make them available. Eriksson believes that prisons must compete with other employers to recruit and retain able employees. The mechanical efficiency of the premises adds much to the employee's impression of the importance of his job, the capability of the administration to plan rationally, and the general progressiveness of the organization. Further, a technologically modern prison reduces the number of employees needed for drudgery, thereby eliminating the need for that class of employee. With centrally operated locking devices, television surveillance of walls, two-way portable radio communication for prison officers on patrol duty, and two-way intercommunication between control stations and cells, Eriksson has virtually eliminated the key-jangling, tower-sitting officers of the conventional prison. The new Swedish prison officer is a man who can be realistically recruited and trained for the task of constructively influencing human behavior. The juice of aspiration will not have been drained out of him by monotonous years on a wall, nor will his goodwill have been soured into cynicism by incessant contention with large crowds of unruly and hostile prisoners. He will still be assigned to tasks of control, but he will not be expected to become an automaton. There will still be unattractive assignments; not much can be said for the task of sitting in front of a battery of blinking television tubes connected to cameras trained on the walls and gates of the prison, but it is a vastly more comfortable monotony than trudging through the snow around those walls throughout a Swedish winter.

Finally, and perhaps most important, is the principle of the small group. The new Swedish prisons house no more than two hundred inmates. The old prisons at Langholmen and Malmö had populations of six hundred and sometimes more. Maintenance of conditions which did not violate the basic concepts of resocialization was virtually impossible. From his experience in juvenile institutions, Eriksson concluded that successful correctional institutions had to be much smaller. Already Sweden had acquired considerable experience in the management of forest camps containing fifty inmates.

The values of the small living unit were firmly accepted as essential to resocialization. But when closed institutions of this size were built, it was soon discovered that the cost of services would be prohibitive, except for highly specialized programs. Thus, the elegant and famous institution for youthful disturbed offenders at Roxtuna was built at a cost of about $11,000 per bed, and the daily per-capita cost is close to $15. Even in the affluent society of Sweden such costs cannot be incurred by the prison administration without stimulating public criticism.

Eriksson has dealt with this dilemma by making the prison an aggregation of physically separate small living units. At Roxtuna, the cottages are spread over a fairly large reservation and house nine inmates each, a figure which results from experience with living groups of several different sizes. More than ten in the unit produces more interactions than inmates of this kind can manage or the staff can keep track of. Fewer than eight seems to produce an unfavorable environment. For an establishment intended for psychiatric treatment an institutional design of this kind is acceptable in Sweden. For the con-

finement of the ordinary adult offender, it may still be an ideal to be
sought by the visionary, but hardly an aim for the practical administrator. Eriksson has settled on a larger, less costly model. The new
medium-security institution at Norrtälje and its twin at Tidaholm exemplify his compromise with expediency. Both institutions are built
around living units of twenty; each unit is half of a divided pavilion
of forty. Staff are permanently assigned to each living unit in the expectation that eventually these units will become treatment entities.

Such considerations are deceptively simple. The exact optimum
size of a unit and its architecture are issues to which the prison archi-
tect gives little attention. The literature about the size of a primary
group as related to its effects on the group's objectives and its impact on its members is scanty. Most people will agree that a small
group is better than a large group, but how much better? In the planning for the effectiveness of the correctional apparatus few questions
can be more urgently in need of solution. Eriksson and his colleagues
have proceeded from a foundation of common sense and the impressions of personal experience. That they have been able to persuade
the Swedish public of the validity of views so based speaks well for
the confidence in which they are held.

Common sense and experience have also settled on a ceiling for
the number of units to be contained in one institution. Here the focus
has been on the prison's director and the number of operating staff
he can hope to supervise while at the same time allowing him time
for his administrative duties. This ceiling is set at six units of forty
inmates each, plus a reception unit of eighty. Specialized institutions
such as Roxtuna, for disturbed younger offenders, and Mariefred, for
aggressive, acting-out younger men, are much smaller. Eriksson justifies the high per-capita costs of such establishments by pointing to
the special problems that each is expected to solve, and the need for
appropriate conditions in which experimental programs can be undertaken.

We have seen that the management of Swedish prisons has been
rationalized to the extent that common sense and the meager lessons
of experience will permit. To maintain needed centralized services,
the Royal Prison Board has its offices in Stockholm. Planning, management controls, and the contacts with parliament required by law
are carried out here. Four prison regions are established for ordinary correctional operations. Each region has the broad range of in-

stitutions necessary for its responsibilities; it is arranged that the director of the region will superintend the central facility from which allocations are made to an assortment of satellites, for whose supervision he is responsible to the Prison Board. Each region is thus a self-contained system for ordinary prisoners. Three additional nation-wide "regions" have been set up; one each for youth prisoners, for preventive detention, and for female prisoners. Each nation-wide "region" is provided with a range of institutions for security and for special treatment.

Although Swedish correctional institutions are notable for physical design and for full employment, Eriksson and his associates are dissatisfied. After-care is primitive in comparison with the provisions in the institutions. A strengthened probation service, perhaps to be merged eventually with the Prison Board, is in prospect. At present, the system has to rely on voluntary probation officers, described elsewhere.

Neither vocational nor academic education are compulsory in prisons. These activities are maintained as services of which inmates may avail themselves after hours. No staff is assigned to carry out such programs; reliance is placed on local educational services. Youth prisons have vocational training shops and are seen as primarily educational institutions.

Religious service is optional and casual, as in most Scandinavian countries. Chaplains are recruited from the local clergy and appear to be expected mostly to provide a weekly chapel service. There is no established provision for religious counseling, nor was there any evident concern that such provision should be made.

Probably most serious is the deficiency in psychiatric and psychological services. Coming from a country in which amenities available at Roxtuna would be hardly conceivable, we thought it disconcerting that at that institution the superintendent was a woman psychiatrist, chosen not because someone thought a woman psychiatrist would be peculiarly appropriate for the treatment of disturbed delinquents, but because she was the only psychiatrist who could be induced to consider the job. Her principal assistant was a young psychologist, a recent graduate who had not been trained for clinical psychology but who, it seemed, was the only candidate for the post. That both clinicians were clearly performing capably and enthusiastically was only fortuitous. The selection of the only candidate available for a creative task usually results in bureaucratic ignominy.

Swedish prisoners are allowed to receive visitors fortnightly and granted furloughs as a matter of right. The fortnightly visits are, with very few exceptions, unsupervised. They may take place in the prisoner's room and may last for several hours. No measures are taken to prevent or discourage sexual intercourse. Verification of the marital status of the visitor is evidently casual.

Furloughs are granted for periods of seventy-two hours, plus travel time, after four months of confinement, and quarterly thereafter. The system is available for all prisoners except for those who have more than three years to serve. In the latter case, application must be made to the Royal Prison Board, which has the final power to approve.

Because Sweden's system of home leaves appears to be the most liberal in use in any Western country, we inquired about its success. Generally, both staff and inmates thought that it was operating well, and that such hazards as necessarily were encountered were well worth the gains in tranquillity and general friendliness. The most specific study of its success was made by Hugh Kenyon, then an assistant commissioner of the British Prison Commission. In a study of 297 home leaves granted by the Southern Region in 1955, Kenyon found that abuses took place in only 34 cases, and of these 22 had merely failed to return to the institution on time. Five had committed new offenses, one had attempted to smuggle in contraband on his return, and the rest were drunk.[39]

The least that can be said of these procedures is that, by all accounts we could gather, the incidence of homosexuality is reduced to the behavior of those persons who were homosexual before confinement. The degrading preoccupation with this subject, the provision of safeguards to prevent it, and the damage wrought on those who are introduced to the practice as a feature of confinement, all these consequences of the conventional prison of England and America are unknown in Sweden.

But beyond this gain, it is at least possible that the program of home leaves and unsupervised visiting preserves values in family and community life which are grossly distorted by the complete isolation

---

[39] Hugh Kenyon, "Report on Scandinavian Prisons," unpublished manuscript, 1957, pp. 128–129, 192, in the author's possession.

of the prisoner from the community. The bridges to the community which are artificially provided at great administrative expense in some American programs exist quite naturally in Sweden. No doubt better advantage could be taken of the home-leave program in particular, but, even without the field services which could strengthen it so much, the home leave must have values for the prisoner offsetting the minimal hazards to the community. Its introduction in a geographically vast area such as the United States would have to be safeguarded by different precautions. Nevertheless, its use as an incentive for the assumption of responsibilities, as a test of the progress of treatment, and as an alternative to some of the unfavorable aspects of conjugal visiting it is long overdue for experimentation.

JUVENILE INSTITUTIONS IN WASHINGTON

A correctional program for adults which is designed to facilitate social restoration to the extent that we found in Sweden is a wonder to behold. It should be less wonderful to discover a comparable program for juvenile offenders. The notion that children must be treated constructively toward responsible roles in the community is old in all Western countries. It is basic to the juvenile-court laws and consistent with the prevailing ideas of child welfare. At Barnbyn Skå in Sweden, we saw a talented psychiatric staff welding into a therapeutic community a manic conglomeration of highly disturbed children. At Valkenheide in the Netherlands an imaginative pedagogue had combined a population of delinquents with an equal number of nondelinquents in a vocational training program which seems to have been so successful as a program as to submerge the problems of delinquency. We have already described the carefully conceptualized methods applied by John Gittins at the Aycliffe approved school in England. The Canadian transplantation of borstal philosophy effected by S. Rocksborough Smith and George Warnock at New Haven in British Columbia must be regarded as a step ahead of which Sir Alexander Paterson would have been proud.

But, over-all, conventional thinking in juvenile institutions is nearly as predominant as in adult corrections. Men of great distinction superintend, plan, and manage such establishments. It is encouraging to observe competent therapists in the remote correctional institutions. It is not nearly so often that supporting talents are found in headquarters offices in the capital cities. The consequences are to be seen in the institutions for juvenile offenders: Large institutions with large living units; heavily custodial staffs; programs emphasizing remedial and vocational education — these are the hall-marks of the contemporary training school. Some remarkable things are attempted in such places; it may well be that such institutions are for some kinds of juvenile offender the best that can be done.

Nevertheless, they seem like prisons for children. With all the hopes and ideas for their planners, boys and girls in such institutions are doing time and filling it in with a training program.

Is there any alternative? We have already mentioned the conviction of Heman Stark of the California Youth Authority that "there has to be a better way." That better way may be the Community Treatment Program described earlier in this chapter. It may be discovered in some other experiments in the treatment of juveniles. It seems unlikely that it will be found in the huge training schools in which hundreds of children are processed through well-meant but impersonal programs. There are clearly ways in which maximum advantage can be taken of facilities of this kind. But the limits are reached when numbers are so great that significant inmate-staff interactions can no longer take place. A version of the inmate culture so familiar in adult institutions takes over.

This persistence of the American institutional planner in the development of vast correctional communities is general throughout the industrial states. An excellent example of an uncompromising organization of juvenile institutions is to be found in the state of Washington. There, under the general direction of Dr. Garrett Heyns, the leadership exercised by Maurice Harmon has so far succeeded in rigorous adherence to principles as they are understood.

Washington, a middle-sized state, only recently afflicted with the problems of growth, is accustomed to small institutions; it has not been difficult to persuade the legislature and the public that increased demands on the system should lead to more small institutions rather than the expansion of existing facilities. It remains to be seen whether this principle can be maintained indefinitely against the economizers, as Washington proceeds toward ever more concentrated urbanization. But for the present, at least, we can see in this fortunate state the structure of a correctional apparatus for juvenile offenders which embodies the currently admired structural optima.

Small institutions are not necessarily good institutions. Let us begin with the Green Hill School at Chehalis which has had a turbulent career during more than seventy years of history. Looking at it now, a visitor is first impressed with small, well-designed cottages, neatly grouped around an unassuming administration building. The effect would be suited to a small boarding school if the nucleus of the original school did not loom above the new buildings. This consists of two large units for thirty-five boys apiece, side by side, so that rivalry between these houses can be continuous and expressed in catcalls and insults. The nights are thus often made hideous, but no more hideous than these repressive-looking structures were built to be in the first place. It is virtually an obsession with the Green Hill staff that somehow, some day soon, these dingy monstrosities must be replaced. One can sympathize with them; the comparison between old and new expresses volumes about the changing concepts of correctional treatment.

Green Hill is built to accommodate 176 boys and is usually overcrowded. Boys stay about nine months. The program is vocational training, with an emphasis on group-counseling. The structure for the group aspects of the program was clearly laid out for us by Superintendent Robert Quant:

> Our job is similar to what you would find in most training schools of our type. It's a matter of returning them to the community in such a shape that they will stay out of difficulty. We're operating a milieu-type program, with added socialization goals. It's not an intensive individual psychotherapy situation. But we have a large program of group discussion, conducted by our caseworkers and our clinical staff. Our consulting psychiatrist has been working with our personnel and with our cottage supervisors in techniques of handling groups. We hope to have our cottage supervisors leading discussions centering on cottage and institutional problems, with no real goal of insight therapy. Such sessions will be for the discussion of problems that the kids encounter. As we find boys who are showing us that they can use a group session well, we will move them into groups with our casework staff in which we will discuss social problems. It's here that we hope that some insight will be developed. Then we have a third group, an exit group, into which we move boys along about the time that parole can be anticipated. Here we discuss the situations the boys will run into after they leave the institution; there'll be a considerable amount of role-playing, beginning with board appearances and leading up to the touchy problems to be expected at home.

We asked whether the plan to use cottage supervisors, unversed in professional concepts, was a matter of expedience or of choice. Quant replied:

I think it's the latter. We're quite pleased with the progress we're making with our cottage personnel. In years past, the cottage staff has been looked at as some sort of bums who knew nothing. But our staff has made real progress as a result of our training program. They're getting some clinical awareness of which they weren't thought capable. We're making counselors out of them with a design in mind. After all, they're the ones who live with these kids; for the most part, they're the ones who do the most work with them. I think the main thing that has come out of this program is a status that the cottage parent never had before. Much more than he ever was before, he is now an important person. He realizes that when the administration talks about his importance — as training school superintendents have done for generations — we're not merely talking. He sees *why* he is important, and as a result feels important. Because he knows that he can contribute more, he *does* contribute more. He becomes more concerned with the kids he is working with.

We have cautioned our cottage staff that there are limitations on what they can do. We ask them to maintain the discussion on the level of problems that the kids are living with in the cottage and in the institution. We don't get off on "my mother," "my father," or family issues outside. We deal strictly with the living problems that we find here and how we feel about them.

Washington's new institutions are built around the cottage for sixteen inmates. We asked Quant how the planners arrived at this standard. His answer was typical of the solutions which are adopted for this problem in every place where we enquired:

At one time we were going to build cottages for twenty-four. But some of us felt that this was too large a unit for one man to supervise and do much more than the functions of a guard. From the first we were interested in the development of close relationships between cottage parents and kids. Referring to the publications of the Childrens Bureau we found that twelve was recommended as an ideal number. We thought that this was too small to justify for a large outlay. We settled on sixteen as a compromise figure and held to it. It has worked out beautifully for us, and we see no reason to change, even if we haven't arrived at it scientifically.

I like our new units. They all have individual rooms. The kids can be gregarious if they want to, but if a kid wants to be alone, he can really withdraw from the group. They're rather homey looking, comfortable — some people have said they're plush — and yet if the cottage is disturbed and upset they can be closed down into formidable bastilles. They're flexible except for size — you just can't put more than sixteen boys in them.

How long should a boy stay in an institution like this? Quant thought that this difficult question was not yet solved theoretically, but the Green Hill School is grounded on a practical solution:

It's rather an arbitrary thing with me. We know that óne kid can be ready to go home as soon as he walks in the door, and another perhaps should be here for twenty years. But I think that on the average if we could have kids for about eleven or twelve months — given the right staff — we could get them to the place that we really could be doing some good work with them. With our present program and staff, I don't think we could accomplish a great deal by keeping kids longer than we now keep them. Once we have a boy who has some awareness of his problems, some insight into them, and some ideas at least of how he can prevent their recurrence, well, if he has an acceptable and adequate parole plan we're ready to let him go.

But the Green Hill program begins before the boy arrives. Like many other correctional systems which involve several units, Washington's Bureau of Juvenile Rehabilitation begins its program at a Diagnostic Center, now located in new quarters in the metropolitan area of Tacoma. At the time of our survey, this part of the operation was implausibly located in a deactivated army post on the remote tip of the Olympic peninsula at Port Townsend. This large establishment, Fort Worden, is still in use as a treatment institution. Taking advantage of space and a profusion of well-maintained military buildings, the staff has surprised itself with the effectiveness with which they have been able to conduct a program in quarters never intended for correctional purposes. From the beginning, much thought was given to the first impressions created for the whole system by the first impressions of Fort Worden. It was foreseen that the distance, the long ride through unfamiliar and wild looking country, the forbidding and austere appearance of an old army post would be unnerving to a newly arrived boy or girl. Superintendent E. G. Lindquist summarized for us the problem and its solutions:

This is a forbidding looking place. When kids are driven in here and they see these huge buildings, the very size of the place is frightening. So I think that it's very important in this facility — which isn't pretty to look at — that the staff approach to the kids should communicate from the first what we want them to know. Kids will behave the way you honestly expect them to.

The kinds of things you concentrate on as a staff will be the kinds of things that get their attention. If you concentrate on runaways, you get runaways. If you concentrate on an individualized approach to kids they'll be very much aware of this. The touches which you can give to the cottage unit to produce a home-like, pleasant atmosphere are important. What we have tried to accomplish seems to be working. There's a grapevine from which we get a lot of help. When we first started, two years ago, and the word was not around, kids were frightened of the place. It sounded like Siberia and looked a little like it too. But now the kids know, if they know anything at all, that Fort Worden is not a place where they are going to get beaten up.

We've been concerned about the nonverbal communication of the institution. In the physical renovation of the plant we've tried for a pleasant atmosphere, repainting the olive drab with bright colors. The return communication from the kids has been favorable. We've had no destruction of furniture. Runaways are such a minor problem that we hardly think about it — we've had only twenty-four in the last twelve months.

Not only the delinquents sent to Fort Worden have been affected by this approach. Mr. Lindquist went on to tell us:

It has to be said that there's also a parallel grapevine among the juvenile court judges and staff. When the training schools were operating as they did ten years ago, the attitude of the juvenile court judges when they committed a boy was, "we're kissing you good-bye, sonny." There has been a tremendous increase in the acceptance of our program, so that instead of the judges reflecting a community rejection of the kids as they talk to them, they are actually promoting our program. The initial shove the kid gets is positive experience. It was only a few years ago that the judges were saying, "Well, we put you on probation a few times but you didn't make it. You're no good and now we're going to send you down the river. When you get a taste of that, you'll wish you'd behaved yourself." By and large they're telling them now that when they get here they'll get help from a psychiatrist or a caseworker. There is still a little guilt on the part of the probation staff at actually having to institutionalize a kid, so sometimes they sugar-coat the process so much that it's misleading.

From this point, the chief of the Bureau of Juvenile Rehabilitation, Maurice Harmon, extrapolated a conclusion with which not everyone will agree:

I think that instead of being the last resort, our institutions now increasingly being seen as the best result. Instead of keeping kids on probation for year after year and offense after offense, maybe long after they themselves have felt that they needed to be contained, the courts are sending kids to us when they begin to feel that they need an institutional experience of the kind that we can offer. We're getting kids at a younger age than we used to; I don't think it's simply a direct relationship to an increase in the population of younger kids, but rather a willingness to commit them when commitment is needed. This should mean a great deal in terms of the impact on the eventual prison population. We can help many of these kids at twelve that we can't really touch when they're sixteen. If we're right about this, the penitentiaries won't be getting them at twenty.

What is sought in the elaborate process of diagnosis that goes on at Fort Worden? Superintendent Lindquist and his assistant, Robert Tropp, thought that practical distinctions should be made. Mr. Tropp put it this way:

We're not particularly using the standard nomenclature of the American Psychiatric Association as a primary tool, except when by coincidence it happens that we have a neurotic kid and we're sure of it. Usually we consider a boy's stay here as a fair sample of his behavior in different situations; we try to pull together our observations of that behavior in different situations; we try to pull together our observations of that behavior in as many ways as we can.

We try to think about problems, and about programs that are relevant to the problems. It's difficult to be highly specific, especially when you're sending a kid to another institution. We can be specific about a kid needing a private room instead of a dorm, for example. We can sometimes spell out the particular kind of staff person to whom we think a kid will respond. Then there's school — can he profit from it? Should he go for just part of the day or all day? And we have to think about whether it would be a good investment of clinical time to put the kid into intensive counseling. What I'm talking about is our effort to examine the total facets of the kid's personality, making use of all the professions and skills at our disposal.

What use can be made of all this subtle information? The program choices are not numerous. Green Hill provides a vocational training program with a varied group-counseling experience. Luther Burbank School provides mostly remedial education. Fort Worden itself has an intensive treatment program and an "annex" into which overflow (beyond the quotas provided at the other institutions) can be accommodated. Finally, there are four forestry camps, providing programs of vigorous work assignments and group counseling.

But the distribution of juvenile clients among these institutions is based on a careful differentiation of their needs. The foundation of success is that the children themselves *feel* understood because they *are* understood. Not all advanced programs are nearly as concerned about the question of diagnosis but focus on other aspects of correctional treatment. It is characteristic of the Washington program that all aspects receive meticulous attention. Thomas Pinnock, the superintendent of Maple Lane School, the handsome girls' institution, in considering the comfortable but elegant appearance of that establishment commented:

It's my feeling that the children at any institution should know what's going on administratively, especially in the financial area. The children who come to us feel that the community is down on them, that they're here because nobody else wants them. The State of Washington has no use for them so they're put in Maple Lane. But even these children can grasp that when the state will spend $5,555 a year on each that they're not exactly being rejected. I use this information positively. The citizens of Washington *do* care about you! Why would they build a cottage for $110,000 for sixteen girls? They built it for you because they think you're worthwhile.

The same care that goes into the design of buildings at Maple Lane goes into the clinical studies at Fort Worden and the training and counseling programs at Green Hill. The maintenance of professional conditions and attitudes toward clients creates a reciprocal expectation of positive results. Washington has shown that through a combination of professionalism and generosity some long steps can be taken toward solving the problems of delinquents instead of containing the offenders.

THE SHORT-TERM PROGRAM FOR THE JUVENILE OFFENDER

Most correctional terms for adults are short, and not much can be said for them. The deterrent effect of a few weeks in a noxious lock-up surely exists, but research has nowhere been applied to finding out what kinds of offenders are deterred. Because the short term of correction for adults is a problem with little interest as compared to that of the major criminal and his predicament in serving a long sentence, the jail has neither been studied nor has its treatment potentiality been seriously exploited.

But for some kinds of juvenile offenders, correctional professionals feel, the short term is relevant.

Earlier we described the British detention center. Here, in an effort to achieve a deterrent effect, some additional gains have apparently been made. First, it has been shown that the long and complex borstal term is unnecessary for some classes of delinquents; the detention centers get at least as good results as the average borstal with a class of delinquent not demonstrably different from the borstal boy.[40] Second, the detention center seems to have shown that a three months' interruption in a delinquent career may be all that is required for some younger offenders, granted some support by the casework staff. Third, the detention center creates a social situation in which interactions among individuals are so brief and superficial that an inmate culture cannot be created.

These propositions are merely tentative; besides, we are aware of the adverse criticism of a system which must for many delinquents oversimplify the problems which caused their behavior. However, this simple system of institutional care does achieve positive results for some unclearly defined classes of delinquents. This finding should spark an examination of the appropriate enrichments of the short term for specific categories of juvenile offenders.

At this point in the fairly recent development of such programs, we are not really able to show that anything which occurs in the course of the short term is peculiarly effective in producing any special consequence. It may well be that the process of subjecting the delinquent to an experience of control is more important than anything which has yet been designed to occur in the course of that experience.

Three enterprises in short-term confinement illustrate some of the possibilities, though in none of them can a finding be made about the content of the program.

We begin with Highfields in New Jersey, without attempting an exhaustive description of an establishment so thoroughly studied.[41] We are interested here in relating Highfields to a movement toward constructive short-term residential care for delinquents. The reader unfa-

---

[40] It must also be allowed that there has been no showing that many detention-center inmates might not have function just as well in an adequate probation program, or in the California Community Treatment program, aimed at much the same kind of delinquent.

[41] Lloyd W. McCorkle, Albert Elias, and F. Lovell Bixby, *The Highfields Story* (New York: Holt, 1958); H. Ashley Weeks, *Youthful Offenders at Highfields* (Ann Arbor: The University of Michigan Press, 1958).

miliar with this profoundly significant program is urged to refer to
the basic sources.

Highfields opened in 1950 as a residential center for twenty seriously
delinquent New Jersey boys, generally limited to sixteen and seven-
teen-year-olds. Occupying a large country home, it aims for an identity entirely different from the conventional correctional institution.
It does not attempt to be a self-contained unit. The residents are on
probation rather than committed to terms of incarceration. So far as
can be arranged, they are kept in contact with the community for
such services as the community can afford them.

The center is a residence, as its official name — the Highfields Residential Treatment Center — implies. Boys live and receive treatment
there, but they are neither out of sight nor out of mind. During the
four months stay which is standard, they go under escort into Hope-
well, the nearby town, for church, movies, haircuts, and sociability.
They are allowed week-end furloughs home at least twice during
their stay. Absences from the Highfields grounds must be in the company of a responsible adult, but such occasions are fairly frequent.

All residents work at the New Jersey Neuropsychiatric Institute, not
far from the Highfields grounds, mostly at farm labor. The pay is
fifty cents a day, and the work is intended to be reasonably arduous.
This employment is not considered a training experience; boys learn
no skills at Highfields. But it is an essential part of treatment, partly
as an introduction to relationships which develop on any job, and
partly because it provides interpersonal relationships which the boys
discuss in evening sessions of "guided group interaction."

The evening groups meet nightly in two sessions of ten. Boys are
free to absent themselves if they choose; when we visited there were
no absences. The term, "guided group interaction," has been adopted
to distinguish it from group therapy, but at Highfields practice seems
to have conferred on it an identity of its own. The focus is on the
daily life of the community. The irritants of interaction among the
members of the group are plucked from the day's events for frank,
and sometimes rather heavy-handed discussion. The model of guided
group interaction is simple, but essential to its ideology is the conviction that as groups pass in and out of Highfields they themselves
participate in adapting it. When we visited the center, the residents
had adopted a pattern about which the director, Albert Elias, was not
too happy. Each resident had his day in the group, a day in which

he spoke freely about how he felt about everything happening to him at Highfields; in reply, the rest of the group was expected to say frankly how they felt about him. One boy, approaching the end of his stay, discussed his plans, while the rest of the group, also not far from the time of their release, criticized them freely and skeptically. At the end of the session, one member asserted, "Well, *I* think he's ready!" No one else voiced a dissent, and presently another member asked, "How about you, Mr. M——, do *you* think he's ready?" The staff leader grinned and nodded, at which point a modest pandemonium broke loose, with congratulations, pounding on the back, and hearty embraces.

The administrative limits on intake to Highfields are in principle defined. Age, legal status as a first offender, absence of gross clinical abnormalities (such as mental illness, mental defect, or sexual deviation) are the principal technical criteria. The staff in informal discussion is by no means sure of the theoretical position of these or other criteria. For example, one boy was referred to in a group session as "too crazy for us — he sure don't belong in Highfields." (The boy belonged to the other group, he was not present for this appraisal.) The staff agreed that the residents had correctly evaluated the boy as psychotic beyond ordinary acceptance. It seemed that he had been incorrectly diagnosed, and that the court, though aware of his bizarre and unpredictable behavior, had wanted to send him to Highfields to avoid a more severe and potentially damaging commitment to a reformatory or to a mental hospital. But though the difficulties in accommodating him to the Highfields program were almost immediately manifest, so too were the benefits. Mutely resistive at first, the boy unexpectedly responded to the daily life of the group and calmed down. At the time of our visit, when he had been with the group for a couple of weeks, he was able to contribute to discussion and seemed to be becoming an adequate group member. "It's this kind of experience, happening to all sorts of marginal people that we get, which leads us to an almost mystical faith that the group is omnipotent," Elias told us.

Acting on this faith, Highfields staff offers no individual treatment. Boys approaching staff members with problems are urged to solve them in the group. This works. In the group a boy with a problem will be faced with a profane skepticism, a needling, almost jeering criticism, all grounded on what seems to be solid, virile concern. Implicit in the proceedings is the image of the Highfields youth, a masculine, tough, worldly-wise young man. His attitudes and values will not have changed as a result of the Highfields experience, but he will be "wised up" to the realities of a society in which certain kinds of behavior will foul you up more than the satisfactions are worth. To face these realities as required by success in this society requires the shedding of rationalizations and the recognition of reactions to frustration for what they are. Perhaps one of the most successful features of correctional group-counseling is the intolerance of such groups for the rationalization and their ready perception of the frustration reaction. These attributes are found in abundance in the Highfields model.

The implicit ideal of the Highfields youth who stands up like a man, who scorns the use of such crutches as rationalization, projection, and self-pity, and who is trying hard to keep from getting fouled up again, is an image which contributes more than an example to the Highfields resident. It offers a certain self-confidence, an assurance that comes from knowing the truth about the world and oneself. For some youths, this is all the help needed. For others, this image is an ingredient of the required assistance. For still others, it is probably irrelevant.

In his analysis of the Highfields program, Jenkins [42] distinguishes between adaptive and maladaptive delinquency. Adaptive delinquency is defined as "goal-oriented behavior based on design and skill." Maladaptive delinquency is "response to frustration." In Jenkins' view, adaptive delinquency must be thwarted, while maladaptive delinquency must be corrected by reducing the frustration which caused it. Immersion in this culture of virile interdependence will attack maladaptive delinquency by proving that a person can do without rationalizations. For the adaptive delinquent it offers the satisfactions of the gang and the hard-boiled self-respect which comes from a determination not to "mess up" again. Since each boy at Highfields has something of each delinquent component within him, it is reasonable to expect that the program will have an impact on him from both directions.

So far as it goes, in creating for stigmatized and delinquency-oriented boys a credible and acceptable means of complying with social norms, Highfields has provided an alternative to psychotherapy. No longer are the cliches of "acceptance," "rapport," "complexes," and

---

[42] Weeks, *ibid.*, pp. 149–156.

the like given professional circulation in the absence of relevant ter-
minology. What the boys hear in the group and work situations is
natural, purposeful, and practical. The program stands on its own,
without explanation or rationalization by the staff. As an exercise in
social science elegance it is not equaled by many other exploratory
programs.

Its success in the terms of over-all recidivism, which are inevitably
applied to corrections, is not outstanding. Compared with its control
group at Annandale, the New Jersey State Reformatory conventionally used for this age group, Highfields is significantly more effective for Negro boys only. Its Caucasian releases are about the same
for serious law violators.[43] However, when boys returned to court
as unsuitable for Highfields are eliminated from the data, the contrast
between Highfields and Annandale becomes significant: Eight of every ten Highfields boys complete the first year after release without
unfavorable incident, compared with only five of every ten Annandale
boys. In this subanalysis, the differential in favor of Highfields is 17
per cent for the white boys and 50 per cent for the Negro boys.

Weeks does not attribute the difference in performance between
Highfields and Annandale Negroes to any selection factors. No identifiable difference can be traced between the two groups. Jenkins finds
a satisfying explanation in the contrasting situations of the Negro youth
in the conventional northern prison and in Highfields.[44] In the former,
rationalized hostility to white authority produces motivations for aggressive behavior which are rewarded by status. This is a combination which, as Jenkins notes, can hardly be expected to result in a
rehabilitative effect.[45] By contrast, at Highfields, antagonism toward
authority, the law, and the white race, too, is reduced by friendly
contacts in fairly intimate groups with Caucasian youths who have
had some of the same experiences and feel some of the same requirements. For the Negro youth, the image of the tough guy who dis-
dains the crutches of projection and rationalization may be even

---

[43] For a full analysis of the data of Weeks, *ibid.*, pp. 118–128.

[44] *Ibid.*, pp. 154–155.

[45] It might also be added that for the Negro who is not equipped to succeed in
aggressive behavior, the consequences of a term in such a setting may be even
more disastrous, resulting in a retreatist adaptation in which failure is even more in
prospect than for the aggressive youth because all incentives to social goals have
proved inapplicable.

more nourishing than for his white contemporary. The "cool stud" who is widely admired in Negro urban life is not necessarily an overt delinquent.

Weeks therefore cautions against a segregated Highfields. Inter-racial interaction is certainly a necessary condition for the success of Negroes; it may also help white residents. The delinquent act is seldom an inter-racial event, but delinquency is a phenomenon to which all races are subject. The intimacy with Negro youths required in Highfields, requires the white youth to give attention to the universality of his problem, to forget the particular situations which seem to get him into trouble and which provide the starting points for new rationalizations.

Based on the success of Highfields, New Jersey has proceeded with the development of additional residential treatment centers, including one for girls. Skeptics may argue that once the pioneering novelty of the experimental phase has passed, bureaucracy will set in and the discrepancy between the results of Highfields and Annandale will no longer be so apparent. Yet it is difficult to overlook the economic and social differences between institutional control of the offender for four months, as at Highfields, and his confinement for a year or so at Annandale. In money cost to the state, the care of the youth at Highfields is about a third as expensive as at Annandale.

Much further research should be done on the Highfields model. Now that it has been replicated in a circuit of such centers, it should be possible to mount an attack on such questions as differential effects of the program on different classes of delinquent, and on the nature of the process by which these effects are achieved. In addition to research into the process, further attention should be given to the persistent problem of bridging the transition from the institution to the community, which afflicts Highfields as much as the conventional correctional institution. In the residential treatment center New Jersey has contributed a valuable model to the future of corrections. It is not complete, and its full utility cannot be established until the process is fully understood and complemented by an adequate after-care system. But in the meantime it is of great service to delinquents fortunate enough to have been selected for the experience.

The maintenance of some integration with the whole community is a challenge which has been picked up by a related program, the Pinehills experiment of Provo, Utah. Directly inspired by Highfields' success, its designer, Dr. LaMar T. Empey, reduces the components of the program to productive work and guided group interaction; the boys are left at home. From the first, this enterprise has been paralleled by a massive research program rigorously based on a research design which logically enough compares the Pinehills population to control groups of boys placed on probation or in the Utah State Reformatory. No attempt is made to limit the population to any particular classes of any typology. On a random basis, the juvenile-court judge selects boys for Pinehills after the decision whether commitment to an institution or to probation has been made. Age limits are fifteen to seventeen, and the length of stay varies between three and six months. Results are not yet available, but a full description of the program has been published.[46] The ultimate place of the Pinehills model in the correctional armamentarium is yet to be decided. The assumption, common to Highfields and Pinehills, is that guided group interaction, by removing peer support for delinquent behavior, will produce conforming behavior not at variance with working-class culture. This is an assumption which is likely to be more effective with delinquents who feel that the culture around them supports their delinquency. To the extent that delinquency results from psychological rather than social problems, the effect of such programs is likely to be diminished.

We should not conclude this discussion of short-term programing for the juvenile offender without some reference to the New Haven Borstal Institution of South Burnaby, near Vancouver, British Columbia. After World War II, when juvenile delinquency increased, many persons in government and the courts who had seen military service overseas were familiar with the British patterns of institutional care. It was decided that youths should not be confined in the old and highly conventional Oakalla Gaol if it could be avoided. Agreed that a borstal should be established, the nucleus of a borstal staff was recruited in England; under this arrangement, S. Rocksborough Smith was invited to initiate this enterprise. Smith was a disciple of Sir Alexander Paterson and a veteran of the North Sea Camp borstal, well known for the strenuous regime it imposes on both staff and inmates. The pattern adopted at New Haven was more moderate. A large and

---

[46] LaMar T. Empey and Jerome Rabow, "The Provo Experiment in Delinquency Rehabilitation," *Proceedings of the 90th Congress of Corrections* (Denver, Colorado: 1960), pp. 304–316.

comfortable old house was chosen as the center of the establishment. Dormitories and work shops were added, built so far as possible by the boys. A greatly modified borstal regime was designed, based on a length of stay varying from six to nine months for youths between the ages of sixteen and twenty-three. At first the capacity was set at fifty; later, experience seemed to indicate that forty was the limit for the intimacy of contact and the sense of community on which the program was to be built.

A staff of sixteen carries out the British Columbia version of borstal treatment. The roles provided for include the director, an assistant director-housemaster, a social worker, vocational instructors, borstal officers, and a clerical person for typing, filing, and miscellaneous duties. No formal counseling or casework in the conventional sense seems to take place. Instead the emphasis is on purposeful communication in daily life, with much variety of activity. Vocational training fills up much of the day, but with a twist of emphasis which puts it in an unusual light. Mr. J. P. Davies, the assistant director, and a man who has been with the borstal from the beginning, told us:

New Haven is meant to be a character-building institution rather than a vocational training center. We use the trades as a therapy, just as a hospital uses them for convalescents. Our aim is to develop in the young man who comes here some leadership qualities if we can, and reliability if we can't. We use the shops, the farm, and the kitchen as therapies to take them through to attainment of the qualities of a good worker.

The result is a vocational training philosophy which sets a premium on self-reliance, initiative, and resourcefulness. Built into the tasks are awkward problems to solve, or challenges to exercise some originality in design or in technique. Hobby and interest groups together with an active athletic program complete the treatment plan.

From the first, release planning is stressed. For New Haven, the plan is based on a Borstal Association of more than a hundred volunteer sponsors scattered throughout the province. Where possible, a sponsor works with the boy from the time he has completed orientation to the time of discharge. For boys from remote parts of the province an interim sponsor is provided. Under the general direction of a social work staff, the sponsors are expected to help with job-finding, housing, and getting the boy as well-established as possible in the community. Because New Haven sets such store by this arrangement a degree of enthusiasm for the program is achieved which seems unusual for volunteer activities in corrections.

The spirit of New Haven is evident in other ways. At the time of our observations, the director was the most recently employed member of the staff. Nearly everyone else was an old-timer, good-humoredly grousing a little about being underpaid but obviously proud of participating in an institutional program which demands teamwork and craftsmanship from the staff. As in any really good correctional institution the staff climate is optimistic, fascinated with the variety of problems encountered, and delighted with opportunities for shop talk.

But the most impressive evidence of the institution's complete cohesion is the New Haven Alumni Association. Unique, so far as we know, this association called itself into being as a response to an emergent threat to the survival of the borstal. In 1958, with the activation of the Haney Correctional Institution, the provincial government proposed the closing of New Haven. Haney is a British Columbian adaptation of California necessities — large, complex, and specialized establishments for the confinement of considerable numbers of offenders. Its existence was a controversial expenditure of public funds: it continues to be the focus of debate about correctional policy in the province. A group of young men who had a common feeling of gratitude to New Haven formed an *ad hoc* association to prevent its closing. The movement gained momentum with speeches by members before church groups and luncheon clubs, culminating in fifteen thousand signatures to a petition opposing the end of New Haven. The association's objective was won, but it remained in existence and at the service of the borstal.

Some members become eligible for the sponsorship of inmates and licensees through the Borstal Association. Others participate in monthly "fireside chats," at which the practice problems of inmates awaiting their return to the community are discussed, and without any staff present. The unprecedented loyalty of these former inmates to a correctional institution which served them well is an unplanned asset to the operation of New Haven. It is a powerful reinforcement of the morale of staff and inmates alike and a capitalization on common loyalties familiar in colleges and schools, but encountered only as a subterranean force in correctional situations.

Between the development of a strong probation system and the need of Haney for amenable inmates the character of New Haven is chang-

ing. More and more it is being seen as a treatment resource for the
emotionally disturbed offender. The staff, confident of the basic sound-
ness of what they are doing, views this trend without alarm. With
the consultation of a psychiatrist and the presence of a psychiatric
social worker on the staff, there is no doubt in this community that
it can handle effectively whatever comes its way.

The confrontation between Haney and New Haven is a dramatic
example of the contemporary correctional dilemma. Huge, modern,
efficient, magnificently equipped, yet impersonal in spite of sincere
efforts to individualize treatment, Haney is the answer to the problem of numbers. What other problems it can answer has yet to be seen.
Small, idiosyncratic, and comparatively expensive New Haven is the
British Columbian concession to a social conscience which knows that
containment can never be enough, and that the values of a good
family and community life which most delinquents have missed can
never be gained in the corridors and cell blocks of a large correctional
facility. That this dilemma can be resolved in favor of treatment
rather than containment is seen in localities as far apart as Sweden,
New Jersey, Utah, and British Columbia. It all depends on the vision
and magnanimity of the community.

FROM EXILE TO CORRECTION

The roots of the modern correctional institution are deep in the
retributivist traditions of the race. The prison as a place for punishment is a place of banishment in more respects than correctional administrators like to face. When offenders could no longer be executed
or transported, they were banished behind secure walls where they
could offend no more nor could they be seen. From the time that
rehabilitative services were first introduced in prisons there has been
an implicit movement to modify the banishment to the extent that
this could be safely done in the interest of solving the offender's problem rather than perpetuating it. Probation, parole, and various other
remissions have vastly reduced the numbers of men, women, and children exiled from the community. We are now searching for a form
of correctional service which will maintain more control than the
field services afford but which at the same time keeps the offender
as close to the community as security will allow.

Such devices as the Huber Plan of Wisconsin have for many years
kept offenders at productive work in the community, usually for pri-

vate employers, while requiring them to reside in jail. Some California sheriffs, notably in Marin County, have provided for week-end confinement so that employed offenders need not give up their jobs. Such devices are not belittled if they are classified as enlightened deterrents. Although far less destructive than the conventional jail, if only because the productive life of the offender is not disrupted, these plans are still punitive. Punishment is still necessary for the maintenance of social control, but its refinement is a matter of expedience rather than design. To our knowledge none of these plans attempt to use the time in confinement for administration of a treatment program. Still, they break hard and fast forms of punishment and modify them into patterns which conserve the offender. For some classes of correctional clients these plans seem to be all that is necessary; they serve their nights or week-ends in jail and sin no more. The question persists, of course, whether even this vestige of confinement really performs a useful function in society. It would be valuable to examine the issue in terms of the comparative effects of these plans on offenders with delinquent identifications (as for example, traffic-law violators), and on those who have to some extent committed themselves to a criminal pattern. Pending the interesting research which could be done, the value of the Huber Plan and its derivatives is in the demonstration that exile need not be total.

This demonstration has certainly contributed to the development of the hostel or halfway-house idea. In the evolution of the hostel, the English seem to have been the leaders, though adaptations of the idea can be found elsewhere in Europe. The beginnings seem to have been in the probation hostel, a special adaptation of the probation system, designed to help the young man or woman who is without a suitable home and in need of detachment from the scene of the delinquency.

Because the probation hostel is hard to staff and difficult to run, it has very limited application. A unit of the Home Office supervises the probation hostels, but most are operated under religious auspices. Situated in the large cities, they accommodate about twenty each, between the ages of sixteen and twenty-one. Generally the hostel's purpose of separating the youth from his usual haunts is accomplished by taking only boys who live at an inconvenient distance.

At St. John's Hostel in Leeds, for example, most residents are Londoners, with a sprinkling from the Midlands and from Liverpool.

Occupying a large old home in a still middle-class neighborhood, the hostel accommodates nineteen boys. A warden and his wife and daughter provide a comfortable home-like setting. They are assisted by a student on leave from Oxford and a cook. The Catholic archdiocese of Liverpool takes a benevolent interest in the establishment, providing volunteer services and assisting the warden to some extent in finding employment for his charges. The hostelers are placed under the supervision of the Leeds probation office and usually remain for about nine months. The maximum length of stay is a year.

Boys are required to work at employment found for them by the warden and to pay their way from their earnings. They are allowed fifteen shillings a week in pocket money; the rest of their earnings must be saved. Most boys save about £35 during their stay, which is thought in itself to be some assurance against further delinquency.

The hostel's formal program is divided among group discussions, religious instruction, and recreation. The warden and his assistant try to maintain a friendly counseling relationship with each hosteler, but neither is equipped to function at a level of formal treatment.

It is a benign, well-intentioned program which must be moderately helpful to the few boys to whom it becomes available. The warden could give us no data on the per-capita cost, though supplementation of the boys' room and board at a rate of £3 per head suggests that the figure must be more than £150 a year. But the economics of hostel operation is not the crucial factor. The problem has been to find competent people willing to live the abnormal lives required of hostel wardens. Even with some relief, the hostel warden finds himself at work primarily during the leisure hours of everyone else. Confined to his establishment, he finds his social life limited to the company of his charges. Without a professional identification with either the probation service or other occupations, his is a lonely existence. Many simple solutions to a problem which drastically limits the usefulness of the hostel as a treatment device could be advanced and have doubtless been considered. At this time, however, the inherent opportunities for the design of a therapeutic community are going begging.

A much more lively application of the hostel idea is found in the prisons. Under the Criminal Justice Act of 1948, the system of preventive detention was set up as a separate punishment stream. The long terms meted out were divided into three stages, the last of which could be served in a hostel in which the prisoner worked in industry residing in a special unit set aside on the prison reservation. These units are rather self-consciously "deprisonized," but achieve an austerely individualistic appearance. Quite unlike any other living accommodations we can think of, we suppose that the time will come when someone's cheerfully bare but obviously remodeled quarters will be compared to a prison hostel.

From its origins in the preventive-detention system, the hostel has spread to most of the large prisons in the metropolitan centers. Its operation has been kept simple. Each hosteler is approved for placement by the prison board of visitors. As soon as a job is found for him, he can be placed in the unit, there to serve out the remainder of his term. Selection is based on capricious standards; the boards of visitors being made up of local magistrates, the inclination is for each board to set its own operational standards, although, of course, the rules of the Prison Commission cannot be overstepped. This allows considerable latitude. In our occasional observation, the tendency of the boards was to rivet their attention on the past and to assume that the future would be more of the same. Thus the comparatively mild recidivist with a still loyal family would be afforded a hostel plan which he neither needed nor particularly wanted as a concession to his deserts, whereas an unattached drifter without plans for the future would be denied the hostel as a judgment on his lack of worth. To some extent prison governors used the hostel arrangement as a means of providing an incentive for conforming behavior during the dreary years of preventive detention.

Hostelers are required to save, and some save notable sums. It is not uncommon for a man to accumulate as much as £200, which gives all concerned a confident feeling about the future as he leaves the hostel to go on his own. Aside from attention to the economics of hostel life and a requirement that a fairly simple set of rules be followed, the men are left on their own. It is here that an opportunity seems to be missed. In talking to many of them it was apparent that leisure time was a serious problem, that life in this kind of a group presented strains which were difficult for individuals to discuss. They were especially difficult for the inarticulate, thoroughly institutionalized "old lags" fearfully emerging from seemingly endless careers at such prisons as Parkhurst or Chelmsford. Isolated from each other by distrust and years of indoctrination in doing one's own time, each man clung with fervor to the simple faith that this time he was going to make it because he had to, but each man was equally sure that few, if any of his mates would be equally successful. In a group discussion with several of them we elicited the expected agreement that all prisons were terrible and destructive places, but that this was especially true of the prison from which the individual speaking had come. Particularly with the preventive detention hostelers was it true that the past looked barren and bleak while the future was grounded on hopes irrelevant to the past. Though group-counseling has become a significant part of the Prison Department's program, the opportunity to use it as a means of making the hostel experience a dynamic one rather than one last impediment before release has not been taken.

Nevertheless, faltering though it is, and without statistical evidence of success, the hostel idea appears to be a step ahead. The program goes on with hardly any unfavorable incidents; the trouble which hostelers get into occurs after their departure from this meager shelter. Its use as a reward for good behavior over a long term confounds its improvement. In an understandable desire to make one means serve as many ends as possible, the Prison Department has introduced the hostel to reward those "good" prisoners who are also being rewarded with a remission of time, while denying it as a treatment device to the "bad" prisoners who are denied this remission. Because correctional practice so seriously needs to explore new means of reducing the terms of exile for major offenders, it is to be hoped that the Department will examine the hostel in terms of its differential effects. Its probable benefits for the resocialization of the recidivist are obvious but still potential. Neither the method of selection nor the program itself are conceptualized as treatment and considered in terms of the trains of events to be expected from each choice of action. Instead, as in so many correctional innovations, the whole enterprise has been approached with the slap-dash enthusiasm which half-bakes an idea but fails to install the means of determining whether the idea is good or how its execution could be improved.

Concern about the problem of the released prisoner has brought forth yet another new service in England, this time under private auspices. Confronted by the bleak future of the released recidivist, the Norman House movement has accumulated some impressive experience in the operation of small hostels for unattached former prisoners. Under the zealous but hard-headed leadership of Merfyn Turner, a conscientious objector who had seen much prison life during

World War II, a small community and a considerable tradition has been built around the notion that in the recidivists' isolation lies the source of his successive defeats. Beginning in 1955, with ideas brought to England from Denmark and Sweden and support provided by the London Parochial Charities, Norman House has grown into a model for a number of such communities throughout England and Northern Ireland.

Turner has reported on the Norman House experience with warm and thoughtful detail in *Safe Lodging*,[47] but without making excessive claims in its behalf. He has focused on a defined feature of the crime problem, and in Norman House has proposed a solution which depends heavily on good will as well as on relevant method.

Norman House stands for involvement. We who live and work there are not social surgeons who diagnose the illness and prescribe the remedy. Neither do we at the other extreme . . . condone criminal behavior, unless by condonation is meant the acceptance of the offender as he is while offering him and ourselves the chance, through living together, of becoming something better than we are. The inability to form deep and satisfactory relationships is an important factor in the failure of the inadequate offender. Crime is not often his first choice. Often it is not even his last choice, but the last link . . . in a personal-economic-social chain of factors over which his control is but relative.

The homeless men . . . who come to Norman House . . . need to learn to live with their fellow men. In the past, the process of learning has not proceeded far because they had no anchorage, nobody to help protect them from their own immature reactions to simple situations which well-integrated members of society take in their stride. Norman House offers that anchor. Living in a state of belonging, accepted as members of the family, and not . . . as society's rejects and objects of charity, they see for the first time in their lives, the true nature of "going straight."

To accomplish this involvement, Norman House consists of a "warden" and his immediate family living with the former prisoners, usually numbering about fifteen. Dire predictions of early failure preceded its establishment. Five eventful years later, Turner was able to report:

. . . almost two hundred men had lived at the House . . . and only one of them returned to prison while he was still living with us. But what was hap-

---

[47] Merfyn Turner, *Safe Lodging* (London: Hutchinson, 1961).

pening at the House was something much bigger than the problem of crime and prison. For us it had become a lesson in living. Crime brought us together. Its renunciation kept us together. Crime was a symptom of maladjustment and disturbance. The appearance or the disappearance of the symptom was of secondary importance in relation to the work we were attempting to do.

Turner tells us that the length of stay at Norman House varied from twenty minutes to twenty months. But the value of the experience was to be found in the sense of involvement in a community in which concern was a common denominator. Whether the gains thus made can survive separation from the house remains to be seen; Turner is not sanguine on this point. But the experience does seem to demonstrate that this is the kind of support which former prisoners can use to good effect. Turner tells us why:

We had often wondered whether the cult of non-involvement, which still commands a strong following among social workers, was advanced less by the force of scientific argument . . . than by considerations for the emotional comfort and well-being of the social worker. Involvement in the life of the offender sometimes meant recovering emotions from the condition of refrigeration into which the offender had placed them. Criminal behavior was the only contact some offenders had with society. . . .

Our experience taught us the paramount importance of our relationship with the offender. . . . It seemed to us self-evident that men who had been deprived in their childhood, and whose criminal behavior was in part at least a manifestation of it, needed to be compensated for their loveless upbringing before adjustment could begin to assume the shape of reality. Punishment, with which they familiar, and which they had long before learnt to accept as a natural consequence of the things they did, could achieve nothing. It hardened their attitudes toward society. Even if by some unexpected chance it ended their criminality, it could do nothing to make them happier men and acceptable citizens.

Interest in the transition between prison and community expresses the intuitions shared by many that the contrast between the regime of dependency required by the institution and the independence which is the essence of life outside. Norman House represents a bridge for that gap which is available at least to a few. Its principal ingredient cannot be allowed for in a public budget; the concern and sense of involvement which it demands from staff are beyond fiscal value.

Nevertheless, some options are available to the public service. Although the interaction on which Norman House is based depends on the presence of people who can look at their own lives and the lives of others in ways which are spontaneously concerned, it can also be conceded that half a loaf is better than none. Drawing on the experience of mental-health organizations, the California Department of Corrections is proceeding with plans for "halfway houses," in which the disillusioned loneliness of the parolee in a flop house is supplanted by residence in somewhat less septic conditions and within the context of official supervision. As envisioned at the time of this writing, the halfway house will be the nucleus for a community correctional center in which as many functions of the correctional apparatus as possible will be kept in the community rather than carried out in banishment behind stone walls. On this line of development the next advances toward the correctional future seem most likely to be made. How far they will carry us toward a a rational equilibrium of needs and resources will not be seen for years to come. But there is nothing in the basic design of the community correctional center that would exclude Merfyn Turner. The essential problem would be to find the source of such people in a community still focused on the market place rather than on man himself.

CONCLUSIONS:

In this chapter we have sought to describe the steps toward correc-tional advance: The first step is to describe the problem in terms of its human dimensions. Some new departures in the realm of typological classifications have been discussed. Further activity along these lines is needed, particularly in cultures other than Anglo-Saxon.

The second step is the development of new correctional models. We need not be forever frozen to the conventional institution of restraint mixed with middle-class helpfulness, to the probation and parole organization coping impossibly with caseloads beyond reasonable possibility of organization. Rather than accommodating treatment to the exigencies of institutional structure, we must design new kinds of correctional structure built for the treatment method adopted. In many described examples, this process, so obvious in conceptualization, so difficult in application, has been evident. The Community Treatment program of the California Youth Authority, which we have studied as an example of the use of a descriptive typology as a basis for correctional advance, brilliantly demonstrates the process of fitting organizational form to treatment process. Similarly, programs such as Highfields, Pinehills, and the Belmont Social Rehabilitation Unit are examples of good organizational architecture.

It is obvious enough that many new ideas will need new packages to be of any use. The Highfields design will not fit Trenton Prison; the Community Treatment program could scarcely function in an ordinary parole office. In every country we visited there was a legacy from the past, a durable structure of stone and reinforced concrete which defied modernization and was too expensive to replace. Many such structures are beyond the capability of goodwill and ingenuity to alter. Usually they are operated by a staff attached to traditions of practice hardly less durable than the cell-blocks themselves. We have seen how the introduction of a new process, such as classification committees or group-counseling can eventually change roles to a point where traditional practice changes and the character of experience imposed by the obsolete design of the prison is ameliorated out of all recognition. We cannot conclude from this observation that correctional administrators are not justified in following the lead of Swedish innovators by replacing the obsolete with new and functionally designed buildings. It is just that some good ideas can be accommodated to old and apparently decrepit packages.

In the scattering of innovations which we have described, one common factor stands out. This is the lack of integration. A good institutional treatment program loses effectiveness because of floundering support in the field services. An imaginative field program suffers from a separation from supporting institutional services under which mutual support is hampered. Throughout this volume we have referred to the need to lead correctional services into a unified apparatus. No single correctional innovation will be a significant gain unless such a rationalization of all correctional services is attained. Nowhere has this been done. The requirements for such an apparatus must cope with many apparently incompatible elements. There must be the centralization required for coördinated planning and the dispersion of authority needed for local decision making; there must be the degree of bureaucratization necessary for the maintenance of performance standards; and there must be wide latitude for individual initiative. A high degree of professionalism in program administration will be essential to an increasingly complex battery of treatment methods, but at the same time provision must be made for the irreplace-able services of interested and zealous amateurs. The objectivity of the social scientist cannot be compromised in correctional research and engineering, but the element of concern for human beings in great trouble must be preserved.

These and many more paradoxes must be balanced to achieve the rational equilibrium of the correctional apparatus. Evolution of social institutions toward goals such as we have indicated must always cope with dilemmas of this kind. No social institution ever resolves them all. The forces which produce social change will always deny us entrance into Utopia. But in the exercise of reason, the conflicts between man and his social environment can be limited in the damage they do to any single human being. Toward this end, the correctional field has made immense strides in this century. The way is open to greater advances than ever through the application of rational innovation to the treatment and control of offenders.

V

THE ISSUES IN

CORRECTIONS

If the future of corrections is to become a forward thrust rather than an expedient drift, some major issues must be settled. In an ideal state, these issues should be resolved by a consensus of all concerned: the courts, the police, the correctional administrator, and the offender himself.

Unanimity will never be so complete as to eliminate the need for compromise. So long as society relies on the dread of prison to maintain control of the unruly instincts of a sinful race, correctional theory must allow for the effects of deterrence on the client to be treated. Until the general public and the persons concerned with the client are more convinced of the efficacy of correctional programs, confinement will be expected to incapacitate as well as to rehabilitate, and the field services will be expected to control as well as to help.

Thus stated, these expectations seem so incompatible as to leave no hope for reconciliation. But the gains in the countries of the West since World War II have been impressive and general. Less than two decades after the closing of the last concentration camp, agreement is general throughout East and West about the permissible limits of punishment. Minimum standards of practice have been established by such organizations as the United Nations Social Defense Section and the American Correctional Association with good effect. The next steps ahead are operable agreements on objectives. They will be compromises, but they will be better compromises if the practice theorist is clear about the positions from which he can make concessions and still expect to treat correctional clients effectively.

Agreements on objectives by the correctional professions require the formulation of an internally consistent theory. Such a theory is almost in sight; its general outlines can be inferred from the trends in advanced practice which we have described. It will be a theory which will replace the accommodation of conflicting interests — of the "irrational equilibrium."

What is a theory? For our purposes in this chapter, we can define it as a set of logically related principles based on empirically verified propositions. These principles should be applicable to practice. They would account for the behavior of the correctional client, prescribe a regime by which he can be restored to function in general society, and account for the efficacy of the regime. With any offender, reference to the theory must enable the diagnostician to establish the factors which caused the offense. On the basis of this analysis, the classifying organ must be able to assign him to a program designed to facilitate optimal return to the community. Most important, the theory must account for the change which the apparatus is to bring about which will reduce the likelihood of further offense to a level which the community can tolerate.

Such a theory does not now exist. The forces which produce the criminal identification of the street hoodlum can be enumerated in terms of anomic subculture and defective ego structure and other social and psychological factors. We still do not know enough about these forces or about the community which generates them or the human material which is eroded by them to prescribe with confidence the regime which will neutralize them and mend the damage they have done.

In the preceding chapter we have identified various programs as "advanced practice." We think that these programs are clues to the elements of such a theory. Hardly any of the propositions which they support have been verified. Reputable practitioners will dispute the validity of each. But with the establishment and refinement of these propositions into principles of practice, we shall have the base for a unified theory of corrections by which a profession can be exercised. It will then be possible to make confident judgments regarding the procedure for restoring a client to the community safely, economically, and with assurance that his positive potential for contributions to society will be at least as well mobilized as that of the nondelinquent citizen.

Contrast this distant ideal with what now exists as standard practice. In the irrational equilibrium we have described, practitioners are principally concerned to determine when enough punishment has been administered to minimize the likelihood of future misbehavior by the offender. Treatment is largely palliative. To reduce the damage done by social degradation, confinement, and surveillance, the correctional apparatus borrows from analogous practice in other professions. The decision maker hopes to discern when the combined impact of punishment, training, therapy, and changed social conditions suffice to restore the offender to a community which, on the whole, would prefer to have none of him. In the light of these considerations, various programs are undertaken in institutions and agencies. Many are of considerable sophistication and value. But in the world of standard correctional practice, treatment is like an extraterritorial concession in a backward country, rather than an integral element of the culture. The prevailing theme of the culture is still punishment; treatment is allowed to coexist because it fills in the time and eases many management problems. The physician in the clinic, the teacher in the school, the works foreman in the shop, and even the psychotherapist with his enigmatic groups are all welcome and valued. Tolerance for their efforts and the facilitation of their occasional success have made possible the research and development on which a theory can be based. But there is little to show that what any of them is doing in ordinary correctional agencies is sufficient for the goal of social restoration.

To avoid misunderstanding: no correctional administrator has the power to design his services to his heart's desire. It is scarcely conceivable that the day will ever come when the correctional client can be marshaled through an institution or an agency with only those things done for him which need to be done, but everything done which would suffice to make him a good member of the community. This is an ideal to be approximated, but we shall never come close without a theory to guide us.

Such a theory must be sufficiently dynamic to allow for social change and sufficiently flexible to incorporate new findings about man and his social environment. We must learn to live with provisional theories which we are ready to revise.

The way to the component principles of the theory is through rigorous answers to questions designed to locate the elements of practice. When these questions are answered, when the theory is logically and empirically airtight, we could expect that many of the present features of the correctional apparatus will survive. We would, however, be more certain of their applicability to any specific kind of offender. The practice of corrections will continue to have its failures, but the post-mortems will be definite. Defects of practice will be traceable to identifiable gaps in theory.

The questions which follow are those to which administrators, social scientists, and practitioners must address themselves. The little questions which obsess the agency director making up a budget or the researcher framing a proposal are essential to the daily life of corrections. As in any bureaucracy, enormous amounts of administrative energy must be expended on maintenance of the present position in corrections. Preoccupation with the trees tends to make a view of the forest a luxury for correctional management.

But self-respect and increased success depend on greater attention to the issues on whose resolution depends the construction of a cohesive theory. We are not in a position to formulate such a theory. But in stating the questions we expect that a strategy for assembling the principles will emerge.

THE CLIENT

By their identification with the classical or positivist schools of their discipline, criminologists have concentrated attention on the choice between making punishments fit the crime or the criminal. This has been a useful pair of alternatives to consider, but at this stage in the development of corrections is unnecessarily restricts the horizon. Instead of attending to crime and punishment, or the event and its just consequences, we are beginning to think about social deviation and its management, or a condition and its remedy. The distinctions thus made lead to important differences in social control.

In this way, offenses which have traditionally led to confinement are now seen as symptomatic for mental-health management. Public drunkenness is one example of this trend. There are indications that the use of narcotics, most sexual offenses, and some violent crimes will be seen as symptoms of conditions requiring psychiatric care. Other crimes have been removed from the class of offenses requiring long incarceration. Increasingly, forgery and theft are seen as more appropriately and economically handled by a short-jail sentence or by probation. But the trend may not go entirely in the direction of less confinement. In the United States, traffic offenses have been typically punished by fines, but the Scandinavian experience with mandatory jail sentences for some kinds of motor-vehicle violations seems to be successful. More experience is needed, but the principle may hold true that for offenses in which there is no question of criminal identification, the punitive effect of confinement may have special values in providing negative reinforcement for behavior to be proscribed.

Such clues lead us to ask whether our experience may not have reached a point at which we can best define the identity of the correctional client in operational terms. In the professions of medicine, law, or education, the nature of the service to be rendered determines the status of the patient, the client, or the student. If the patient can neither be cured nor made more comfortable he is not an object for medical care. The client without a cause and the student who will not be taught have no roles with the lawyer or the teacher. The services which these professions have to offer are well understood through the long history of civilization with them. The services which the correctional profession has to offer are hardly understood at all. As we gain in knowledge of their potentialities we shall be able to define the kinds of people who can benefit by them and in what forms they can most appreciably profit from the experience.

If the identity of the correctional client is to be sought in terms of the services which the apparatus can render, what is the substance of these services? In this chapter we are trying to define the issues; neither a consensus on the answer to this question nor the data to support one exist. More research will be needed before we can say that the capabilities of the correctional apparatus have been defined. But we can propose the elements of such a definition. They consist of variable degrees of control, ranging from complete restriction of all movement to cursory surveillance. The variable manipulation of the social structure produces the different levels of physical control which are characteristic of penal systems in all forms, from the most barbarous to the most enlightened. This is a combination of considerable power to produce behavioral change. Its limits have scarcely been studied. Obviously it is an implement whose uses are specialized. It is inappropriate for some purposes, as for example for many kinds of psychiatric care, although in conditions where the maintenance of control is essential, it combines well with the required treatment. In such cases, it may well be questioned whether the use of control is subsidiary to the need of a patient for medical treatment. Where this is the case, the agency administering the treatment should probably be considered an organ of a mental-health apparatus. Perhaps this issue would be decided by considering whether principal reliance is placed on the use of control or the use of psychotherapy to produce the changes needed for social restoration.

If we can construct from the capacities of the correctional apparatus a definition of its clientele, some of the men, women, and children now under its control can be channeled to psychiatric care. Aged delinquents can be given home care, perhaps wholly apart from confinement. Juvenile offenders more in need of educational opportunities than of control might be routed to residential schools. There surely is no reason why society should limit access to this kind of education to the most and the least privileged children in the community. Many others between the extremes can profit from some boarding-school experience at some phase of adolescence.

These subtractions from the caseload would leave the group of people who have violated the law and who can be defined as able to benefit from some form of control better than from any other form of social service. It does not presume that any kind of offender will go free simply because neither the correctional apparatus nor any other instrument of society is capable of benefiting him. The correctional apparatus will continue to catch most of those is now confines. It will not have to catch all.

From the foregoing we can extract questions about the identity of the correctional client not in terms of the crimes he has committed, or even in terms of his status as a criminal, but rather with regard to the capability of the apparatus itself. We have indicated a definition of the correctional system in terms of various combinations of physical and social control. These combinations allow for a virtually infinite number of provisions for the client. Just as in determining who the client is in the first place, the system should determine what it can do for him; similarly, to decide what kind of a client he is, it should settle what kind of provision it must make for him to reach the objective of social restoration.

The professional correctional administrator must answer the basic question: what needs to be done? This question answered, the correctional service can restrict itself to doing only those things which no other service can do, rather than attempting to do badly what others can do better. The various forms of control which are at the disposal of the apparatus are needed by certain offenders, and certain offenders only. To be sure who these offenders are, it will be well to consider the questions pertaining to the structure of the apparatus itself.

THE INSTITUTION

The correctional world today is confused by a variety of prisons, jails, reformatories, colonies, training schools, borstals, and centers. If we are trying to determine what a correctional institution at its best can do for its inmates, we should keep in mind the best correctional institution we can devise and describe it in terms of its optimal dimensions. If we can aim our research in the direction of these optima, we should be able to predict what benefits an institution can confer on its inmates. Profound changes are wrought upon the inhabitants of these involuntary retreats from a disordered world. Whatever else may be said of the "total institution," [1] it will influence the nature of inmates and staff alike. But though these influences may be vast, there are limits to their kind and their extent. Through an examination of the dimensions of cultural institutions we may arrive at some notion of where the limits are.

How large should an institution be? In answering this question the administrator compromises between economy of operation and efficiency of program. To our surprise, we found in this survey that neither administrators nor researchers had better guidance to offer than the impressions gained from day-to-day operation. Nearly everyone thought that the institution he was running, whether its population was 5000 or 500, or even less, was too large. One superintendent thought that no institution should be larger than its superintendent's ability to remember the names of its inmates; in his case, this principle fixed the maximum at about 250. An experienced clinician thought that everyone should be able to maintain a realistic contact with everyone else, but that everyone should be allowed some privacy; he thought this would fix the figure at about 100. The superficial and stereotyped contacts possible in very large living units are well known; the influences of the institution in such circumstances appear to be deterrent at best. [2]

---

[1] For a definition of this term and an account of its influence, see Erving Goffman, *Asylums* (New York: Anchor Books No. 277, 1961).

[2] See Donald Clemmer, *The Prison Community* (New York: Rinehart & Co., 1958), and Gresham Sykes, *The Society of Captives* (Princeton: Princeton University Press, 1958). Both of these well-known studies of the conventional prison are intended to make somewhat different points than the one we are making here. However, they

The few studies which have been conducted in institutions in which numbers have been kept to reasonable levels indicate that a deeper and more positive interaction is possible where the structure is designed to facilitate the goals of the staff rather than in the interests of pound-foolish economy.[3] The contrast between these two kinds of institutional design suggests that it will be worth while to design an institution in terms of what is needed to produce favorable interaction. Much is known, and there are ways of learning more, about the scale of a man's attention span in terms of the number of people he can know at various levels of knowing. Age, duration of institutional care, social background, and institutional program will be only a few of the variables for which allowance must be made. But a living unit based on this number seems a reasonable point to find and on which to begin.

From the living unit, the next consideration is supervisory. How many such units can a supervisor manage? If the program is simple, the number can be larger than if the supervisor is responsible for the effectiveness of individualized activities. Finally, the size of the institution depends on the capacity of the administrator to maintain purposeful contact with middle-level supervisors.

Whatever the number arrived at by the application of some such formula, only the first questions will have been answered. A small institution can have a noxious as well as a favorable impact. A second subsidiary question at least as important as the problem of size deals with the question of time. The determinate sentence predicts too soon the response to the regime to which the client is to be subjected. The indeterminate sentence presumes the evaluation of the client's response by instruments of evaluation which have neither been standardized nor even tested. The problem has scarcely been analyzed. Here we can only indicate some hopeful paths to explore and mention that hardly anyone has trod them.

What factors should determine the time which offenders should serve? We must assume that for a good while to come the public will insist that incapacitation and retribution will play their parts in setting

---

both demonstrate in abundant detail the superficiality and the meaninglessness of prisoner interaction as it might relate to resocialization. Eventually, as Clemmer demonstrates, this interaction for the sake of cohesiveness against the captor leads to the apathetic isolation of the recidivist.

[3] See Oscar Grusky, "Organizational Goals and the Behavior of Informal Leaders," *American Journal of Sociology*, 65 (1959), 59–67.

terms, but the correctional administrator should be ready with appropriate answers about the optimum duration of confinement when factors other than the effects of control can be disregarded. What can be taken as evidence that the control exercised by the institution has been sufficiently internalized to warrant social restoration? Researches are urgently needed.

When the study of term-fixing can be removed from policy, the tools are ready for a rational approach to standards. In the establishment of base expectancies, in our accumulating experience with typologies, we already have in crude form, at least, the instruments with which a specific treatment can be applied to a specific client with the means to appraise the outcome. Guided group interaction can be applied to clients whose delinquency patterns are related to manipulation, for example. If a significant group of those so exposed can be shown to have succeeded in larger proportions than anticipated by their base expectancies, clues are available by which terms can be systematically varied to see when guided group interaction seems to be enough. The structure of the time problem is capable of providing for various other important factors, such as economic conditions, family situations, and subcultural influences. The massive accumulation of time-setting examples which has piled up in the century past is beyond our evaluation. We now have the tools to make a system out of an inequitable chaos; the criminologist therefore should find ways of putting them to work.

A third dimension of the correctional apparatus is classification. Many major reforms have been effected through classification dating from the separation of men from women prisoners and of child prisoners from both. We have little difficulty with the principle that each client should be subjected to systematic study for a determination of the kinds of treatment he needs to achieve a durable restoration to the community. The intuition of the nineteenth-century prison reformer told him that hardened criminals should not be housed with first offenders. This principle has been intuitively refined to provide for the separation of many classes of criminals from each other: The bright are housed away from the stupid; the coöperative are kept away from the recalcitrant; the homosexuals are secluded from all except each other. Perhaps the British borstal system carries classification to its furthest, though most logical extreme. Using the base expectancy system in combination with personality appraisals a continuum has been established by which the correctional barrel is layered into nearly air-tight divisions, from a top where all social systems are sweetness and light or nearly so, to a bottom in which fists fly on all sides. Unpublished studies suggest that if the contamination of the good is to be avoided, the bad must be concentrated on the bottom.

Other students incline to a belief that attitudinal classifications of this kind should be eliminated. Though the prospects of the hopeful may be enhanced by exposure to each other, the gains may hardly be worth the deterioration incurred by the inmates on the bottom. In conventionally organized institutions this kind of separation is a necessity. Where inmates are left to their own devices, an antitherapeutic, anti-restoration community will result. The most that can be done in the traditional institution is to maintain order.

In the opinion of the proponents of the therapeutic community, there are now instruments available by which the focus on social restoration and mutual aid can be sufficiently reinforced by staff-inmate interactions to produce a regime in which the social and personality differences among inmates become unimportant. Obviously the means of accomplishing this end in a large physical structure which has to be filled up are not yet in sight. The fact that a mutual-aid culture was developed in Highfields, Pollington Borstal, and the Inmate-Staff Community Project at the Deuel Vocational Institution establishes the existence of the opportunity. It does not tell us the limits of the situations in which the culture can be successfully replicated. Especially it does not tell us the tolerance of the new correctional community for the recalcitrants. Clearly the way is open for many new explorations in correctional community building.

The final dimension of the correctional facility to study is its boundaries with the outside world. We have previously commented on the prison's use as a place of banishment and incapacitation. Until we can think of alternate programs for dangerous offenders, the prison will have to continue receiving exiles. As long as this purpose must be served, the boundary should clearly be airtight. But for the majority of offenders, the purpose of the correctional facility is not exile; but social restoration. The success of modest probation programs demonstrates that the boundaries may not be needed. For some Russian prisoners, a correctional institution is a specialized place of work for mandatory labor. For a Highfields boy the institution limits exist but are permeable. For Swedish prisoners the frequency of furloughs out and visits in is so high as to transform the nature of the correctional experience. And in a very few American jails the correctional facility has become a place of punitive residence rather than of incapacitation. Halfway houses and hostels exist or are planned in many American and English communities. Few principles can be yet derived from these devices to substitute process for exile. The intuitions of the innovators, not their empirically validated findings, have guided them in the establishment of new boundaries between the client and the community. We must now test these boundaries with different classes of correctional client. From the short, sharp shock of the British attendance center or detention center to the life-long dependence on the apparatus which Danish and Finnish correctional planners foresee is a long range to provide for. It is probably a necessary range, with many variants to be established in between. It can hardly be said that a means of systematically studying the clientele and the range has been conceived. But society has much to gain from getting on with this job; when it is completed, the economic and social costs of the correctional apparatus should be immensely reduced.

The aggregation of the four areas of study proposed in this chapter should set up many model institutions to make up the correctional apparatus of the future. The dimensions of each will be specially pertinent to treatment. From such models we can make some determination of the maximum benefits to be expected from confinement in a correctional institution. We shall also be able to assess the minimum damage to be expected for commitment to such models. We may never arrive at an organization of criminal justice in which the correctional administrator will be able to limit all inmate programs to doing what is necessary to resocialize the individual. But with an appraisal of the four dimensions we should see the day when the specialist in corrections can reliably advise courts and judges as to the most favorable disposition of prospective clients.

THE FIELD SERVICE

Because of the sociological interest in prisons, more study has gone into their dimensions and potentialities than into the probation or parole agency. Because of the complex tasks of the probation officer, he has scarcely begun to exploit the possibilities. The process of deciding the dimensions of the agency should help to decide what clients can be benefited by field management alone or by some combination of institutional and field management. The dimensions which seem most relevant to a solution of this problem are time, level of contact, and program content. These dimensions must be fitted to a typology of problems looking to an answer for each client to the question of what treatment strategy can be put into the most significant effect by an official agency. We have seen how the Community Treatment Project of Sacramento depends basically on the classification of the caseload into nine personality types. Age, subcultures, and other social factors will further subdivide the types into specialized problems.

With respect to time, we must look for criteria enabling us to judge when enough is enough. For some clients a life-long casework relationship with the agency would be beneficial, for others a brief admonitory interview.

Every probation officer we talked to felt that his caseload should be smaller. Besides, the level of contact needed for different problems was rarely clear. If optimum caseloads and contacts can be established, different caseload sizes will result, depending on what the officer needs to do. This principle seems obvious, but such issues are resolved by negotiations from one intolerable level to another just barely less intolerable. Even for so sophisticated a project as Community Treatment no attempt has yet been made to relate the size of the caseload to the nature of the task to be done.

Different things need to be done in the field agency, and widely varying levels of skill are needed to do them. Where contact with a cooperative probationer is needed to meet a legal obligation, a minimum service is required for which the skill of a trainee or a case aide is enough. It should not be an encumbrance on a skillful caseworker or group counselor. The vocational guidance which so many correctional clients need is a speciality which might be worth developing even at the cost of relieving the specialist of a professional responsibility for correctional casework. For a long time, now, there has been a controversy in the probation field regarding the specialization of the investigatory function. So evenly balanced are the arguments on both sides that some agencies permit their officers an option whether they will specialize. A number of other specialized services exist or can be built into the structure of the correctional field agency. Hardly any of them has been fully exploited simply because the probation officer has typically been expected to operate simultaneously at widely varying levels of skill. The

consequence is that he seldom has an opportunity to attain full pro-
ficiency at any of the difficult tasks. By the time he has become a capable counselor he is usually ready for promotion to supervisory responsibilities. The correctional practitioner who is in significant contact with
his clients is either a man who has not been promoted, or one who is in
the earliest phase of his career. Under the circumstances, practice is
rarely illuminated with excellence. While this condition prevails in the
institutions as well as in the field agencies, it is probably more significant in the latter because we lack any test of the capabilities of the field
agency performing at its best. The essence of the field agency task is the
quality of contact between agent and client. Until we know how well a
trained agent can perform, we shall not know the capabilities of a field
agency. Various pilot operations in the institutions have already given
us some perceptions of the capabilities of residential care beyond the
present general level of correctional practice. But the improvement of
field practice by differential caseload planning is long overdue. The
mere reduction of caseloads will never produce a lasting improvement
in practice.

Most field agencies provide services within the traditions of the occupation and a caseload of from fifty to seventy. These dimensions will
generally produce a service consisting of investigations, surveillance
contacts, counseling contacts, employment contacts, referrals, and
emergency procedures. Some California studies notably the Special Intensive Parole Unit project (SIPU), have shown that a reduction in
caseload coupled with some specialization of service, primarily directed to the issue of surveillance or counseling alternatives, will produce some improvements in recidivism. New California projects under the Increased Correctional Effectiveness program will be based on
more sophisticated models; some of the assumptions propounded in
this chapter will probably be tested.

However, the content of the field-agency program has not yet been
sufficiently examined. On the negative side:

First, who should be afforded probation or parole services? Some
communities have tended to make of probation a service which attends
to nearly all social-welfare problems arising from the work of the criminal, juvenile, and domestic-relations courts. This is particularly true in
England, where probation officers find themselves assigned to marriage-
counseling, adoption, and divorce problems. The diversity of practice
thus converging on the agency is usually not specialized. It is accepted

because it is work which needs to be done, but it is seldom made the object of careful agency planning. Indeed, with all the disparate demands made on agency and officer, nothing less than a full-scale operations research study would suffice to determine how the work might be optimally organized. But before such studies are undertaken, some preliminary studies should be made of the comparative effectiveness of the probation service as an arm of the court specializing in correctional practice as compared to the present all-purpose agency.

Second, studies should be made of the surveillance function of field service. A huge amount of agency resources are devoted in Anglo-Saxon countries to the process of "checking up." Is this properly a part of the probation officer's duties, and if so why and to what extent? Why should not the police, whose role is clear in investigation, arrest, and reports, be relied on to carry out assignments which are not related to the treatment and social restoration of the client? There are strong arguments on both sides of this issue, and though the phrasing of our questions may suggest our stand, we do not plead a case. We simply want studies to be made which will clarify a muddy issue. The fact that apparently successful probation and parole agencies in various parts of the world exemplify both approaches to the role of probation suggests that it might not be difficult to make some preliminary soundings.

Third, we need to study the auspices under which probation is most successfully carried out. Should the probation officer be an officer of the court, responsible to it, and governed by its policies? Should he be an independent agency in the community, responsible like other public services to the policy-making body? Should he, as in some northern European countries, be a representative of a philanthropic agency, privately financed but publicly supervised? Or, to propose a fourth alternative, should this service be an integrated feature of the national correctional apparatus, so that probation and parole caseloads are merged and at least some of the work is directly integrated with institutional practice? Traditions, vested interests, and sincerely held beliefs have supported each of these alternatives. They have also tended to block studies which might demonstrate optimum administrative solutions.

On the positive side, we find ourselves concerned with a variety of techniques which might be and in some places have been added to field-agency practice. Implicit in the questions raised by these techniques is the need to answer clearly the negative questions, which will provide some structure to the role of the field agency. If this agency is seen as a community service directed at the social restoration of offenders, many new services become clearly necessary. If, on the other hand, the field services are primarily a specialized arm of law enforcement, then some new agencies must be invented to provide the various forms of official help which will continue to be needed — in many communities more than ever, as urbanization proceeds faster than techniques of social organization can be devised to keep us.

Assume, then, that the field agency is to become a specialized resource of the correctional apparatus primarily intended for the social restoration of offenders. Several questions arise concerning the components of service.

First, we must ask how the field agent can be armed with skills to enable him to devise a favorable social structure for his client. We must define the essentials of such structure-building for the different classes of client which can be found in a correctional typology. There is work for many pilot studies in this area before we shall have a model which we can standardize for training and practice. Because of the compulsory features which at least can be established in the correctional services, the contributions of workers in this field may be significant for the other social services. It is important that projects in this area be launched with no more delay than is necessary to find able personnel and to crystallize a concept into a model for pilot operation.

Second is the exploitation of the interest in halfway houses and hostels. It is evident that the intuitions of professional leadership in the field and of offenders concur on the values of this kind of residential experience in their present form. They must be clarified from experience. Such experience must be related to a comparison of effectiveness of such programs concerning various kinds of offenders. We must account for the comparisons we make.

Third, we must examine the relevance for the correctional field services of the group techniques currently popular. Data are needed which tell under what circumstances the group-counseling approach to field supervision is appropriate; whether it makes a crucial difference; if so, what makes the difference. Is it possible that a counterpart of the institutional therapeutic community can be constructed in field situations? Is it worth doing, and, if so, why? The enthusiasm generated for group methods in all phases of correctional practice should be exploited. But enthusiasm is no substitute for data and logical analysis.

It is at least probable that these methods will benefit some kinds of offenders more than others. We should like to see some hypotheses reflecting this probability and with them the means to put them to the test.

The experience of the past two decades suggests that in correctional service an equation exists between benovolence and economy. The most richly staffed field service is much cheaper to provide than confinement in the most economically efficient institutions. Pressure is exerted in many places to increase probation and parole caseloads by removing various classes of offenders from institutions. No one in the correctional apparatus is now in a position to say how far this process can be safely carried. Because there is no apparent end to the increases in the cost of institutional care, it is important to the correctional administrator to use his resources to arrive at some tentative formulation of the optimum field caseload. He should certainly not have to rely on hunches drawn from the experiences of his colleagues in other fields of professional endeavor.

EVALUATING CORRECTIONAL SERVICE

Increasingly, the criterion of success or failure of the correctional apparatus is recidivism. It may be refined into various kinds of experience. Its definition may be specialized to meet the demands of a particular research problem. But it is the most understandable gauge applicable to correctional programs. It is so clear that it may tempt both professional and layman to the belief that it is the only possible gauge.

We do not propose that recidivism should be abandoned as a measurement. But we question whether the messages conveyed by tables of recidivism can be clearly understood in their present forms. The efficacy of correctional service is only one among many forces impinging upon the offender after his release. It may play no part in his success, it may play a limited part, or it may have a crucial influence. It is necessary to establish expectations for different kinds of offender. Through the use of base expectancies and prediction tables a beginning has been made. For the highest and lowest groups on the expectancy continuum we know what to expect from the man and from his environment. Significant deviations for the group may be charged to the service. For the large middle group we are little better off than we were without such a device at our disposal. When, for example, it is necessary to return a youngster to the delinquent subculture of the city slums from which he came, his nearly inevitable failure is much less indicative of correctional effectiveness than the failure of another offender for whom more favorable choices exist. Yet both failures must be counted as statistically identical items.

Besides, how long can the influences exerted by the apparatus be expected to shape the behavior of clients? Some offenders may be changed or deterred by their experiences for the rest of their lives. Others undergo more fleeting changes. The calculus of correctional effectiveness is a perplexing problem in social engineering. Its solution lies in the application of scientific method to correctional data. So far, realities have fallen short of scholarly aspirations. Treatment variables have been applied to one group and withheld from another. The resulting data have been zealously tabulated. The comparisons have been inconclusive. The confidence of some, at least, in correctional research has been shaken.

The trouble is based on a persisting indifference to the conduct of the kind of observations needed to define a variable. New activities are launched on the basis of reasonable assumptions. They are subjected to control-group study in the name of classical scientific method. A significant difference between control and experimental groups is sought to support or cancel the activity.

Now, whatever the worth of a control-group study may be for the evaluation of procedures designed to influence human beings, it is always necessary to state a hypothesis to test. Such a hypothesis must be grounded on a clear analysis of the procedure to be introduced. The independent variable must be sharply defined. Such gross entities as "group-counseling," or "intensive after-care," or "psychiatric treatment," will resist the most ingenious test. Only variables which have been minutely observed can be conclusively compared.

But because the criterion of recidivism is always available, tables can be set up to compare any crudely differentiated groups. Under such circumstances the lack of statistical significance is not surprising. Until correctional research can more reliably distinguish apples from oranges, it will never be able to decide what fertilizer to use to increase the size of either.

More observation is needed in correctional research. Connections between events and consequences are left to speculation; the events themselves are neither accounted for nor related to the results they produce. Indeed, they are not even described or recognized for what they are. Without the causal links between group-counseling transactions, for example, and their impact on offenders, we cannot construct hypotheses about the expected effects or any assumptions about group counseling. But the laborious business of observing, recording, and classifying these transactions is beyond the economic means of correctional research. Because we have conducted so few observations, few researchers know how to conduct them. It is much easier to classify input and output, make comparisons, and draw conclusions. So "global" studies of the consequences of introducing this or that procedure as an independent variable are undertaken without concern about the meaning that can be extracted from the results a few years later.

These questions about research are too advanced for most correctional systems we have visited. In few places have the procedures of elementary statistical accounting been installed: the staff and the equipment needed for laboratory work in the social sciences exist in less than a dozen places in the world. Our simple demands far exceed the capacities of administrators whose hands are full trying to keep their programs afloat. It is useless to urge that they distinguish the various meanings of recidivism, that they state clearly what they expect to accomplish, or that they make detailed observations of process before they undertake an elaborate statistical analysis of programs. Our demands will not be met in many quarters, but we can take cold comfort in the certainty that no elaborate statistical analyses will be prematurely undertaken, either.

So it is no wonder that correctional research so often seems a frantic attempt to take advantage of a golden opportunity to plumb every depth before it is too late. The application of scientific method to correctional problems is hardly more than thirty years old. Funds are meager. Adequately trained people for social research are hard to find. When a valid opportunity to do something falls into the right hands, the temptation to try for too much is strong. Observation is a matter of course in medicine and physics. The contrast between the condition of research in the natural sciences with the adjustments of scientific method which go on in the social sciences is not merely the reflection of the relative maturity of method in the two fields, but also a reflection of the disparity of means. Medicine and physics can afford patience; the social sciences cannot. Until resources are available for learning how to study the details, correctional research will probably find that useful generalizations elude its grasp.

THE FUTURE OF PUNISHMENT

We are nearly at the end of our pilgrimage. We have described an instrument of social control which, in spite of local differences, is wielded in much the same way throughout the world. It is an instrument which requires a complex apparatus for its operation. In some places, limited need for its use has resulted in the survival of an antiquated design. In other places, the demands upon it have required improvised changes and adaptations. It looks much the same the world over. The guard at the barbed wire fence of a corrective labor colony near Moscow conveys the same message as the guard in the tower of an American prison. The message is punishment.

We are often enough told that man has always needed to punish and always will, if only to maintain control over the vicious urges which lurk in every breast. The arguments are familiar, and we shall not attempt to refute them. The question is whether alternatives to punishment may exist which can be implemented in a social order that falls short of Utopia.

The limited experience drawn from the advanced practice of corrections seem to indicate the existence of alternatives. The history of punishment in the past century and a half shows that punishment has always been excessively used. It is only one hundred and fifty years since Lord Chief Justice Ellenborough warned the House of Lords against an attempt to eliminate the death penalty for thefts of more than five shillings: "Your Lordships will pause before you assent to a measure so pregnant with danger for the security of property. The learned judges are unanimously agreed that the expediency of justice and public security require that there should not be a remission in this part of the criminal law."

This admonition is cited usually as an example of the wrongheadedness which at the time went into the making of the criminal law. The same kind of heartless thought goes into the framing of our criminal codes. We punish because we must, and we assess the punishments, in large part, at as high a rate as the public conscience will bear. That the public conscience will no longer tolerate sheep thieves on the gallows redounds to its credit. Public conscience is the only check to the public sense of outrage.

But punishment has been in retreat during the past century. Prisons which prescribed silence, solitude, and hard labor for their captives have been replaced by probation, parole, and correctional facilities which subject their inmates to treatment, training, and idleness. It is easy enough to belittle the changes represented by this gradual replacement of undisguised infliction of pain with increasing admixtures of positive measures. Yet their meaning for us is profound. Punishment alone is so ineffective that it cannot survive for long without compassion. In the form of sentimental leniency, compassion is dangerous and usually inequitable. In the form of a program directed at the objective of social restoration, compassion requires intelligence and discrimination, as well as generosity.

We do not mean to say that compassion may be enough, nor can we legitimately ask whether punishment can now be eliminated from correctional practice. The question is: *What is the minimum punishment needed to maintain control and the maximum which can be tolerated by the objective of social restoration?* Implicit in this question is the recognition that for no two people can the answer be the same, but that a good system must establish the margin for error.

It must also take into account the unanswered questions about punishment — unanswered because unasked. What are its effects in the correctional situation? In the thought of B. F. Skinner,[4] and G. C. Homans,[5] punishment is *negative reinforcement* of behavior; its effects can be experimentally studied and compared with those of positive reinforcement through a system of rewards and incentives.

Homans, after describing experiments in the negative reinforcement of the behavior of pigeons, concludes that punishment is unsatisfactory because it is too costly. He states the consequences:

Suppose there is an activity that we find undesirable but that nevertheless gets some reinforcement. Unless we are in a position to punish the activity every time it appears, it will soon reinstate itself. If accordingly we disapprove of a certain activity, let us say in our children, and want to get rid of it, we had better use, if we can, some other method than punishment. We had

[4] B. F. Skinner, *Science and Human Behavior* (New York: Macmillan, 1953).

[5] George Caspar Homans, *Social Behavior: Its Elementary Forms* (New York: Harcourt Brace and World, 1961).

better use extinction, and see that the activity goes without reward: if a child cries to get attention, we should see that he does not get it, though we may run risks in doing so. Or we should reward an alternative activity, praising him for not crying rather than punishing him for crying. But let us face it: this is not Pollyanna's world. Control may be necessary at times when the only means of control at our command is punishment, however, unsatisfactory. These times may also come less often than we think.[6]

Advocates of tradition may at first have little trouble with Homans. Punishment may not always be satisfactory, but it is our only means of control.

Control of what? If our objective is the control of crime, then we had better heed Homans' warning that an activity which gets positive reinforcement will reinstate itself unless always punished. If we think of the positive reinforcements associated with most crimes, it seems probable that punishment is an insignificant support to social control. It communicates to the criminal that his act is disapproved, but it presents no alternative route to the satisfactions which the crime conferred on him. If these satisfactions were the consequence of various patterns of delinquent identification, or the release of hostility toward a society which conveyed rejection to him, or simply the easy money at moderate risk which many forms of theft offer, then the negative reinforcement of prison will hardly suffice for a change of life. Coupled with a desire for respectability and an opportunity for attaining it, in other words, some form of positive reinforcement, punishment plays an unknown part in the resocialization of many a "hardened" recidivist.

The problem, as expounded by Skinner and Homans, is to extinguish criminal behavior by seeing to it that it goes unrewarded, and to reinforce some more acceptable form of behavior. According to Cloward and Ohlin,[7] the problem is to detach the offender from an illegitimate opportunity structure and to relate him to a normative opportunity structure. In the language of the analysts of subcultures, Albert Cohen, Walter Miller, or Milton Yinger, the problem is to relate the delinquent to the cultural norms of the community. Psychologists hope to strengthen ego structure. However the process of social restoration may be stated, the objectives are identical and the means are positive. Punish-

---

[6] *Ibid.*, pp. 26–27.

[7] Richard Cloward and Lloyd Ohlin, *Delinquency and Opportunity* (Glencoe, Illinois: The Free Press, 1960).

ment is still in the process, and rightly so, to provide us with a means of controlling the offender when we don't know what else to do. It is enormously expensive. It gets in the way of our positive measures of resocialization. In most situations it must be offset while it is being administered. The task of correctional advance is clear: to reduce to an absolute minimum the use of punishment through alternative positive measures.

There is a long way to go, as we have seen. The benefits to society will not merely consist of the replacement of the present irrational equilibrium in corrections by an effective apparatus. The association of correctional experience with success rather than failure will have an impact on the prevention of delinquency. For if correctional experience can be expected to contribute to successful living rather than to failure, effective behavioral technology can be applied to predelinquents rather than the present expedients to keep them in homes and on streets which offer only anomie and anxiety.

We have allowed ourselves the luxury of a vision. But more than most human institutions, corrections needs a vision to work toward. The day-to-day routines are monotonous, often depressing, and the rewards are infrequent and nebulous.

The first step toward the attainment of that vision is to reopen the dialogue on the great issues.

The second step will be courageously to act on the consensus.

With the forces which always in the past have produced crime, intensifying as ever-increasing urbanization and mobility of the race combine to intensify the forces which produce crime, no modern community can afford to do less.

INDEX